AN APPEAL TO HEA
DON'T TREAD ON ME

AMERICA IS

THE HERITAGE

MY COUNTRY

OF A FREE PEOPLE

HARRIETT M. BROWN · JOSEPH F. GUADAGNOLO

With the editorial assistance of Howard R. Anderson

HOUGHTON MIFFLIN COMPANY

HOUGHTON MIFFLIN COMPANY

The Riverside Press Cambridge PRINTED IN THE U. S. A.

TO THE READER

My country, 'tis of thee,
Sweet land of liberty,
Of thee I sing;
Land where my fathers died,
Land of the pilgrims' pride,
From every mountain-side,
Let freedom ring.

When you pick up a new book, you usually wonder what it is about and whether it will be interesting. As its title indicates, this book is about your country. Most of the material in it deals with patriotism, or love of country. Among other things it tells about the symbols of our democracy, our national documents, our monuments and shrines, our patriotic songs, poems, and holidays.

As you read AMERICA IS MY COUNTRY, you will learn about the high ideals on which our nation was founded. You will learn what it means to be an American, and what your rights and freedoms are as well as your responsibilities as a citizen. May your reading of AMERICA IS MY COUNTRY deepen your devotion and loyalty to the United States of America!

About the Authors and Editor

THE AUTHORS. Mrs. Harriett M. Brown is a former teacher of social studies in the Los Angeles City Schools. She is co-author of two widely used texts, *This Is America's Story* and *Our Latin American Neighbors.* Mr. Joseph F. Guadagnolo is head counselor at Washington Irving Junior High School in Los Angeles, where he taught social studies for seventeen years. His special interest as an educator has been the teaching of American institutions, ideals, and government for junior high schools.

THE EDITOR. Dr. Howard R. Anderson is the Provost of the University of Rochester, Rochester, New York. Dr. Anderson has become one of the outstanding authorities on the teaching of social studies through his work at the University of Iowa, Cornell University, and the United States Office of Education.

About the Opening Illustrations

The pictures on the first four pages of AMERICA IS MY COUNTRY illustrate the growth of our nation. The first page suggests the birth of America as an independent country. Under the American Flag as it is today are some of the earlier flags carried during our struggle for independence. The colonial minutemen recall the patriots whose courage made our nation free.

The second and third pages illustrate how modern America has developed. Our swift planes and trains, our many schools, our broad farms and busy cities, our bridges, dams, and factories, have grown out of the hard work, skill, and sacrifice of early Americans, who lived very differently from the way we do today.

Page iv points to our government, represented by the two sides of the Great Seal of the United States. This government has developed from the wise planning of the men who wrote our Constitution.

CONTENTS

CONTENTS

CHAPTER 1

What It Means to Be an American

Some time ago there appeared on television a play about an old man who came to America from Europe. He had been persecuted in his own country during World War II because of his race. After the war he had been pushed about from one place to another. He had no home and no country, but he had a dream — somehow to reach America, land of liberty. His son in America had finally located him and arranged for him to come to this country.

When the old man arrived, he was full of fear. He especially feared policemen because their uniforms reminded him of the soldiers who had ordered him about. At first he was afraid to talk freely, even to his son. When he finally realized that he was not being spied upon, he whispered over and over again, "I want to be an American citizen." The play went on to show how the old man gradually lost his fear, and how he gained the citizenship that he had dreamed of.

We Americans who have always lived in freedom sometimes take our precious liberty for granted. Stories like this one bring home to us what it means to be an American. Such stories make us realize what a wonderful thing it is to be able to live our lives without fear, to speak freely, to take part in our government, and to look any man in the eye as an equal. We know that there are many people in the world today who do not have the liberties we enjoy and who live more like slaves than like free men.

AMERICA, PRESENT AND PAST: *Gazing at the Liberty Bell, present-day Americans recall the love of freedom which founded our nation and spurred pioneers to push westward.* (See illustration above.)

America was founded on the idea that human beings are entitled to live in freedom. We believe that our democratic government and our way of life promise more liberty and happiness to more people than any other system of government. We are proud and thankful to be Americans.

This first chapter will point out some of the reasons why our country has become a leader among the nations of the world. In Chapter 1 you will also read about our heritage as Americans, and the importance of being loyal and patriotic citizens.

This Is Your Country

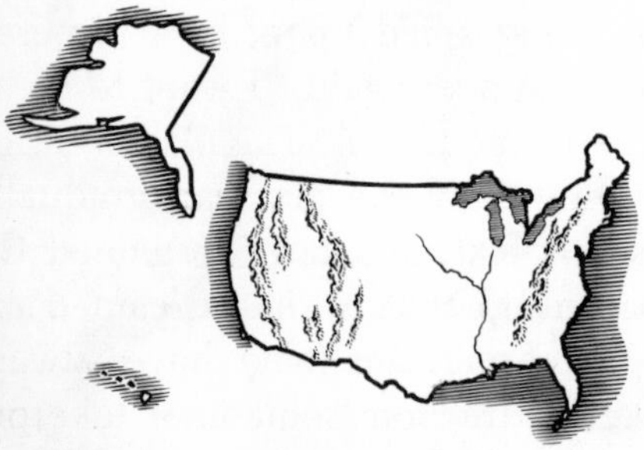

When this nation was born it was given a name, just as you were: THE UNITED STATES OF AMERICA. This is your country's legal or official name, but it is often shortened to *The United States* or simply *America*. Your country's birthday, as you well know, was July 4, 1776. The United States is about 185 years old, a very young age as nations go. Our country is the fourth largest in the world, covering about 3½ million square miles. We have over 180 million people, and so we are fourth in the world in population.

Our Land

We Americans have a rich and beautiful land. Nature has given us magnificent mountain ranges, great stretches of green forest, and gently rolling, fertile plains. Hundreds of lakes, blue and sparkling, add their beauty to our land. Rivers plunge through rocky gorges or flow more slowly through lovely valleys to the sea.

America is rich in natural resources. Our land produces crops and livestock in abundance, more than enough for our food and clothing and other needs. Our mines furnish most of the minerals we need for our industries. Rivers and lakes provide transportation and supply us with electric power, as well as water for many other uses. Our forests supply not only lumber, but other valuable products too, such as resin and turpentine. Most of our country has sufficient rainfall, and our climate makes it possible for us to raise a great variety of crops. Americans have sometimes used their natural resources recklessly. We must remember that our minerals and lumber and other raw materials will not last forever. Nevertheless, we are more fortunate than most countries because we have within our borders plentiful supplies of most of the materials needed to support a great nation.

Our American Nationality

We Americans are different in a very important way from the people of most countries. In England, for example, most of the people are of English blood. Their ancestors have for centuries lived in England. The same thing is true of many other countries. But we Americans do not come from one national stock. We are descended from people of many nationalities — English, Scotch, Irish, German, Scandinavian, Italian, Polish, Russian, and so on. Even in your class at school the pupils may represent several different nationalities.

These forefathers of ours came to America because they wanted freedom and better lives for themselves and their children. They thought that in new and unsettled America they would find opportunities they did not have in their old homes. Only courageous people would leave homes and friends to settle in a strange and far-off land. We are proud of our ancestors, whose courage and love of liberty brought them across the seas to America. No matter where they came from, they became Americans, loyal to the country that had given them freedom and opportunity. We believe that our country is stronger and richer and more vigorous because our people came from many lands. We are proud of our American nationality.

How Americans Built a Nation

Most of you have studied the history of your country. Some of you are studying it now. The story of the growth of the United States from a small, weak nation into a large and powerful one is among the most remarkable stories of all time. Never before in the history of the world has a great nation been built in so short a time!

One of the amazing things about America's story is the way our country grew in size. You remember that even in colonial days pioneers started traveling westward across the mountains in search of new homes. After we became a nation, Americans kept on pushing farther and farther west, across the Mississippi, across the

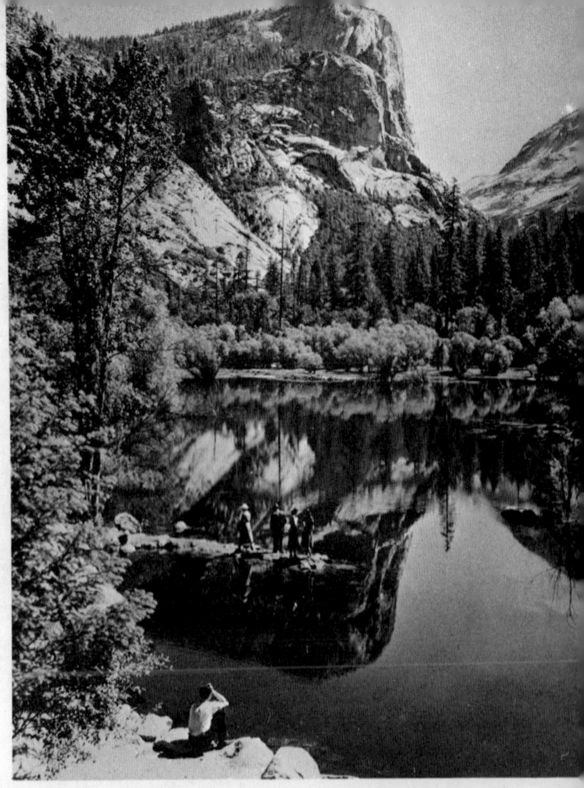

America abounds in natural beauty and grandeur. Here, visitors are enjoying a striking scene in Yosemite National Park, California.

Our country possesses fertile farmlands and rich mineral deposits. These resources, combined with hard work, skill, and scientific knowledge have made America a world leader in agriculture and industry.

Rockies, until they reached the Pacific Ocean. Wherever there was good land, Americans moved in to settle on it. And as the stream of pioneers moved westward, one territory after another was added to the United States. The little country on the Atlantic seacoast grew until in 1850 it stretched from ocean to ocean, from Canada to the Gulf of Mexico! In less than 100 years Americans conquered a wilderness and built a nation.

Today huge cities and towns stand where the Indian once stalked his game. Farms and ranches cover the plains where buffaloes used to roam. The land that was once a wilderness has become the home of our great modern nation. A network of highways and railroads, of telegraph and telephone lines, unites our huge land. The food we raise feeds not only our own people, but people of many other lands also. The United States has become the greatest agricultural country in the world.

By 1900, the United States had also become the world's most important industrial country. We have invented new tools and machines and new ways of getting work done. Our mills and mines and factories turn out such quantities of goods and machinery that we have enough to send to all parts of the earth. Trucks and trains, ships and planes transport our products over the entire globe. Our tremendous production has made the United States a world leader in trade as well as industry.

Our Place in the World Today

As our country grew strong at home, it also grew in power among the other nations. You all know that today the United States is a leader in world affairs. Long ago, when we were a small, weak nation, we believed that we should keep out of the affairs of Europe and the rest of the world. Since we were separated from Europe and Asia by two great oceans, this seemed easy to do. But the telephone, the radio, and the airplane have brought the countries of the world closer together in recent years. The farthest corner of the earth is only a few minutes away by telephone or wireless, and only a few hours away by plane. Gradually, Americans have come to realize that no nation can live by itself. Nations today depend on each other for trade and friendship.

Twice in the 1900's we have fought in world wars because we believed that we had to defend our own freedom and should help other nations to keep theirs. Today our wealth, our great industrial strength, and our strong desire to prevent war have made us the leader of the free nations of the world. We do not want the possessions of any other country. We do not wish to rule other people. Along with other free nations, we hope for a world where people can live in peace, a world whose resources and scientific discoveries are not wasted in war but are used to make a better life for all mankind.

Cities and towns, where more than half our people live, are centers of business and industry. Here you see a freighter making its way amid the towering skyscrapers of Chicago.

GALLOWAY

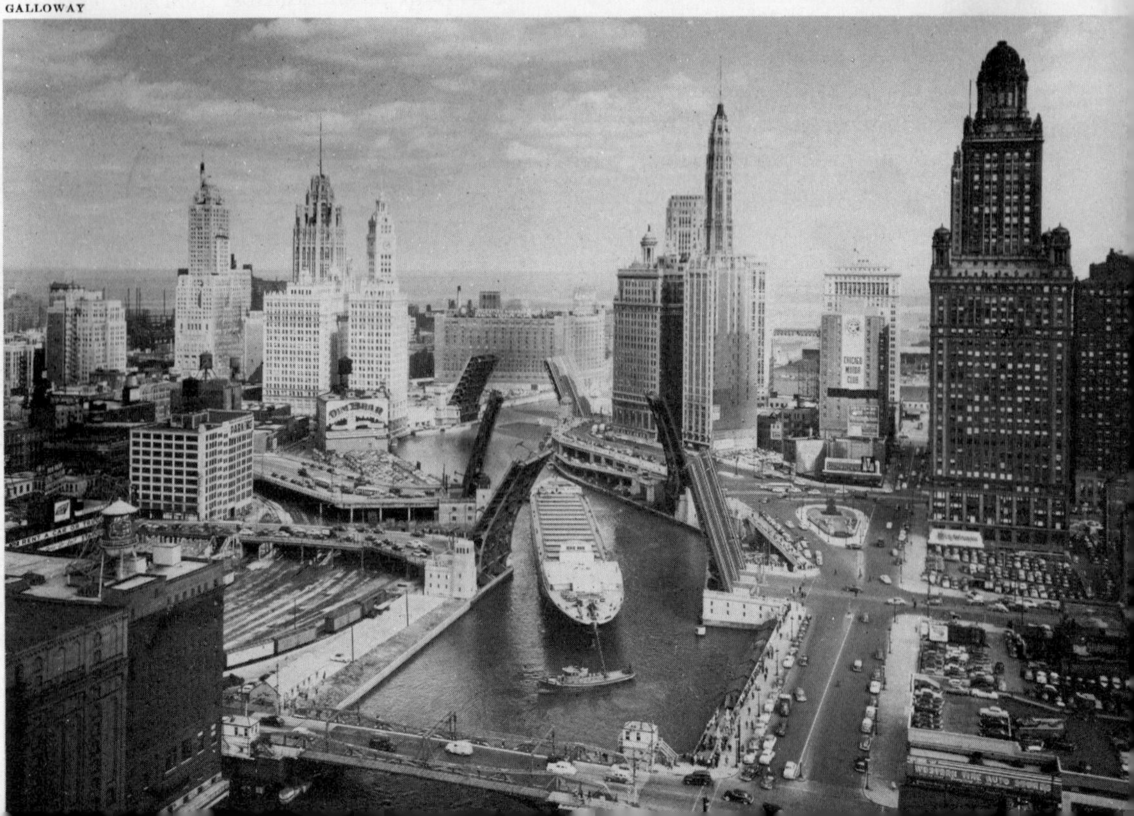

We Are Proud of America and What It Stands For

We Americans have a right to be proud of our great nation and the people who built it. We have put labor and skill into developing our rich natural resources, farming our land, pumping our oil, cutting our timber, working our mines. We are constantly inventing and using better tools, machines, and labor-saving devices. Nowhere else in the world have people put machinery to work on such a large scale, and nowhere else do so many people have so many comforts and conveniences. Visitors from abroad look in wonder and envy at our many household appliances — our toasters, washing machines, electric irons, and vacuum cleaners. Visitors to our country can scarcely believe that so many American families can own not only these things, but also one or two cars and a television set, too. Our high standard of living is the result of hard work, inventive genius, rich resources, and tremendous industrial production.

But our country is more than a huge industrial machine turning out comforts and conveniences for us. Throughout history men have struggled for freedom and justice and the right to govern themselves. In many countries these ideals have never been achieved, but in the United States they are the very foundation of our government and our way of living. We are proud that this is so. We are proud of the democracy and the freedom for which America stands.

America Stands for Freedom

Liberty has been strong in the hearts of Americans from the time the first colonists came to our shores.

Busy factories across America make all sorts of products, some to be used at home, some to be traded overseas.

The right to be heard in court before a jury of twelve fellow-citizens is one of the most precious parts of our American heritage.

Patrick Henry expressed the American love of liberty when he cried, "Give me liberty or give me death!" Our well-loved song, *America,* calls our country "sweet land of liberty" and speaks of "freedom's song" and "freedom's holy light." Liberty is and has always been the very spirit of America. It was written into our Declaration of Independence and into our Constitution. Our Constitution with its Bill of Rights, as you know, guarantees us individual liberties which no man or government can take away. Indeed, liberty is part of our way of life. It means our right to vote and hold office, our right to free speech and religion. It means our right to take sides on any question and to stand up for what we believe. Liberty is our birthright and the most precious possession of every American.

America Stands for Equality and Justice

Hand in hand with the idea of liberty goes the belief that *all* men have a right to it. Under our Constitution and our laws all citizens have equal rights. Our courts stand for equal justice for all. It makes no difference what a man does for a living, to what race or religion he belongs, or how much money he has — he is the equal of any other citizen in the eyes of the law.

In the United States the individual is important, no matter who he is. His welfare is important, his job is important, his family is important. We Americans believe that everyone

Interesting Facts about the United States

It has:

7% of the world's land (fourth largest country)
6% of the world's population
65% of the automobiles
53% of the telephones
66% of the television sets
35% of the electric power production
30% of the cotton production

should have an opportunity to get an education and a job, and the chance to make a decent life for himself and his family. We have done a great deal to make these things possible for all Americans. Although some of our people still do not enjoy equal opportunities, we are working toward our ideal of "liberty and justice for all."

America Stands for Democracy

Abraham Lincoln described the government of the United States as a "government of the people, by the people, for the people." We believe that people are capable of making decisions for themselves. As you know, we elect the men who run our government and make our laws. If we are not satisfied with the men we have chosen, we are free to go to the polls in the next election and choose other men to represent us. Our government is based on the will of the people. The plan for that government was set down in the Constitution about 175 years ago. This plan has worked so well that in all that time only twenty-two amendments (or changes) have been added to the Constitution. Under our Constitution America has become a symbol of liberty and democracy to all the world.

"In God We Trust"

These words on all of our coins remind us that we are a religious nation. The United States was founded by men who had a deep belief in God. In our Declaration of Independence there are many references to God. The speeches and sayings of our great men show a strong religious faith. Even our national songs, like *America* and *America the Beautiful,* have a religious spirit. We all remember such lines as, "Protect us by Thy might, great God, our King," and "God shed His grace on thee." You could find many others.

Religion also has an important part in our national life today. Those of you who watched or listened to the inauguration of our President may remember that several prayers were given during the ceremony. The men who said them represented the chief religious faiths of our country — Protestant, Catholic, and Jewish. Since the time of George Washington, it has been the custom for our President and other important officials to take the oath of office with one hand on the Bible, and to finish with the words, "So help me God." It is also our custom for sessions of Congress and the Supreme Court to be opened with prayer. Of course, these customs do not mean that we have a national church or a national religion in the United States. We all know that the Constitution guarantees to each person the right to worship as he pleases.

What Patriotism Means

Some of you may have read the story of *The Man Without a Country*. It takes place in the early 1800's. At that time the idea of a United States was still strange to many Americans, especially those who lived in the frontier region of the lower Mississippi River Valley. The story is about a young army officer named Philip Nolan, who served out West. Nolan had been found guilty by a military court of taking part in a scheme to seize control over United States territory in the Southwest. When he was asked if he had anything to say about his loyalty to the United States, he cried out in a burst of anger, "D—— the United States! I wish I may never hear of the United States again!"

Nolan got his wish. He was ordered to sea on an American warship and from that time on was transferred from one warship to another, so that he never reached an American port. Nolan spent the rest of his life at sea. No one aboard ship was allowed to speak to him about the United States, or about matters having to do with our country. All conversation about America stopped when he appeared. As years went by, Nolan's feelings about his country changed completely. He died aboard ship without ever seeing the United States again. But before his death he said, ". . . there is not in America . . . a more loyal man than I. There cannot be a man who loves the old flag as I do, or prays for it as I do, or hopes for it as I do." The "man without a country" had learned at last the meaning of patriotism.

Patriotism Means Unselfish Service

Every American worthy of the name loves his country and respects the Flag. But patriotism is more than a feeling. It is a willingness to serve America, to put the nation's welfare above our own. Our history is filled with stories of American patriots who devoted their lives to their country.

You are all familiar with the loyal service given by such well-known

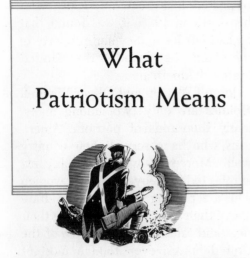

The Man Without a Country Longs for America.

Americans as George Washington, Benjamin Franklin, and Abraham Lincoln. There are other patriotic Americans you may not know so well. For instance, Dr. Joseph Warren, a young surgeon of Massachusetts, was one of the patriot leaders in the early days of the Revolution. It was Warren who arranged the signal from the Old North Church that sent Paul Revere and William Dawes riding to warn the Massachusetts farmers that the British were marching. Dr. Warren volunteered for service in the American army and was killed in the Battle of Bunker Hill. History tells us that when a friend urged him not to take part in the fighting, the young patriot replied, "It is sweet to die for one's country."

Oliver Wendell Holmes, an American patriot of more recent times, served his country in many ways. He was a Justice of the United States Supreme Court from 1902 to 1932. He started his distinguished career on the Supreme Court when he was sixty-one years old, an age when most men begin to retire from hard work. For thirty years Holmes helped to decide cases before the Supreme Court and to interpret the Constitution of the United States in the way he thought was right and just. He finally retired at the age of 91, admired and respected as a great American. After his death in 1935, it was found that he had left his money and property to the land he loved — the United States of America.

Joseph Warren and Oliver Wendell Holmes are only two among many, many thousands of patriotic Americans who have served their country well. Moreover, we have many examples today of loyal men and women who are putting the nation's welfare above their own. They are giving their time and talents to the service of the United States, even though most of them could be earning more money in business or in a profession. Hundreds of thousands of young Americans have served or are serving their country in far-off lands. Many Americans have given their lives so that the land they loved may remain strong and free. Nor should we forget to mention the millions of ordinary people who love America and serve her by being good citizens day by day.

Joseph Warren at Bunker Hill

America Needs Our Loyalty and Cooperation

These are difficult and troublesome times for our country and for all freedom-loving people. The safety of the United States and other free countries is threatened by nations whose leaders do not believe in freedom and democracy, but in force. Today, more than ever before, the United States needs the loyal support of her citizens. Free people are always stronger than people who are ruled by fear. As citizens of this great democracy, we owe America our wholehearted loyalty and service.

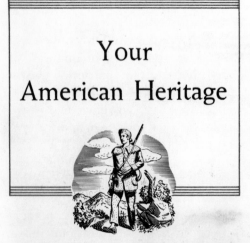

Your American Heritage

A teacher once asked her pupils this question: If you were given the choice between being poor in a country where people are free, or being very rich in a country where people have no freedoms, which would you choose? At first several pupils made the second choice. But as they discussed the question, they changed their minds. One girl summed up the ideas of the class when she said, "What good would a fine car and clothes and a beautiful home be if we didn't dare to speak our thoughts or read what we wish or go to our own church? Money wouldn't make up for losing the rights and liberties we have in the United States."

She was right. We Americans have something that money cannot buy. We sometimes call it our American *heritage,* because it is passed on to every American child as his birthright. What is our American heritage? It is made up of many things. It is our love of freedom, for which Americans have fought from Bunker Hill in Massachusetts to Bunker Hill in Korea. The Declaration of Independence, our ideals of equality and justice, our representative government and democratic way of life — all are part of our heritage. Our heritage also includes our great and bountiful land and the Stars and Stripes that fly over our nation. It is made up of little things, too — songs that stir our hearts, poems that have caught the spirit of America, and the brave words and deeds of gallant men.

Our American heritage is the free gift of all those who helped to build America, from the humblest citizen to the greatest. The men who died for freedom, the men who lived and worked to make democracy come true, have passed on this heritage to you. It represents the hopes and sacrifices and achievements of millions of Americans. It is yours because you are an American. Your heritage is your share of America and all that it stands for. You will learn more about your American heritage in the chapters that follow.

CHAPTER 2

We Americans Honor the Symbols of Our Democracy

What do you think of when you hear the name of your country, the United States of America? Do you think of the government? Of the American Flag? Of the land? You probably think of the Flag first. Much as we Americans love our country, we find it difficult to show our patriotism toward such general things as democracy and government. We find it easier to honor and respect certain *symbols* which represent the United States.

We have many patriotic symbols. For instance, we honor our Flag because it stands for our nation. The Liberty Bell symbolizes our freedom. Throughout the years various other symbols have become dear to the hearts of the American people, such as the Great Seal, the Statue of Liberty, the American eagle, and Uncle Sam. All of us should know the stories of our national symbols. In this chapter you will study the backgrounds of our national symbols and learn how they came to be honored and loved by Americans.

AMERICA, PRESENT AND PAST: *The lofty Statue of Liberty stands as a symbol of the freedoms which have brought millions of people to America's shores.*

Our Flag

What American does not feel a thrill of pride at the sight of the Stars and Stripes waving in the breeze? Our Flag, with its brilliant colors of red, white, and blue, stirs the hearts of all Americans. Our deepest feelings of patriotism are connected with the Flag. Why? The reason is that our Flag, more than any other one thing, is the symbol of the United States of America. Our Flag represents the very soul of our people and our nation.

Suppose we let the Flag speak for itself. "Americans! I am your Flag. I stand for the United States of America — for the government, for the Constitution, for the Declaration of Independence. I stand for the brave men and women who built this nation. Above all, I am a symbol of your liberty. I was created by men fighting for their freedom. For about 185 years I have waved proudly over this free land, a symbol of liberty to all the world. My stars and stripes are stained with the blood of gallant men who gave their lives to keep me flying. Remember that when you honor me, you are honoring their memory. Remember that when you are loyal to me, you are loyal to your country and all it stands for."

The Stars and Stripes Have a Meaning

While we all know in a general way what our Flag looks like, probably few of us could draw an exact picture of it. If you study the picture at the front of this book, you can count thirteen stripes running horizontally across the Flag. As you see, there are seven red stripes alternating with six white ones, with red stripes on the outside edges. In the upper quarter next to the staff is the blue field, or *union,* as it is called. You can see that it extends to the lower edge of the fourth red stripe from the top. In the blue field there are fifty five-pointed white stars arranged in five rows of six stars each, alternating with four rows of five stars each. Notice that each star is the same size and is placed with the point straight up. It is easy to see why the Flag has been given such names as "The Red, White, and Blue," "The Star-Spangled Banner," and "The Stars and Stripes."

Every part of our Flag has a meaning which we American citizens should be able to read. The blue field and its fifty white stars stand for the Union of our fifty states, that is, for the United States of America. The thirteen stripes of red and white stand for the thirteen original colonies, which became the first thirteen states of the United States. The colors of the Flag are also symbolic. For hundreds of years red has been the color

This inspiring picture of United States Marines raising the Flag at Iwo Jima reminds us of the sacrifices of young Americans in defense of freedom.

for courage. The red in our Flag represents courage, too — the courage of our forefathers who fought for independence, the courage of patriots who died for their country, and the courage of all the brave men and women who helped to build our nation. White stands for liberty — the spirit of America. Blue, true blue, is the color of the heavens and stands for loyalty — the loyalty of all Americans to their country and their Constitution. Courage, liberty, loyalty — this is the message that the "Red, White, and Blue" has for us.

The Stars and Stripes Have a Story

You have all heard the story of Betsy Ross, the pretty seamstress of Philadelphia who is said to have made our first flag. There is no definite proof that this story is true, because neither Betsy Ross, nor George Washington, nor anyone else living at that time wrote any account of it. But the Betsy Ross story has become dear to Americans, and it will probably continue as one of our national legends. Although we are not sure exactly how our first flag was made, we do know something about its early history.

When the thirteen colonies first started their struggle for independence against England, they did not have any one colonial flag. Instead, they carried dozens of different banners into battle on land and sea. Some of their flags represented the individual colonies, some belonged to certain regiments, and others represented cities and towns. Some of the colonial flags (first page of this book) showed the resentment the colonists felt toward England. There were the "pine tree" flags of New England, which bore a lone pine and the words, "An appeal to heaven." Some colonial flags expressed defiance of England with pictures of crawling rattlesnakes and the warning words, "Don't tread on me." Even the flag of the mother country itself was carried by the colonists early in the war!

From this confusion of flags, one came to be recognized as truly American. This was the "Grand Union" flag. It had thirteen red and white stripes, which to the colonists represented the thirteen colonies. In the upper quarter were the red and white crosses on a blue field which make up the flag of Britain. This may seem surprising to you, but in the early days of the war the colonists felt they were fighting for their rights and not to gain independence from the mother country. They still hoped that their grievances could be settled without separation from Britain.

In 1775 the new Grand Union flag was hoisted for the first time by John Paul Jones on the flagship of the new American navy. He called it the "Flag of America." George Washington later adopted the same flag for the new Continental army. Records show that on the first or second of January, 1776, it was hoisted over Washington's headquarters in Massachusetts in honor of the "United Colonies." The Grand Union flag was recognized as the colonial flag for the next year and a half.

With the Declaration of Independence in July, 1776, the colonies finally broke with the mother country. Then the thirteen new states no longer wanted a British emblem on their flag. So on June 14, 1777 the Continental Congress, which governed during the Revolution, adopted a new flag for a new nation. The Congress kept the thirteen stripes of the Grand Union flag, but changed the British crosses to thirteen stars in a circle on a field of blue. Today we still celebrate June 14 as Flag Day.

Each State Has a Star

Our Flag has grown with our nation. When Vermont and Kentucky became states in the late 1700's, two new stars and two new stripes were added to the Flag. By 1817 there were five more new states. Of course, we could not keep on adding stripes without spoiling the beauty of the Flag. In the following year, Congress passed a law limiting the number of stripes to thirteen. The law also said that for each new state, a star was to be added to the Flag on the Fourth of July following the admission of the state to the Union. So the number of stars in the blue field of our Flag continued to grow as our nation grew.

By 1912 there were forty-eight stars in the Flag, arranged in six rows of eight stars each. In 1959 and in 1960, the Flag changed again to make room for two more states. Alaska and Hawaii were admitted to the Union, and their stars were added to the blue field of the Flag. On July 4, 1960, the first fifty-star Flag was flown.

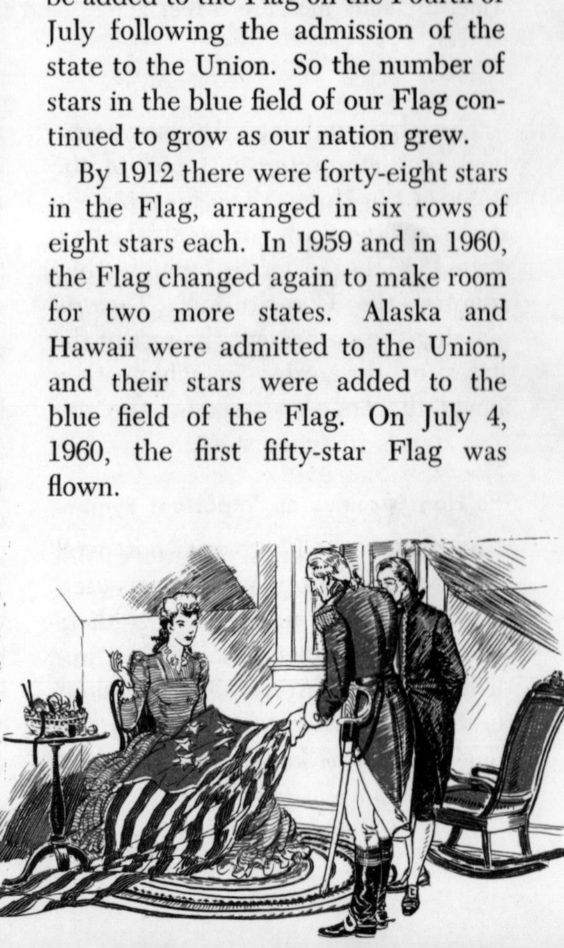

Betsy Ross

Interesting Facts about the Flag

First School Flag

The first American Flag to fly over a public schoolhouse in this country was flown over a log house at Catamount Hill, Massachusetts, in the year 1812. A tablet now marks the place where the little schoolhouse stood.

Capitol Flags

It may surprise you to learn that two Flags fly day and night over our Capitol building in Washington, D. C. These Flags above the east and west entrances are never lowered, except when new ones are needed. Flags are raised above the Senate and House wings of the Capitol also, but only when Congress is in session.

White House Flag

The Flag flies over the White House from sunrise to sunset when the President is there. If he is out of the city, the Flag is not raised.

Largest Flag

As far as is known, the largest United States Flag in the world is the one owned by the J. L. Hudson Company of Detroit, Michigan. It measures 90 feet by 230 feet and weighs 900 pounds. The stripes are 7 feet wide, the stars measure 5 feet across, and the blue field is 48¾ feet by 64 feet.

The chart on page 18 shows you how each star represents one of the states of the Union. The first thirteen stars represent the original thirteen states in the order in which they adopted the Constitution. The remaining stars represent the rest of the states in the order in which they joined the Union. Look for the star that stands for your state.

The Flag Becomes an Important Symbol

At first, our Flag was not well known among our people. It was used by our Navy, but in the Army soldiers still carried regimental flags. Not until 1834 did the Army officially adopt the Stars and Stripes. Gradually the Flag came to be known and loved by Americans. The beautiful and inspiring words of *The Star-Spangled Banner,* written during the War of 1812, called America's attention to the Flag. Soon other songs about the Flag began to appear. Poets glorified it and artists painted it.

Today our Flag flies over the schoolhouses of the land, over every government building, and on every American ship at sea. It can be seen on forest ranger stations, on public libraries, on post offices, and on every military post. The polling places where Americans vote are marked by the Flag. The nation shows respect for important public officials who die in service to their country by flying the Flag at half mast. On our national holidays the

Flag is raised over the homes, stores, and business places of America. It is flown in patriotic celebrations. And the Flag is honored by the military forces of our nation as part of their daily routine. The clear notes of the bugle sound out for *reveille* (rev′ eh-lee) in the morning, and all men at military posts assemble for the raising of the Flag and roll-call. At night the Flag is lowered while the bugle sounds *retreat*. The Flag has become an important part of American life.

Americans Show Respect for Their Flag

We all wish to show respect for our Flag, but not all Americans know the proper way to do so. Whenever the Flag is being raised or lowered, or when it is being carried past us, we should stand at attention and salute. Men and boys salute by removing their hats and holding them over their hearts. Women and girls place their hands over their hearts. Saluting the Flag is not an empty, meaningless ges-

Flag Etiquette

Here are some rules to follow in using or displaying our Flag:

We should always show respect for the Flag.

The Flag should be flown only from sunrise to sunset. It should be raised briskly and lowered slowly and with ceremony.

Always keep the Flag from touching anything beneath it, such as the ground or the floor or water.

Display, use, and store the Flag in such a way that it will be kept clean and undamaged.

Keep the Flag and flag poles free from any lettering, design, drawing, or advertisement of any kind.

Place no object or emblem of any kind above the Flag.

The Flag should not be used as a decoration to drape tables or walls. Use red, white, and blue bunting instead, with the blue on top.

The Flag should never be worn as part of a costume. It should never be used on such articles as handkerchiefs, cushions, paper napkins, and so on.

In displaying the Flag in a window or against a wall, keep the union of stars to the observer's left. When we look at the Flag, it should "read" "Stars and Stripes" from left to right (stars always first).

Our Flag represents a free people, and should always be left to fly freely to the wind.

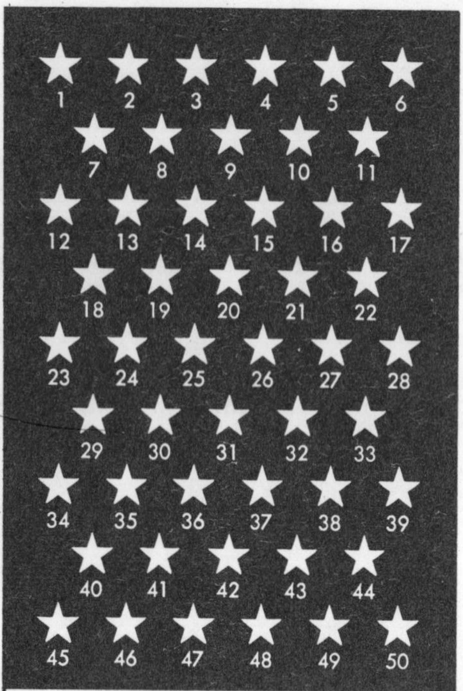

1. Delaware
2. Pennsylvania
3. New Jersey
4. Georgia
5. Connecticut
6. Massachusetts
7. Maryland
8. South Carolina
9. New Hampshire
10. Virginia
11. New York
12. North Carolina
13. Rhode Island
14. Vermont
15. Kentucky
16. Tennessee
17. Ohio
18. Louisiana
19. Indiana
20. Mississippi
21. Illinois
22. Alabama
23. Maine
24. Missouri
25. Arkansas
26. Michigan
27. Florida
28. Texas
29. Iowa
30. Wisconsin
31. California
32. Minnesota
33. Oregon
34. Kansas
35. West Virginia
36. Nevada
37. Nebraska
38. Colorado
39. North Dakota
40. South Dakota
41. Montana
42. Washington
43. Idaho
44. Wyoming
45. Utah
46. Oklahoma
47. New Mexico
48. Arizona
49. Alaska
50. Hawaii

Each State Has a Star

ture. We salute the Flag to show our love for our country and our pride in being Americans.

Because it is a symbol of our country, we should always handle the Flag with respect. It should never be allowed to touch the ground, nor should it be left carelessly about. There are certain rules about the respect due the Flag and about displaying it which we should all know. On page 17 you will find more information about what we call flag etiquette.

The Pledge of Allegiance

As you rise from your seat in the schoolroom each morning to pledge allegiance to your Flag, do you ever think of the millions of pupils all over our nation who are repeating the same words? With hands on hearts, young Americans face their Flag each school day and speak these words:

I pledge allegiance to the Flag of the United States of America and to the Republic for which it stands, one nation under God, indivisible, with liberty and justice for all.

Adults also repeat the Pledge at public meetings and patriotic rallies, but it is the schools of America that have made the Pledge a part of their daily programs. Nowhere else in the world, so far as we know, do young citizens rise and pledge their loyalty to Flag and country as ours do.

When you repeat the Pledge each day at school, do you think about the *meaning* of the words you say? A *pledge* is a promise to do something; *allegiance* means devotion or loyalty.

So when you give the Pledge, you are promising to be loyal to your Flag and your country. You are also saying these things: "I believe that our Flag stands for our country. I believe in a republic where the people choose those who govern them. I believe that our Union of fifty states cannot be divided. I believe in liberty and justice for all Americans." This is a great deal of meaning to be included in one sentence. Let us remember to recite the Pledge thoughtfully and reverently, as Americans who love our Flag and the country for which it stands.

The Great Seal of the United States

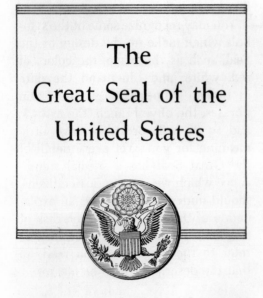

Have you ever noticed the designs on the back of a one-dollar bill? Do you know what they are? The average American doesn't realize that these circular designs represent the two sides of the Great Seal of the United States. Yet, next to the Flag, the Great Seal is the most important symbol of our nation. Every civilized country in the world has a national seal. It represents the authority of the government. Our Great Seal is more important than the signature of any man, even the President. In fact, the Great Seal might be called the "signature" of the United States government.

How the Great Seal Is Used

The Great Seal is shown on page iv at the front of this book. To stamp the Seal on government papers, there is a circular die or design of metal about three inches in diameter, showing the eagle. This Great Seal is used by the Department of State, and according to law the Secretary of State is the keeper of the Seal. It may be used only on important documents, such as treaties with foreign countries, and on all laws of the United States signed by the President. Of course, when the Seal is stamped on documents, it does not appear in color as in the picture in this book. It is merely pressed into the paper. The Seal can be seen in large size and full color above the entrance to the official headquarters of our consuls and ambassadors in foreign countries.

The Story of the Seal

Before we study the Great Seal more carefully, let us see how it came into existence. It is interesting to know that the Great Seal was considered so important that plans for it were started the very day on which the Declaration of Independence was adopted. Late in the afternoon of July 4, 1776, the Congress at Philadel-

The Great Seal of the United States shown here is over the entrance to the American Embassy in Rome.

phia appointed a committee of important men to design an official seal for the new nation. You will recognize their names — Thomas Jefferson, John Adams, and Benjamin Franklin. The first designs were not satisfactory, and other committees worked on the seal. Finally, a design using the eagle was submitted to Congress by two men named William Barton and Charles Thomson. The members of Congress approved of the description and explanation of the seal, and it was adopted in 1782. In 1789 Congress passed a law making this seal "the Seal of the United States."

The Great Seal Has Two Sides

Now let us turn once more to the picture of the Great Seal. When the Seal was adopted, no illustration had been made of it, so the exact design had to be worked out by artists from the written description. This picture shows the design that was finally decided upon. You will notice that the Seal has two sides, or disks. The main or front side is called the *obverse*. The dictionary will tell you that *obverse* means the principal or most important face of a coin or medal. The other side is known as the *reverse*, meaning opposite. It is the obverse of the Seal which is used as a stamp for documents.

You may recognize some of the symbols which make up the design of the Seal, such as the eagle, the colors of red, white, and blue, and the date in Roman numerals. But the Latin phrases, the olive branch, the arrows, and so on will probably have little meaning for you. Yet every detail of the Great Seal has a special significance which we, as American citizens, should understand. Here is an explanation of the symbols on each disk of the Seal. It would be a good idea to refer to the picture as you read, so that the description will be clearer.

Obverse of the Great Seal

The crest. You will notice at the top of the Seal a circular design, which is called the *crest*. Our nation is represented here as a new constellation, or group of stars, in the sky. The thirteen five-pointed stars on a blue field stand, of course, for the original thirteen states in our new nation. The ring of light breaking through the white cloud which surrounds the stars symbolizes God's guidance and protection of the new nation. It is interesting to know that the five-pointed white star found on our Flag and on our Seal is also used on the military planes of our country, and on military insignia. The entire obverse of the Great Seal is worn on the caps of military officers, and appears also on the uniform buttons of army officers.

National coat of arms. The rest of the Seal makes up the coat of arms of the United States — the eagle, the shield, the scroll with its motto, the olive branch, and the bundle of arrows. All or part of the coat of arms is used by various departments of the government for seals, letterheads, and decoration.

The American *eagle* was selected as the bird which would best represent the United States because of its proud appearance, size, and strength. The original description of the Seal called for "an American eagle with wings expanded," which is what you see in the illustration. Of course, no bird could possibly assume this unnatural position! The eagle itself has become the national emblem of the United States. You will read more about it later in this chapter.

The *shield* on the breast of the eagle has a bar of solid blue, which represents Congress. The thirteen vertical stripes of white and red represent the first thirteen states. The red, white, and blue on the shield are, of course, our national colors.

Notice the *motto* that appears on the scroll held in the eagle's beak. The Latin words *E Pluribus Unum* mean "One out of many," and refer to our Union of many states. The motto reminds us, too, that we can be a strong nation only if we work together as one for our country's welfare. *E Pluribus Unum* is stamped on most of our coins.

You notice that the eagle clutches in his right talon an *olive branch.* For many centuries the olive branch has been known as the symbol of peace. A bundle of thirteen arrows in the eagle's left talon stands for our determination to defend ourselves in case of war. The number thirteen again represents the thirteen states. As a whole, the obverse of our Great Seal has this meaning: "We are a new and sovereign nation, a strong Union of many states, with a belief in God. We are powerful like the eagle. While we want peace with all nations, we are ready at the same time to defend ourselves against attack."

Reverse of the Seal

The pyramid. The pyramid in the center of the reverse side of the Seal represents the strength and stability

"In God We Trust"

Our national motto appears on all our coins, from pennies to silver dollars. It was first put on our coins in the 1860's. Earlier than that, our faith in God's guidance and protection was stressed in the design of the Great Seal. The same trust is stated in the last stanza of our National Anthem.

of our government. It was left unfinished to show that the new nation would grow in size and strength. Notice that the date when our nation was born, 1776, is inscribed in Roman numerals at the base of the pyramid.

The eye. The huge eye above the pyramid stands for the watchful eye of God. The light around the eye signifies the glory of God. Both sides of our Great Seal remind us that our nation was founded upon faith in God.

Mottoes. The Latin motto over the eye means "God has favored this undertaking." Underneath the pyramid another Latin motto states, "A new order of the ages." Both mottoes refer to our new nation and its democratic government.

The reverse of the Great Seal is not so well known as the obverse. Taken as a whole, the reverse of the Seal means, "Our nation was founded in 1776, with the help of God. It is strong, and will continue to grow in size and power. For the first time in history a nation is established with a government run by the people."

As we have mentioned, both sides of the Seal are found on the back of a dollar bill. The next time you have one, see how many of the symbols on the Seal you can explain.

Interesting Facts about the Bald Eagle

Size	35 to 42 inches long; wingspread 7 to 8 feet
Weight	8 to 12 pounds
Nest	3 to 8 feet across; 3 to 8 feet deep
Food	Fish, snakes, small animals, and birds
Home	High trees or high cliffs near water

The American Eagle

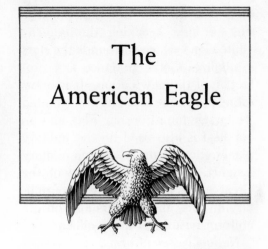

Every American knows that the eagle is our national emblem. But not many of us have ever seen an American eagle, nor do we know the story of how it happened to be chosen to symbolize our nation. In fact, the eagle, once a familiar bird, has almost become a "forgotten" American.

The Eagle Becomes a National Emblem

The eagle became our national bird when it was chosen to appear on the Great Seal of the United States. We were by no means the first nation to use the eagle as a symbol. From early times this bird has been a sign of strength and courage. Centuries ago an Egyptian ruler used the eagle as a symbol of his power. The figure of an eagle was also on the standards of the Roman armies before the time of Christ, and later on those of Napoleon's armies. Many other nations also have used the eagle as a symbol. In fact, Benjamin Franklin objected to the eagle because it had been used in the Old World. Franklin preferred the wild turkey, which was a bird of the New World. But our Congress favored the eagle on the design of the Great Seal, and as you have read, it was adopted in 1782.

The eagle became a popular ornament in the early years of our nation. In addition to appearing on our stamps, coins, and medals, and on military uniforms, it could be seen in almost any home. The eagle appeared in many poses above mirrors and on furniture as a decoration. It was carved from wood and cast in metal for ornaments. Eagles were embroidered on women's sashes and engraved on men's metal buttons. Eagle designs were used on dinnerware and even on buttermolds. Speakers of those days referred to the eagle in flowery words as the emblem of our independence and the guardian of our liberty.

Today we Americans believe that it is not in good taste to put our national emblem on furniture or clothing. The eagle, as it appears on the Great Seal, is now used chiefly on stamps and money, and for government and military insignia. It appears, for instance, on stationery used by the Department of Defense, on military discharges, and so on.

Laws Protect the Eagle

The bird which became our national emblem is known as the American, or bald, eagle. He is a splendid-looking bird, with dark feathers and a white head, neck, and tail. He is called the bald eagle because his white head gives him a bald appearance. The eagle soars at enormous heights on his great wings, which appear to be almost motionless as he flies. In the early days of our country, he lived in high trees along the banks of rivers, where fish were plentiful. But as settlements advanced into the forest regions, and trees were cut down, the bald eagle began to disappear from settled regions. Today there are few bald eagles left in the United States.

In recent years the states have passed laws against shooting the eagle, because there is danger that he may die out altogether. He can still be found in the deep forests of Florida and a few other places. Alaska is a favorite breeding place of the bald eagle, but until recently he was not safe there. Because the eagle feeds on the valuable salmon which swim up the rivers to breed, the Alaskan government permitted the shooting of

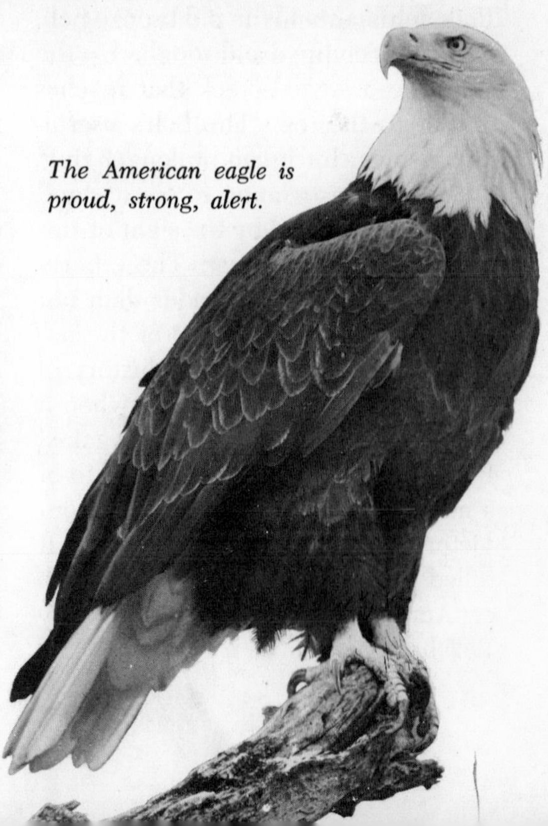

The American eagle is proud, strong, alert.

the birds when they were found damaging other wild life or property. As a result, thousands were killed. Today, however, the eagles are protected in all states by federal law. We do not want the symbol of our liberty to vanish from our country.

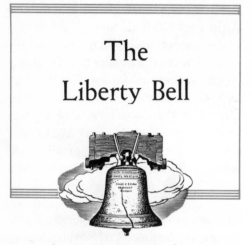

The Liberty Bell

In Independence Hall in the city of Philadelphia stands an old bronze bell. The rim is chipped and rough. Up the side runs a jagged crack that reaches almost to the top. The bell's usefulness is over, for it can no longer ring. Yet Americans who go to see it stand in reverence, awed by the sight of this relic of our nation's past. The Liberty Bell, twenty-five years older than our nation, has tolled for most of the important events in the early history of our country. It pealed loudly when it called the colonists to rise against British tyranny; it rang in the birth of a new nation in 1776; it rang out our victories during the Revolution; it tolled in muffled tones for the death of American patriots. The Liberty Bell has come to be a symbol of the freedom which we all hold dear. Every American should know its story.

The Bell Is Born

Strange as it may seem, in the first part of its life the Bell we honor today was just a plain bell, and not a very good one at that. In 1751 the people of Philadelphia were celebrating the fiftieth anniversary of religious freedom in their colony of Pennsylvania. As a memorial of the anniversary, the Assembly (law-making body) ordered a bell to be made in London, "a good bell, of about 2000 pounds weight." The Assemblymen planned to hang the bell in their new State House or capitol building. They asked that the following quotation from the Bible be put on the bell in "large, round letters":

> Proclaim Liberty throughout all the land
> unto all the inhabitants thereof.
> Leviticus xxv. 10.

Little did the members of the Assembly know that their bell was destined to proclaim liberty from England throughout the colonies!

After the bell arrived from England, it was "cracked by the stroke of the clapper" while being tested for its sound. Two workmen whose names, Pass and Stowe, appear on the Liberty Bell offered to break up the bell, melt the metal, and recast it. They added an ounce and a half of American copper to each pound of the old bell to make it less brittle. Their first bell had a poor tone, so they tried once more, and finally got a bell with a

Measurements of the Liberty Bell

Circumference around the lip	12 feet
Circumference around the crown	7 feet, 6 inches
Lip to the crown	3 feet
Height over the crown	2 feet, 3 inches
Thickness at lip	3 inches
Thickness at crown	1¼ inch
Weight	2080 pounds
Length of clapper	3 feet, 2 inches

satisfactory tone. In 1753 the great new bell was hung in the steeple of the Pennsylvania State House.

The Bell Sounds Defiance of the British

It was not long before the Liberty Bell began to take part in the events of the day. A bell, you know, was very important in colonial times when there were no radios and few newspapers. Bells tolled for all important meetings and to announce special news.

In the 1760's quarrels with the mother country were beginning, and the Liberty Bell called the people of Philadelphia together for one important happening after another. After the Stamp Act was passed in 1765, the Bell called the people of Philadelphia to a town meeting. Here they resolved not to allow the hated stamps to be sold. But the Stamp Act was enforced by British officials. Then the Bell tolled again to announce the "death of liberty," and the people burned the stamps in protest. The Liberty Bell raised its voice against the tea tax, and pealed triumphantly when the ship carrying the "detestable tea" to Philadelphia was turned back. The news of the Battle of Lexington and Concord was also announced by the Bell.

The Bell did not ring on July 4, 1776, when the Declaration of Independence was adopted. On July 8 instead, it called the Congress and the townspeople to hear the Declaration read aloud. We might say that on this great day its voice was heard not only throughout the land but around the world!

We are told that when the people of Philadelphia heard the momentous words that made them free, they were at first serious and silent. To them it was not an occasion for rejoicing. They knew that a grim war must be fought and many lives lost before freedom could be won. But as they left the State House, they tore down the British coat of arms on the door.

The Liberty Bell Continues to Announce Important Events

When General Howe and his British soldiers marched on Philadelphia in 1777, the Bell was smuggled out of

Saving the Liberty Bell

Visitors to Independence Hall eagerly study the Liberty Bell, a vivid reminder of our country's struggle for independence.

town in a wagon and hauled to Allentown, Pennsylvania, where it was hidden under the floor of a church. The next year the Bell was returned to the State House, which was now known as "Independence Hall." It rang out the surrender of Cornwallis at Yorktown, and the peace with Britain in 1783. The Bell tolled solemnly, its tones muffled, for the funeral of the beloved George Washington. It rang to honor those two great patriots, Thomas Jefferson and John Adams, who both died on July 4, 1826. (See page 188 for the story of their deaths.)

Liberty Bell

That old state-house bell is silent,
Hushed is now its clamorous tongue;
But the spirit it awakened
Still is living, ever young.

AUTHOR UNKNOWN

The Bell tolled also for the death of Lafayette, the gallant French general who fought in Washington's army.

But the Bell was getting old; its voice was no longer clear. In 1835 when it was tolling the death of John Marshall, the great Chief Justice of the Supreme Court, its bronze side cracked wide open, and it never actually rang again. The life of the Bell was ended, but not its story.

The Bell Symbolizes the Spirit of Liberty

By 1816 Independence Hall was no longer in use as a capitol building. It was bought by the city of Philadelphia to be preserved as a monument. For many years the old Bell hung in the tower below the belfry, neglected and dusty. Boys in the town were said to hit it with rocks to knock off pieces for souvenirs. Not until 1876 did Americans begin to realize the importance of the Liberty Bell. It was displayed at the Centennial celebration in Philadelphia, marking the hundredth anniversary of our independence. The old Bell was something out of our past that people could see and touch; it was a symbol of our struggle for liberty.

People in other parts of the country wanted to see the Bell, too. From 1885 to 1917 it was sent to world fairs, expositions, and patriotic celebrations in many cities. Americans everywhere crowded to see the historic Bell. In 1917 a new crack developed, and the Bell's travels ended. It was returned to Independence Hall, where it is kept as a cherished symbol of our nation's past. On June 6, 1944, during

World War II, Americans heard the old Bell again. It was struck with a rubber mallet to celebrate D-Day, when the Allied troops landed on the coast of France. (Early in the day, the twelve letters of "Independence" were tapped out; in the evening seven tones were sounded to represent the seven letters in "Liberty.") Because of its historic value, the care of the Bell has been taken over by the national government. It is now in the care of the National Park Service of the Department of the Interior.

Every year a million Americans go to see the Liberty Bell. It stands just inside the doors of Independence Hall under the old steeple where it used to ring. As the picture (page 26) shows you, the Bell is hanging from the original yoke with strong iron supports at each side. The platform on which it rests is set on a four-wheeled truck which can be quickly moved in case of fire or other emergency.

Those who go to see the Bell can clearly read the inscription, the date, and the names of the makers. There are guards who gladly answer the many questions asked by visitors. The guards say that the first thing most people want to do is touch the Bell. Men are expected to remove their hats, but the guards seldom have to remind them. When a man steps into the doorway and sees the cracked old Bell with its chipped rim, he seems to understand that it deserves his respect. The men who founded our nation have long been gone, but the Liberty Bell remains as a lasting symbol of our freedom.

The Statue of Liberty

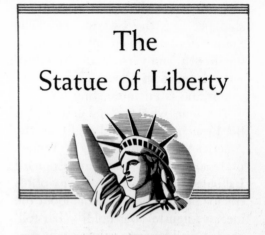

Americans returning home from foreign lands crowd to the rails of their ship as it nears New York harbor. Cries of "There she is!" can be heard, and all eyes are turned to the magnificent statue of a goddess, holding high a lighted torch in welcome. The sight of the Statue of Liberty is one that no traveler forgets. To the American returning home, the Statue is a symbol of his native land and all it means to him. To the foreigner arriving at our shores, it represents the freedom for which our country stands. Since 1886, when the Statue was erected in New York harbor, it has become one of the famous symbols of liberty to Americans and to all the world.

The Statue Has a Story

The Statue of "Liberty Enlightening the World" was a gift of goodwill and friendship from the people of France to the people of the United States. France, you may remember, sent armed forces to help the United States during the Revolutionary War.

Since that time there has been friendship between the two nations. The Statue was built to commemorate the hundredth anniversary of American independence in 1876. The story of the Statue is an interesting one.

The man who first suggested that the French people send a gift for the American Centennial was a French professor by the name of Edouard Laboulaye (la-boo-lay'). Many of his friends became enthusiastic about the idea. Auguste Bartholdi (bar-toll' dee), a well-known sculptor, was sent to the United States to look about and get ideas for a monument. He returned inspired with the idea of erecting a huge statue of the Goddess of Liberty on an island in New York Harbor. A lighted torch in the hand of the Statue was to serve as a beacon for the ships going in and out of the chief gateway to America.

Laboulaye and his friends liked the plan. But it would take a great deal of money. It had been decided when Bartholdi was in America that if the French people raised money for the Statue itself, Americans would furnish funds for a pedestal on which to place it. A committee was formed to interest the people of France in the idea. All over France, people were told about the Statue. As interest grew, bazaars and fairs were held to raise funds. Gifts of money began to pour in from rich and poor, from school children, farmers, and shopkeepers. Soon there was enough to start work on the Statue.

Creating the Statue of Liberty

The Statue Grows

Bartholdi began work on a clay model of the figure he had in mind. After several changes he completed the Statue. It represented the Greek Goddess of Liberty dressed in flowing garments and holding a torch high in her right hand. The torch symbolized the light of liberty. In her left hand she held a tablet, or book, representing the Declaration of Independence. At her feet lay a broken chain to represent the breaking of the bonds between England and the United States. The Statue was enthusiastically approved by the committee. The chief problem now was to enlarge the original five-foot model to 151 feet! Most statues, as you know, are chiseled from some kind of stone or cast from metal. But Bartholdi had a different idea for his figure. It was to be made of copper sheets shaped into parts of the body and riveted together.

You may be wondering how Bartholdi got patterns for shaping the enormous arms, legs, head, and so on. He did it by making a series of models,

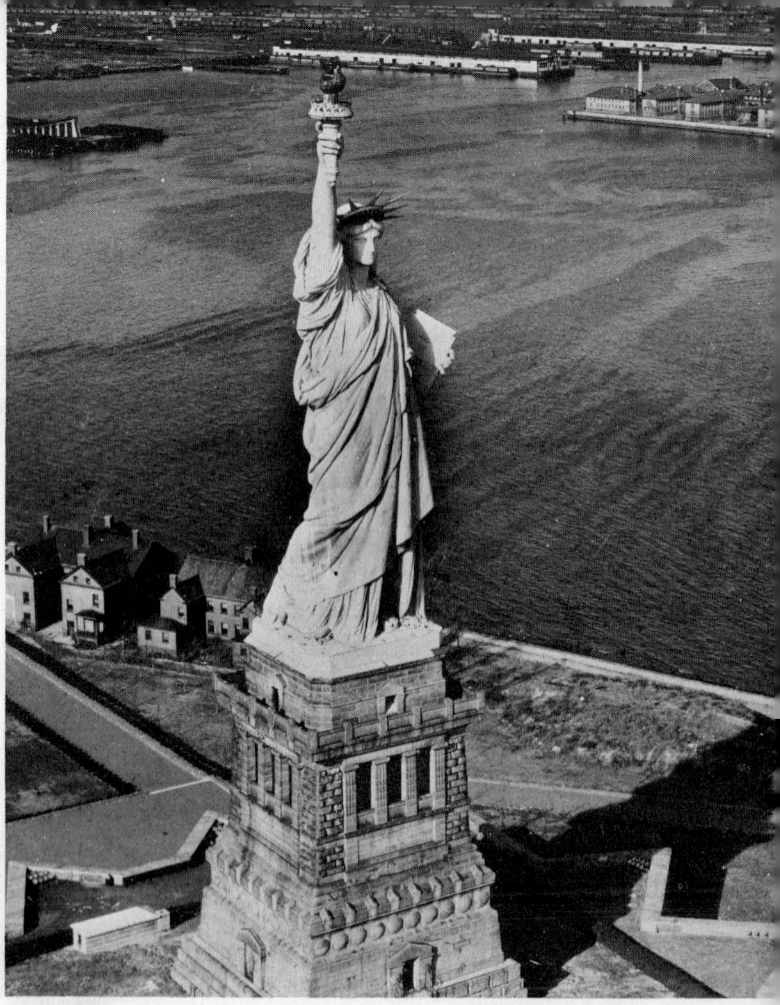

Even when seen from an airplane, the Statue of Liberty towers over New York Harbor. In this picture, the Jersey City piers and Ellis Island are in the background.

each larger than the other until the proper size was reached. He started with a nine-foot model of clay, which he himself made as an exact copy of his smaller original. This model was then divided into small sections, and after careful measuring and figuring, each section was enlarged in proportion to make another figure 36 feet high. This process was continued until the model for the huge figure was at last ready. Then wooden patterns for the workmen to use were carved in the exact shape of the final model.

The final step was shaping the great sheets of copper about as thick as a nickel. These were hammered and pressed and fitted over the wooden patterns until each sheet fitted perfectly. Each copper part — fingers, nose, and so on — was held firm by bands of iron placed inside. This was the "skin" of the Statue. It now remained to fit it over the "bones."

The Statue Is Completed

A great skeleton of ironwork was built to serve as the support for the Statue. The work was carried on under the direction of Alexandre Eiffel (eye'ful), the builder of the famous Eiffel Tower in Paris. Of course, no building would hold a framework 151 feet in height, so the skeleton was constructed in the open. As each copper part was finished, it was lifted onto the iron bone which was to support it, and riveted onto the piece next to it. You can imagine the interest and curiosity of the people of Paris as the great structure began to tower over buildings in the neighborhood.

All this work had taken four years. The committee realized that the Statue could not be completed for the Centennial in 1876, but Bartholdi hastened to work on the great right hand holding the torch. The hand was shipped to Philadelphia in pieces, put together again, and exhibited at the Centennial celebration. Meanwhile, the tremendous task of completing the Statue went on. At last, in 1884, it was ready. It was taken apart, the pieces labelled and packed in over 200 cases, and sent to the United States. There was a great celebration the day the Statue arrived. Flags of the United States and of France flew from the buildings of New York City. Bands played and cannon roared as a United States warship escorted the French ship into the harbor. The President of the United States was in a boat at the head of the procession. The cases were unloaded on Bedloe's Island, a small island in the harbor where the Statue was to stand.

The Statue Finds Its Place

An embarrassing delay followed. Not enough money had been raised in the United States to build the 150-foot pedestal or base on which the Statue was to stand! It seems that Americans had not understood that the monument was a gift to all the American people from the French people. Because it was to be placed in New York's harbor, it was believed that the Statue was a "lighthouse" for New York City alone. An American newspaper man who owned a paper called the *New York World* came to the rescue. Through his paper he explained the story of the Statue of Liberty. He called on the American people to meet what he called "the most generous gesture one nation ever made to another." Money soon started coming in from all over the nation. American schoolchildren, like the French children, gave their pennies to the cause. The pedestal was at last completed and the great Statue erected upon it after a delay of nearly two years.

On October 28, 1886, the Statue of "Liberty Enlightening the World" was dedicated in a ceremony at Madison Square in New York City. People gathered by the thousands on the streets and in grandstands to see the celebration. President Cleveland of the United States, Bartholdi himself, and other prominent persons took part in the ceremony as the Statue was presented to the people of the United States. Later on at Bedloe's Island, Bartholdi pulled aside the French flag which had been draped over the head of the Goddess, and revealed all of the magnificent figure. At last, after many years, the monument which

Interesting Facts about the Statue of Liberty

	Feet	Inches
Height from base to torch	151	1
Foundation of pedestal to torch	305	1
Heel to top of head	111	1
Length of hand	16	5
Index finger	8	0
Circumference at second finger joint	3	6
Size of finger nail		13 × 10
Head from chin to cranium	17	3
Head, thickness from ear to ear	10	0
Distance across eye	2	6
Length of nose	4	6
Right arm, length	42	0
Right arm, greatest thickness	12	0
Thickness of waist	35	0
Width of mouth	3	0
Tablet, length	23	7
Tablet, width	13	7
Tablet, thickness	2	0

Number of visitors a year: over 500,000
Cost of maintenance: $50,000 a year

symbolized the goodwill and friendship of France stood in its place at the gateway to America. Facing the Old World, her light held high, the Statue seems to be welcoming newcomers to the "Land of Liberty."

Storms have beaten upon her, lightning has struck her, but no harm has come to the Goddess. There have been a few changes since 1886. The salt air has turned the bright copper to green, and many electric bulbs have taken the place of the oil lamp which was formerly in the torch. The Statue of Liberty has been declared a national monument like the Liberty Bell and is looked after by the National Park Service. It was made a national monument because our government wished to care for it and make it possible for Americans to visit it. Through the years the Statue has become a symbol of the liberty which is so dear to Americans.

We Visit the Statue

Over half a million visitors go to see the Statue every year. Let us suppose that we are among these visitors. At the ferry landing in Battery Park at the southern tip of Manhattan Island, we take a boat for Liberty Island (as Bedloe's Island is called now). Looking ahead from the boat, we see that the island is not far from the Battery, actually less than two miles. The Statue appears much larger as we approach the island. Once ashore we walk toward it, marvelling at its enormous size. The pedestal is built upon a large star-shaped foundation where, we learn, an army fort once stood.

As we go inside the main entrance to the Statue of Liberty, we notice an inscription. It is the beautiful poem by Emma Lazarus, an American poet who lived from 1849 to 1888. Her parents left Russia to seek liberty in America. Her poem tells how the Goddess of Liberty welcomes the immigrants from "ancient lands" to our land of freedom. Here is a part of it:

> Give me your tired, your poor,
> Your huddled masses yearning to breathe free,
> The wretched refuse of your teeming shore.
> Send these, the homeless, tempest-tossed to me,
> I lift my lamp beside the golden door!

We find that we can either climb stairs up to the balcony near the top of the pedestal, or we can pay a small amount and take an elevator. From the balcony we get a view of the harbor and the famous skyline of New York. We can see the great bridges in the vicinity and the busy cities of nearby New York and New Jersey.

"Give Me Your Tired, Your Poor . . ."

This poem by Emma Lazarus has been set to beautiful music by Irving Berlin, one of America's popular song writers. You may have heard it sung, or perhaps you have sung it in a school music program.

Next we start the long climb up a spiral staircase which will take us from the feet to the head of the Statue. We are glad to stop for breath on the two rest platforms which make the way up the 168 steps a little easier. Puffing slightly, we arrive at last on the platform inside the head, which is large enough to hold 30 people. From here we can look out the windows just under the rays of the crown. It is a wonderful feeling to be 260 feet above the sea, looking down upon the scene below. We are especially interested in seeing the tablet which the Goddess carries in her left hand. In Roman numerals it reads July 4, 1776. We ask about going farther up into the arm, but are told by the guard that the arm is closed to the public for safety reasons.

The trip down is much easier, and we soon find ourselves on the promenade, or paved walk, outside the foot of the pedestal. From here we get an excellent view of the Statue, and can see how the sheets of copper were overlapped and riveted. We see the huge floodlights that light up the Statue at night, so that it appears as a shining Goddess, lighting the way for ships to enter the harbor. We find that we can buy souvenir statuettes, postcards, booklets, and even lunch if we wish. We sign our names in the great leather book which is kept for visitors' signatures. At last we return to New York, tired but content. We realize the Goddess has a lesson for us — that we Americans must never forget to hold high the torch of our liberty.

Our National Characters

Not all our national symbols are serious ones. We Americans have created some humorous characters who represent ourselves and our government. You have all heard of Yankee Doodle and Uncle Sam. Not so many of you know about Brother Jonathan. Let us turn back to the days of the Revolutionary War and find out how these national characters came to be.

Yankee Doodle

The term "Yankee Doodle" is older than our nation. It was first used by British troops in the 1760's to poke fun at the awkward and untrained colonial soldiers. The British considered the colonists simple country fellows, rather crude and unpolished, so they ridiculed them in a good-natured way by calling them Yankee Doodle. Soon a song about Yankee Doodle began to be heard. Its words were set to a popular tune of the day. Although the words poked fun at them, the Americans took it over as a marching song during the Revolution (see page 176). Apparently they didn't mind making fun of themselves, for they sang the words lustily as they marched to war:

Father and I went down to camp,
Along with Captain Goodwin,
And there we saw the men and boys,
As thick as hasty puddin'!
  Yankee Doodle, keep it up,
  Yankee Doodle dandy,
  Mind the music and the step
  And with the girls be handy!

After the war, the nickname Yankee Doodle hung on. New Englanders were often called Yankees. During the War Between the States, the Southerners referred to all Northerners as Yankees. Years later, when we entered the First World War, our troops were called "Yanks" by the Europeans. In Mexico and other parts of Latin America, we are often called "Yanquis." Today the term Yankee generally refers to any inhabitant of the United States. But it no longer means a country bumpkin, as it did two hundred years ago!

Brother Jonathan

Another humorous character, called "Brother Jonathan," appeared during our war for independence. According to the story, Brother Jonathan was Washington's friend, Governor Jonathan Trumbull of Connecticut. When Washington needed arms and materials for the war, he would say, "We must consult Brother Jonathan." This expression came into common use, and before long Brother Jonathan became a symbol of the American nation and people. In 1787 he was the leading character in a play that pictured our new nation.

Brother Jonathan was a crude fellow with little schooling, but he was wide awake and well able to look out for himself. Brother Jonathan appealed to Americans. They didn't mind his seeming, like many of them, a shrewd country lad with little education and social polish. He represented the pride those early Americans felt in their nationality. When artists began drawing Brother Jonathan, they pictured him in different ways. In time, however, most people came to think of Brother Jonathan as a tall, thin, awkward fellow with a long-tailed coat and a high hat. He had a humorous countenance, but you could tell by looking at him that Brother Jonathan was nobody's fool!

Uncle Sam

As time went on, Brother Jonathan gradually disappeared, and in his place came Uncle Sam. Like our nation itself, Uncle Sam is older and wiser than Brother Jonathan. But Uncle Sam, too, stands for the qualities of the American people. He is a good-hearted fellow, honest, hard-working,

A "Yank" tells two Korean children a bedtime story. By their generosity and kindness, American servicemen, often referred to as Yankees, have won the friendship of children in many lands.

and shrewd. He also symbolizes our federal government, and looks after our people with wisdom and goodwill. As you can see from the drawing on this page, Uncle Sam is a "lanky Yankee" with a top hat, striped pants, and a star-spangled vest.

There are several stories of how Uncle Sam came into existence. The most likely story is the one about Sam Wilson, who inspected supplies for our troops during the War of 1812. When he approved the contents of a case, he would stamp on it "E.A.—U.S.," for the name of the contractor for whom he worked, Ebenezer Anderson, and for the United States. A workman jokingly explained that "U.S." stood for Uncle Sam, and people began to use the expression as a nickname for our national government. As years went by, government employees would say, "I work for Uncle Sam." Cartoons of Uncle Sam also began to appear. Those drawn during the War Between the States by a famous cartoonist, Thomas Nast, made Uncle Sam a familiar figure. From then on the idea of Uncle Sam as the tall, thin Yankee became popular. Uncle Sam appeared in parades to represent the government. He was pictured in newspapers and magazines, and referred to in speeches. Uncle Sam represents the pride we feel in our people and our government. He is a personal symbol of our affection and loyalty. It is to be hoped that he will not disappear from American life.

Uncle Sam

★ ★ ★ ★ ★ ★ ★

You have read the stories of our national symbols. In themselves they mean little — a flag, a seal, a bird, a bell, a statue, and a man in a top hat. But to Americans these things have become precious. We honor them because they represent our country and our liberty. They remind us of our glorious past; they symbolize our faith in the future.

CHAPTER 3

Our Documents of Freedom

Below the main floor in the National Archives Building in Washington, D.C., is one of the strongest safes in the world. It is burglarproof and fireproof. Its walls are of fifteen-inch steel; its two doors weigh five tons each. The safe is so strong that if the entire building should fall on it, its contents would not be hurt. Each morning two marble cases are raised from the safe to the floor above by an electric elevator. Each night the cases are lowered into the safe and the great doors closed.

What treasures are these that our government guards so carefully? The words engraved in back of the two display cases give the answer:

THE
DECLARATION OF INDEPENDENCE

THE
CONSTITUTION
OF THE
UNITED STATES OF AMERICA

AND THE
BILL OF RIGHTS

These original documents are our most precious heritage from America's past. They are written by hand in the spelling and style of another day. Their ink is faded by age. In order to preserve them, they have

AMERICA, PRESENT AND PAST: *In the heart of modern Philadelphia, Independence Hall recalls to us the birth of our historic Documents of Freedom.*

been sealed in helium gas and protected from the light by tinted glass.

Visitors may step up to the two cases for a closer look at these old documents. Although their value is beyond price, they are not hidden away from public gaze. They belong to the American people. They mean as much to us Americans living today as they did to the people of the 1700's.

The *Declaration of Independence* proclaimed to the world the birth of a new and free nation. The *Constitution* is the plan of government for that nation. The *Bill of Rights* guarantees certain precious rights to all Americans. These are documents of American freedom, and they contain the ideals on which our nation was founded. Like the men who wrote these documents, we Americans believe in the ideals of liberty and justice and self-government. And like Americans of the past we stand ready, if need be, to defend these ideals.

The Declaration of Independence

"When in the Course of human events," . . . *"all men are created equal,"* . . . *"Life, Liberty and the pursuit of Happiness."* These words are from our Declaration of Independence, the document that announced the birth of our new nation in 1776. When it was published, people in Europe as well as America talked about it. It would have been a remarkable document if it had done no more than declare the independence of the American colonies from Great Britain. But the Declaration of Independence did more than that. It boldly announced the idea of a government in which all men would have the right to freedom, to equality, and to a voice in their own government! It declared the intention of the American colonies to break away from England and establish such a government. In a world where kings and emperors ruled much as they pleased, this was indeed a bold step. The Declaration of Independence became an inspiration and a hope to all men that they too would one day be free. It is one of the most famous documents in the history of mankind.

America Started as a Land of Freedom

The story behind the Declaration of Independence is a familiar one, for it is the story of the thirteen English colonies in America and how they became free. Although we shall not try to retell in detail the early history of our country, it will be worthwhile to review briefly the events that led to our war for independence.

You will probably remember that some colonists from England and other European countries came to the

New World in search of adventure and riches. Most of the colonists, however, wanted freedom — freedom to worship as they pleased, freedom to earn a decent living for themselves and their children, freedom to live on land which they could call their own. In America the settlers found the freedom and the opportunities they had dreamed of. They worked hard to make a new life in the wilderness. They cut down forests and planted crops; they built towns, started small businesses, established schools.

England was a long way off, so these men and women had to depend on themselves if they were to survive in the new land. By the 1700's a way of life had grown up that was quite different from the old civilization of Europe. The colonists had worked out their own ways of doing things and their own ideas. For instance, they judged a man by what he could do rather than by his wealth or the position of his family. They also believed that his religion was his own business, not the business of the government.

The American colonists had other very definite ideas, too. They had brought with them the English belief that the people should have some say in their government. Although all the settlers were subjects of the British king, the voters of each colony chose representatives to take part in running the affairs of the colony. By 1750 there were thirteen colonies in America, each one governed separately, but all thinking alike as far as their rights were concerned. The colonists were loyal to England, but they had become American in their ways of living and thinking.

The Colonists Resent Taxation by England

The men who ran the British government, including King George III, did not know much about the independent, liberty-loving men and women who lived in America. In fact, few English leaders had ever been in America. Perhaps that is why they made such a bad mistake in trying to tax the colonists. Their reason for doing so was that England had spent a good deal of money on her American colonies. The colonies had to be protected against attacks by the French and Indians, and troops for this purpose cost money. So Parliament (the law-making body in England) decided it was only fair to tax the colonists to help pay expenses. But in 1765, when Parliament passed the Stamp Act to raise money, trouble started. The colonies refused to buy the stamps. They argued this way: "We are not represented in the British Parliament, therefore it has no right to tax us. Only our colonial assemblies in which we *are* represented have the right to tax us. We will not pay taxes voted by Parliament."

Everywhere people were talking against "taxation without representation." The colonists raised such vigorous protests that the Stamp Act was repealed. But soon there were new taxes. The angry colonists hit back where it hurt the most. They refused to trade with Great Britain. Finally these hated taxes were also repealed, though Parliament kept the tax on tea just to show the colonists who was "boss." In a famous "tea party" the people of Boston dumped the cargoes of tea in the harbor to show the British how Americans felt about taxation. But if the colonists were stubborn, so was King George. Boston was punished by having its port closed to all shipping, and Massachusetts was placed under strict military government. The punishment of Boston aroused all the colonies. They began to think and talk about their rights and liberties as they never had before.

An angry meeting in Boston's Old South Church led to the famous Tea Party in 1773.

The First Continental Congress Complains to the King

If King George had *wanted* to bring the thirteen American colonies together, he could not have found a better way than by taking away the rights they believed were theirs. Up to this time the colonies had not worked together much. But because patriots in all colonies felt the same way about an important matter — taxation — they decided to send delegates to a *Continental Congress* in Philadelphia. In the fall of 1774 the Congress met to decide what the colonies should do about their quarrel with England.

Although all the delegates to the Continental Congress believed that taxation was unfair, they did not all agree on what to do about it. Some said, "In spite of our trouble with the mother country, we are still loyal British subjects. If we do not take any rash steps, this trouble will be settled peacefully." But others replied, "We must stand together to defend our rights, even if it means bloodshed. That is the only way to make England see that we do not mean to give in." Finally they decided to appeal once more to the King for their rights. They sent him a petition, protesting against the punishment of Massachusetts and against unfair taxation by Parliament. The delegates of the First Continental Congress then returned to their homes, little dreaming that the King would refuse even to read their petition.

Under a giant elm tree in Cambridge, Massachusetts, George Washington took command of the colonial army on July 3, 1775.

War Brings the Idea of Independence

All through the colonies men began to talk of what they would do if the King did not recognize their rights. Since they were determined not to give in, they must prepare to fight. In Massachusetts and other colonies, men began to collect guns and powder and to meet for military drill. They hoped that their willingness to fight would show King George how strongly they felt about their rights. Then one day in the spring of 1775 something happened that shocked all the colonists. In the Massachusetts towns of Lexington and Concord, British troops had fired on the colonial militia, and in the fighting that followed the British had been forced to retreat to Boston. War had begun! The men of Massachusetts prepared to defend themselves.

What would the colonists' next step be? England had shown no signs of giving in. In the year that followed, the King not only refused to listen to their grievances but declared them rebels and traitors. The only way to peace would be to surrender their rights. Among the colonists a bold word began to be heard more and more. That word was *independence*. At home, in their churches, at meeting places, there were people who began to talk about independence. Some leading men in the colonies began to speak openly for separation from Great Britain. Since we are already at war, they said, why not fight for independence?

The Second Continental Congress Meets

In May, 1775, delegates from the colonies met again. This time as they rode through the streets of Philadelphia, they were greeted with cheers by the people. The colonies had sent their leading men to the Second Continental Congress. There was the tall, dignified man from Virginia who was later to lead the Continental Army through a long war for freedom — George Washington. There was sober-faced John Adams, the short, stout lawyer from Boston who was said to be in favor of independence. His cousin, Samuel Adams, was there, too. Sam Adams had spoken so loudly and acted so boldly against the British that they considered him a dangerous rebel.

Another delegate was Patrick Henry, the fiery orator from Virginia who had ended his speech in favor of fighting the British with the ringing words, "Give me liberty or give me death!" Seventy-year-old Benjamin Franklin — perhaps the most famous American of his day — was there, too. Franklin's words of wisdom and humor often calmed the heated arguments of the delegates. Another delegate was Thomas Jefferson, a red-haired young man from Virginia, already well known for his gift of writing. John Hancock, wealthy merchant of Boston who rode to the meetings in an elegant coach, was elected President of the Congress.

Altogether, about fifty-six able and hard-working men took over the difficult task of representing the thirteen colonies in their struggle with Great Britain. They appointed George Washington commander of the colonial army, and made arrangements for buying arms and ammunition and supplies for the troops. Throughout the long year that followed, Congress discussed what steps the colonies should take in their quarrel with Britain. They debated long hours about independence, but took no action. The feeling for independence was growing stronger day by day in the colonies, but many people were not yet willing to take the fateful step.

Independence Is Proposed at Last

Finally, on June 7, 1776, Richard Henry Lee brought matters to a head. He arose in Congress and in a clear strong voice read the resolution, or statement, that "these United Colonies are and of right ought to be, Free and Independent States." When Lee had finished reading, he turned to the members of Congress and urged them to delay no longer in declaring independence and forming a new nation.

Lee had indeed proposed a bold step, for there were still some delegates who hesitated to break away from the mother country. So Congress postponed the vote until July 1, hoping that all the colonies would then approve Lee's momentous resolution. But Congress did appoint a committee of five to draw up a declaration which would explain to the world why the colonists were separating from England. Among the men on the committee were Thomas Jefferson, John Adams, and Benjamin Franklin. It was John Adams who suggested that the brilliant young statesman from Virginia be given the job of stating the colonists' case against England.

Richard Lee Proposing Independence

Jefferson Writes the Declaration of Independence

Jefferson was just the man to do this job. He knew what the colonists believed and he understood what they were fighting for. Jefferson himself believed with all his heart in independence. As he sat at his desk on that hot June day, the words flowed easily from his quill pen. He started by saying that when one people separates from another and sets up a new nation, "a decent respect to the opinions of mankind requires that they should declare the causes which impel [force] them to the separation." He described the rights to which all men are entitled:

> We hold these truths to be self-evident [easily seen], that all men are created equal, that they are endowed [furnished] by their Creator with certain unalienable Rights [rights that cannot be taken away], that among these are Life, Liberty, and the pursuit of Happiness.

Jefferson then stated a new idea of government by the people:

> That to secure these rights, Governments are instituted [set up] among Men, deriving [receiving] their just powers from the consent of the governed.

Jefferson then went on to set forth a long list of wrongs and injustices committed by the British King against the colonists. You may turn to the Declaration of Independence on page 226 and read these wrongs as Jefferson listed them for all the world to know. He also told how the colonists had appealed in vain to the King for justice. In the last paragraph, the Declaration states that "these United Colonies are, and of Right ought to be Free and Independent States." The final sentence contains a solemn promise:

> And for the support of this Declaration, with a firm reliance [trust] on the protection of Divine Providence [God], we mutually [together] pledge to each other our Lives, our Fortunes, and our sacred Honor.

In a half-day, Jefferson had not only written a declaration of independence, but he had proposed a new kind of government for the United States of America. This government would be based on the rights Americans believed in — liberty and equality for all men. One of our most valued documents is the first draft of the Declaration in Jefferson's own handwriting with corrections written between the lines. (See illustration on page 43.) What he wrote was so good that John Adams and Benjamin Franklin made only a few changes when Jefferson showed his work to them. Then the Declaration was presented to Congress. But it could not even be discussed until Congress had voted on Lee's resolution for independence.

Independence at Last!

The time was now drawing close for a decision. Would all the colonies vote for independence? People knew that such a step would mean a long and costly war against the most powerful empire in the world, and might well fail. On the other hand, if the colonies won, they would be independent and free to govern themselves. Those colonists who believed in American independence were willing to risk everything for freedom.

At last July 1 arrived. A hot sun glared down upon the statehouse where the delegates were arguing the question that would decide the future of America. By nine o'clock that night, they had not yet taken the final vote. They agreed to wait until the next day. On July 2 the delegates assembled again for the fateful vote. It was to be taken by colonies. You can imagine the tense feeling among the delegates as the roll call started. Lee's resolution passed with twelve "yeas" (yeses) and not a single "nay"! (The delegates from New York did not receive instructions to vote "yes" until July 15, so rather than vote "no" they did not vote at all.) The colonies had made their decision. John Adams wrote to his wife the next day, "Yesterday the greatest question was decided which was ever debated in America; and a greater, perhaps, never was nor will be decided among men."

The Declaration of Independence Is Adopted and Signed

Two more days passed before the Congress could agree on Jefferson's Declaration. On the afternoon of July 4, John Hancock called the members of Congress to order and asked for a vote on the Declaration. One by one all the delegates (except those from New York), in voices shaking with emotion, voted "Aye." The delegates then watched in silence as John Hancock, the President, and Charles Thomson, the Secretary of the Congress, signed their names to the document. The final step had been taken. As Benjamin Franklin had remarked in his humorous way, they must in-

Here is part of Jefferson's original draft of the Declaration.

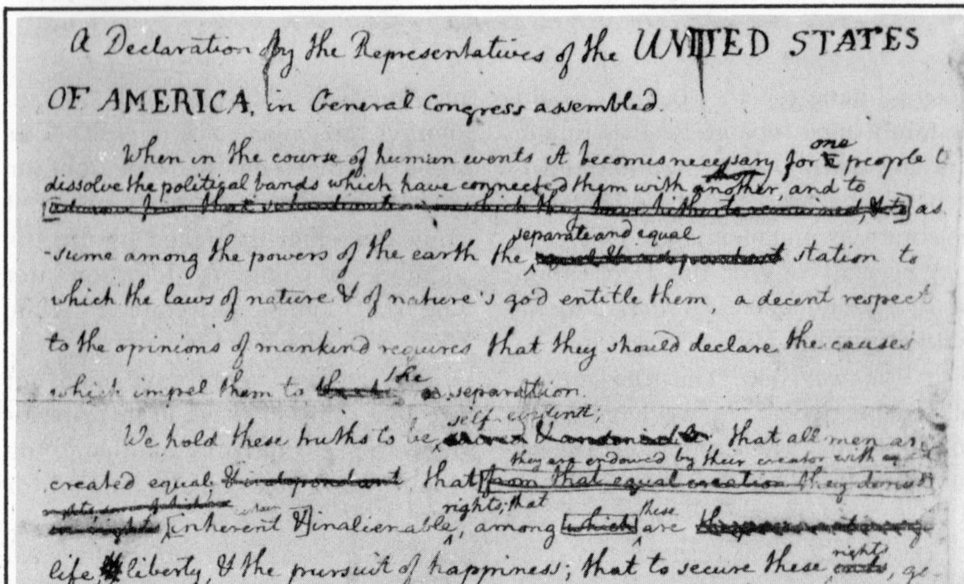

A Declaration by the Representatives of the UNITED STATES OF AMERICA, in General Congress assembled.

When in the course of human events it becomes necessary for one people to dissolve the political bands which have connected them with another, and to assume among the powers of the earth the separate and equal station to which the laws of nature & of nature's god entitle them, a decent respect to the opinions of mankind requires that they should declare the causes which impel them to the separation.

We hold these truths to be self-evident; that all men are created equal; that they are endowed by their creator with inherent & inalienable rights; that among these are life, liberty, & the pursuit of happiness; that to secure these rights, go-

In this painting, the artist has portrayed Benjamin Harrison of Virginia reading the Independence Resolve to the delegates, July 2, 1776.

deed all hang together or they would certainly hang separately! It is July 4, the day when the Declaration of Independence was adopted, that we celebrate as Independence Day.

A special copy of the Declaration of Independence was ordered to be written in large letters on parchment. The title was not "The Declaration of Independence," as we have come to call it, but "The Unanimous Declaration of the Thirteen United States of America." Moreover, the actual signing took place not on July 4, as some people seem to think, but on August 2. On this day the parchment copy was officially signed by fifty-six members of Congress. Jefferson later said that "no hand trembled" while signing the Declaration.

The signers were brave men. It was one thing to *speak* in favor of independence, but quite another thing to put their names on a document for

George III and all the world to see. In doing so, they were indeed risking their lives, their property, and the welfare of their families. Below is the ending of the original Declaration. Notice the size of John Hancock's signature. It is said that he remarked as he laid down his pen, "I write so that George the Third may read without his spectacles." The room where the Declaration was signed and the pen used by the signers can be seen today in Independence Hall.

The Declaration of Independence Is Read to the People

Soon after Congress had adopted the Declaration on July 4, 1776, it was made public. As you read in Chapter 2, the people of Philadelphia were called to assemble in the State House yard by the tolling of the great bell in the tower. At high noon drums sounded for attention, and men removed their hats. Colonel John Nixon began to read in a loud clear voice the stirring words of the Declaration of Independence, "When in the Course of human events . . ."

The crowd was silent and many wept as the inspiring phrases rang out. At the closing words, "And for the support of this Declaration . . . we mutually pledge . . . our Lives, our Fortunes, and our sacred Honor," the Liberty Bell "proclaimed freedom throughout the land" and the crowds cheered wildly. They shouted, "God bless the free states of North America!" Everywhere in the country the public reading of the Declaration was hailed with great enthusiasm. Independence had come at last. It brought the colonists together as nothing else could have done. United in a common cause, Americans stood ready to fight for their liberty.

* * * * * * * *

This is the story of our Declaration of Independence. It was written 185 years ago, but it still has the power to stir the hearts of freedom-loving people. It is good for us Americans to recall now and then the inspiring words of this great document of freedom.

Below are the signatures on the Declaration of Independence.

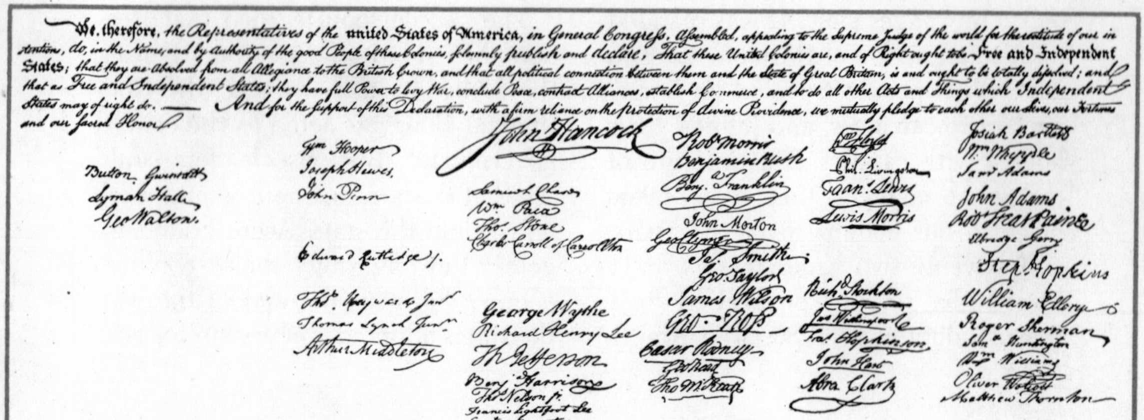
We, therefore, the Representatives of the united States of America, in General Congress, Assembled, appealing to the Supreme Judge of the world for the rectitude of our intentions, do, in the Name, and by Authority of the good People of these Colonies, solemnly publish and declare, That these United Colonies are, and of Right ought to be Free and Independent States; that they are Absolved from all Allegiance to the British Crown, and that all political connection between them and the State of Great Britain, is and ought to be totally dissolved; and that as Free and Independent States, they have full Power to levy War, conclude Peace, contract Alliances, establish Commerce, and to do all other Acts and Things which Independent States may of right do. —— And for the support of this Declaration, with a firm reliance on the protection of divine Providence, we mutually pledge to each other our Lives, our Fortunes and our sacred Honor.

John Hancock

Button Gwinnett, Lyman Hall, Geo Walton.

Wm Hooper, Joseph Hewes, John Penn

Edward Rutledge

Thos. Heyward Junr., Thomas Lynch Junr., Arthur Middleton

Samuel Chase, Wm. Paca, Thos. Stone, Charles Carroll of Carrollton

George Wythe, Richard Henry Lee, Th Jefferson, Benj. Harrison, Thos. Nelson jr., Francis Lightfoot Lee, Carter Braxton

Robt Morris, Benjamin Rush, Benj. Franklin, John Morton, Geo Clymer, Jas. Smith, Geo. Taylor, James Wilson, Geo. Ross

Caesar Rodney, Geo Read, Tho M:Kean

Wm Floyd, Phil. Livingston, Frans. Lewis, Lewis Morris

Richd. Stockton, Jno Witherspoon, Fras. Hopkinson, John Hart, Abra Clark

Josiah Bartlett, Wm Whipple, Saml Adams, John Adams, Robt Treat Paine, Elbridge Gerry, Step. Hopkins, William Ellery, Roger Sherman, Saml Huntington, Wm Williams, Oliver Wolcott, Matthew Thornton

Our Constitution

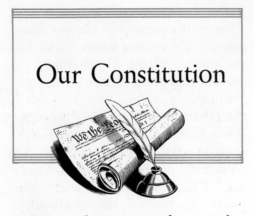

Many of you remember our last presidential election, and the inauguration of the President and Vice-President. Many of you know, too, that every two years your parents vote for members of Congress. But how many of you know where to find the rules for our national elections? The qualifications of the candidates, the way in which they are elected, the date of the President's inauguration, the first meeting of each new Congress — all are regulated by the *Constitution of the United States of America.* Of course, these are only a few of the matters taken up in the Constitution. This document outlines the plan for our entire national government.

If you turn to the back of your book, you will see that the Constitution is only a few pages long. It was planned for a small nation of thirteen states in days when people traveled on horseback or in carriages, and lighted their houses with candles. But in spite of the great changes that have taken place in our country over the years, only twenty-two amendments have been added to our Constitution since it was adopted in 1789. We Americans are proud of our Constitution and the government it gives us. Its story takes us back to the days after independence was declared.

Independence Is Won

The Declaration of Independence was a bold and courageous call for freedom. But it was only a declaration. The new American states still had to fight and win their war against England before they could be actually independent. Until then, in the eyes of England and the rest of the world, they were merely rebellious colonies.

For seven long years the Continental Army with General Washington as Commander-in-Chief fought the British troops. In spite of discouraging setbacks the patriot forces kept up the struggle. At last, they bottled up a British army under General Cornwallis in Yorktown, Virginia, and Cornwallis was forced to surrender. Two years later, in 1783, the Treaty of Paris ended the war and England recognized our new nation, the United States of America. Americans felt they were ready to enjoy the independence for which they had struggled.

The New Nation Faces Problems

The people soon learned that freedom has its problems, too. During the earlier part of the war, the Continental Congress acted as the central government. But wise leaders could see that this arrangement would work only while the states were bound together in fighting their common enemy. So, near the end of the war, the states adopted a new plan for governing the nation, called the *Articles of Confederation.* The Articles set up a rather weak central government, for people considered the states much more important than the national government. In fact, they thought of themselves as Virginians, New Yorkers, and so on, rather than as Americans. We can understand this situation better if we remember that the people of Revolutionary days had good reason to fear a strong government. Because they had resented England's authority, they now feared to give much power to a national government of their own. They thought they could get along with strong state governments and a weak central government. But Americans soon found that this plan would not build a nation.

The war had left the country in bad condition. Farms had been destroyed, industry and trade had suffered, money was almost worthless. Instead of working with other states on their common problems, each state went its own way, paying no attention to the welfare of its neighbor. There were quarrels over boundaries, over trade between the states, and other things. There was confusion everywhere. Indeed, it began to look as though the union of the American states would soon fall apart.

Our country's leaders, however, were not willing to see America lose all that its people had fought for so bravely. They decided to do something. In 1787 they asked the states to send delegates to a convention in Philadelphia to see what could be done about improving the Articles of Confederation. Because the delegates ended by writing a new constitution, this meeting has been called the *Constitutional Convention.*

The Leaders in the Constitutional Convention

It was a remarkable group of men who met that summer to decide the future of our nation. They represented the best the country had to offer in wisdom, ability, and experience. Forty of these men had been members of the Continental Congress and eight of them had signed the Declaration of Independence.

The most famous American at the Convention was George Washington, who had led the Continental Army to victory. He was then fifty-five years old, a calm man with excellent judgment and good common sense. Benjamin Franklin was there to serve his country for the last time. He was now an old man of eighty-one years, so crippled from painful rheumatism that he could scarcely move. But he could not remain at home when the nation needed him. He was the one who pleaded for compromise and told witty stories to relieve the strain that so often developed during the Con-

The British Surrender at Yorktown

vention. In fact, if it had not been for this wise and broad-minded American, our Constitution might never have been written.

Not all the leaders who had worked for independence were present at the Convention. Thomas Jefferson was in France, serving as ambassador from the United States. John Adams and Patrick Henry were not present, either. John Adams was our ambassador to Great Britain, and Patrick Henry was opposed to any idea of making the central government stronger. But there were other men who have become famous for the parts they played in the Constitutional Convention. There was Alexander Hamilton, brilliant and handsome young lawyer from New York, who had served in the Continental Army. Hamilton believed the only thing that would save the country was a powerful national government. Another outstanding man was James Wilson of Pennsylvania. He believed strongly in the right of the people to vote for their leaders. Then there was Gouverneur Morris of Pennsylvania, who thought that only the property owners should have the right to vote.

Perhaps the member of the Convention to whom we owe the most was James Madison of Virginia. He was a gentleman with a brilliant mind, who had made a study of governments. Most of the information we have about what went on in the Convention comes from the journal, or record, he kept of each day's discussion. Indeed, Madison played such an important part in the making of the Constitution that he has been called the "Father of the Constitution." Although they deserve to be mentioned, we cannot name all the patriotic and capable men who took part in the Convention. Altogether there were fifty-five. You will find the names of the signers of the Constitution on page 49.

The Convention Gets Under Way

The Convention met in May, 1787, in the same room where the Declaration of Independence had been signed. George Washington was chosen president. He sat at a simple desk on a low platform in the front of the room. The rest of the members sat together at tables. We can imagine them meeting there day after day, wearing the long coats, tight knee breeches, ruffled shirts, and curled and powdered wigs of the 1700's. The work of the Convention was kept secret. There were guards at the doors to see that only delegates entered. In spite of the summer heat the windows were closed, so that no one could hear what was being said.

A New Constitution Is Needed

It soon became clear to the members of the Convention that the Articles of Confederation could not be patched up. The delegates instead would have to make a new plan for a national government. This new government would need to have enough power to manage the affairs of the nation as a whole. It would need the power to raise an army for defense, to coin money, to regulate trade among the states, to establish post

Washington's Signature on the Constitution

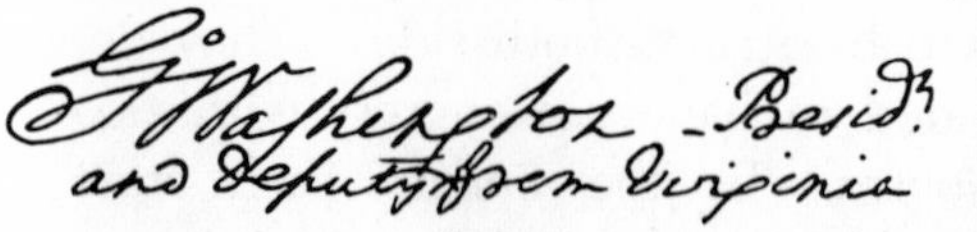

offices and carry the mail, and even to raise money by taxation. This new government must also have the power to pass laws to get these things done.

Of course, a national government with all these powers would then be much stronger than the state governments. Men like Washington, Hamilton, and Madison believed that was the way it should be. But many delegates wanted the states to remain stronger because they feared to give so much power to a central government. Gradually most of the members were won over to the idea that only a strong national government could save the nation. So the Convention voted to write a constitution, or set of laws, for a new government.

A Government of Three Branches Is Planned

What form was this new government to have? The delegates had no pattern to follow, for there was not a nation in the world at that time that had a written constitution! But the members of the Convention knew a good deal about government. They had had useful experience in the various colonial legislatures and in the Continental Congress. The government for the United States of America must first of all be a government in which the people were represented.

Gradually, the members of the Convention developed a general plan. There was to be a *legislative* branch to make the laws, an *executive* branch with a president to carry out the laws, and a *judicial* branch to interpret the laws and see that justice was done. The delegates planned that one branch should not have more power than another. (Perhaps you know that our state and local governments are organized according to the same plan.)

Other Signers of the Constitution

New Hampshire	John Langdon; Nicholas Gilman
Massachusetts	Nathaniel Gorham; Rufus King
Connecticut	Wm. Saml. Johnson; Roger Sherman
New York	Alexander Hamilton
New Jersey	Wil: Livingston; David Brearley; Wm. Paterson; Jona: Dayton
Pennsylvania	B Franklin; Thomas Mifflin; Robt Morris; Geo. Clymer; Thos. FitzSimons; Jared Ingersoll; James Wilson; Gouv Morris
Delaware	Geo: Read; Gunning Bedford jun; John Dickinson; Richard Bassett; Jaco: Broom
Maryland	James McHenry; Dan of St Thos. Jenifer; Danl Carroll
Virginia	John Blair; James Madison Jr.
North Carolina	Wm. Blount; Richd Dobbs Spaight; Hu Williamson
South Carolina	J. Rutledge; Charles Cotesworth Pinckney; Charles Pinckney; Pierce Butler
Georgia	William Few; Abr Baldwin

Attest William Jackson Secretary

Many Problems Face the Convention

It was one thing for the members to agree to the broad outline for the government which we have just mentioned. But it was quite another thing to work out the details. There were many hot arguments among the delegates, for they disagreed violently on a number of points. For instance, how were the states to be represented in the legislature? The delegates from the states with small populations said, "We insist on the same number of representatives as the large states have. Otherwise we would have no voice at all in the Congress. We would be outvoted on every question by the large states." A delegate from Delaware felt so strongly about this matter that he announced he would rather be under the power of George III than under the power of a neighboring state! But the large states had a different point of view. They said, "Your suggestion is unfair. Certainly 10,000 people deserve more representatives than 1,000 people do."

Some of the delegates became so angry that they shouted at one another. It seemed that the large and small states would never agree. In times like this it was Benjamin Franklin who came to the rescue. He urged each side to try to understand the other and to look for a way to compromise. Finally a way was found which satisfied both sides. They decided to have a Congress with *two* houses. In the Senate each state would be equal, with two members and two votes. In the House of Representatives the number of members would be based on population, so that the large states would have more representatives and more votes.

Many other disagreements came up during the summer. There were times when the delegates believed they could not possibly agree on a constitution. One of the biggest arguments was over who should vote. In those days the idea that every citizen should have the right to vote was not widely accepted. Many delegates said that the poor had no right to vote, that only men of property should have a voice in the government. But James Wilson gave a stirring speech on the rights of all men under the law. The delegates finally agreed not to put any statement in the Constitution about who had the right to vote. This decision was instead left to the states.

Another problem was how the President, members of Congress, and Justices of the Supreme Court should be chosen. There were delegates who honestly believed that the people could not be trusted to choose important officials like the President and the judges. Again a compromise was

Franklin Calming the Delegates

reached. The members of the Senate were to be chosen by the state legislatures, and the Representatives by the voters themselves. (The 17th amendment to the Constitution, added in 1913, now gives the people the right to elect Senators as well.) The President and Vice-President were to be chosen by electors from each state (see page 63, Chapter 4), while the judges of the Supreme Court were to be named by the President with the approval of the Senate.

The citizens of Philadelphia often gathered outside Independence Hall while the delegates debated within.

The Constitution Is Signed

Gradually the many differences were ironed out and the Constitution took shape. The final job was to rewrite the entire Constitution in clear language so that its meaning would be plain. A special committee worked on this job. Every word in every sentence was checked and rechecked, so that it could not be twisted into some other meaning. We owe the excellent wording of our Constitution to Gouverneur Morris, who wrote the final copy. Section by section the delegates approved the Constitution as it was completed. After four months of hard work, a parchment copy of the Constitution was ready for signing on September 17, 1787.

When it was read to the assembled delegates, everyone was worried. No one was sure how many would sign, for no delegate was entirely satisfied with every part of the finished document. But just the same, all the delegates knew that it was the best plan of government they could agree on. As soon as the secretary finished reading, Franklin, Hamilton, and others urged the members to forget the parts they did not like and support the Constitution by signing it. For, they said, if the delegates themselves could not all agree on the new plan, how could they expect the people to approve it? All but three delegates rose and signed the Constitution. The signature of George Washington was first. The other signatures were grouped according to states.

At last the delegates could return to their homes. But their work was not yet over. The Constitution would have to be explained to the people in each state, and the men who had made it were the best ones to do the job. Many members of the Constitutional Convention worked hard to get the

Adoption of the Constitution

The Constitution was signed on September 17, 1787. The thirteen original states adopted the Constitution in the following order:

- Delaware
- Pennsylvania
- New Jersey
- Georgia
- Connecticut
- Massachusetts
- Maryland
- South Carolina
- New Hampshire
- Virginia
- New York
- North Carolina
- Rhode Island

The first elections were held in 1788. The new government began in New York in March, 1789. George Washington was inaugurated as first President on April 30.

Constitution adopted in their home states. We Americans owe a debt of gratitude to these patriotic men. They gave us the Constitution which made possible the free government under which we live. They well deserve the name "Founding Fathers," for by their efforts they founded our nation.

The Constitution Is Adopted

The following year was one of great anxiety. Before the Constitution could be put into operation, nine of the thirteen states had to approve it. People of the various states objected to certain parts of the document, just as the delegates had. Would the Constitution be approved by a sufficient number of states? Before the year 1787 ended, news came of its adoption by Delaware, Pennsylvania, and New Jersey. Soon Georgia, Connecticut, Massachusetts, Maryland, and South Carolina adopted the Constitution. One more state was needed! At last, in June, 1788, New Hampshire became the ninth state to give its approval. Virginia followed a few days afterwards. The Constitution was now the law of the land! Later New York, North Carolina and Rhode Island also approved it. Plans could now be carried out for the election of the first President and Congress.

The New Government Gets Under Way

There was no problem about who should be our first President. George Washington was the overwhelming choice. John Adams was elected Vice-President. On April 30, 1789, Washington was inaugurated in New York City and the new government was officially started. The President rode to his inauguration in an elegant cream-colored coach drawn by six fine horses amid crowds of cheering people. He stood on the balcony of the Federal Hall in New York City where all the people could see him. With one hand on a Bible, in solemn tones, Washington then took the oath to "preserve, protect, and defend the Constitution of the United States." It is interesting to know that when President Eisenhower took the oath of office in 1953, he used the same Bible that George Washington used.

President Washington had taken on a big responsibility. He had to make many decisions about questions not covered in the Constitution. Washington's decisions were particularly important because his example would be followed by Presidents who came

Before crowds of his fellow-citizens, George Washington was inaugurated as our first President.

after him. For instance, how should the President live? How should he be addressed? No other nation in the world had a President at the head of it. The aristocratic and wealthy people believed that Washington should live as the kings of Europe did, surrounded by palace guards and servants in livery. They wanted to address him as "Your Majesty" or even "Your Serene Highness"! But Washington was a man of good sense. He chose to live in a simple but dignified style and to be called simply "Mr. President." As you know, this is the way we address our President to this day.

The Constitution does not provide for anyone to help the President in his many duties. Even in the days when our nation was small, one man could not take care of the Executive Branch of the government alone. So Congress set up four government departments and Washington chose men to head them. Alexander Hamilton became Secretary of the Treasury, Edmund Randolph was the Attorney-General, General Henry Knox headed the War Department, and Thomas Jefferson became Secretary of State. These four men also gave advice to the President and were called his *Cabinet.* More departments and cabinet offices were added as the country grew. You will learn about our present Cabinet in Chapter 4.

The Bill of Rights

In addition to passing laws needed to get the government started, Congress had another very important job

A Tribute to Our Constitution

A famous British Prime Minister, William Gladstone, said these words in praise of the Constitution, "The American Constitution is the most wonderful work ever struck off at a given time by the brain and purpose of man."

to do. It had to make some additions to the Constitution! Although the Founding Fathers had drawn up a fine plan for government, they had left out something that the liberty-loving people of America considered most important. When the Constitution was given to the states for approval, people said, "Our Declaration of Independence states that we, the people, have certain unalienable rights. But nowhere in the Constitution is there any guarantee of these rights. We want to be sure that we ourselves and those who come after us are guaranteed free speech, freedom of religion, and the other rights that belong to a free people. We want these rights written into our Constitution!" Many thoughtful men, such as Thomas Jefferson and Samuel Adams, believed that the Constitution should include a "Bill of Rights." In fact, Virginia and Massachusetts did not approve the Constitution until they were assured that when Congress met, a "Bill of Rights" would be added to the Constitution.

The men who wrote the Constitution wisely included rules for amending it. James Madison worked out a list of amendments which guaranteed the rights that the people wanted. According to the Constitution, these amendments had to be approved by a two-thirds majority of each house of Congress. After this, the amendments were submitted to the states for approval. When three fourths of the states had approved, the amendments became part of the Constitution — the highest law in the land. We call these first ten amendments the "Bill of Rights." Turn to pages 237 and 238 to find your rights as an American. These rights cannot be taken away by a law of Congress nor by the President nor by the Supreme Court.

In addition to the first ten amendments, only twelve others have been added since 1791. The Founding Fathers made a much finer Constitution than any of them realized, for it has stood the test of years and changing times.

Understanding the Preamble of Our Constitution

At the end of this book you will find the entire Constitution. Furthermore, in Chapter 4 you will read about the three branches of our government and how they work. But there is something perhaps more important to every American than the *facts* of the Constitution. If we are to be good citizens, we must understand and believe in the *ideas* on which our government is founded. The *Preamble,* or first paragraph, of the Constitution explains in only fifty-two words the purpose of our government and the ideas on which it is based. Try reading it aloud:

We the People of the United States, in Order to form a more perfect Union, establish Justice, insure domestic Tranquillity [peace within our own nation], provide for the common defence, promote the general Welfare [of the people], and secure the Blessings of Liberty to ourselves and our Posterity [descendants], do ordain and establish this Constitution for the United States of America.

The words may be difficult but the ideas are not hard to understand. What the Preamble says is: "We Americans want to work together for a strong, united country. We want a government that looks after the good of the people and gives fair treatment to all. We want to get along peacefully with each other, but we must be able to protect ourselves against outside enemies if necessary. Above all, we want to be sure that we and those who come after us are free people. Because we want these things for our nation, we, the people, agree to this Constitution as a plan for the government of the United States."

What Should We Know about Our Constitution?

The rest of the Constitution is a plan for our government, and a statement of our rights. Much of it is difficult for young people to understand. But there are certain things that every American should know about the Constitution.

1. We should understand that it is the highest law of our land. The Constitution ranks higher than any law of Congress or President's decision.

2. We should understand that the Constitution gives us a representative government. This means that the people govern themselves through the men they elect to represent them.

3. We should know that our government is based on the idea of liberty and equal rights for all under the law.

4. We should know that our Constitution gives us certain liberties which no one can take away, and that the most important of these are freedom of speech, the press, religion, and the right to trial by jury.

5. We should know that no American can be refused the right to vote because of race, religion, or color.

Let us be proud and grateful that we are Americans, protected by the Constitution. Let us remember that we, in turn, must believe in and defend our Constitution if we wish to remain a great and free nation.

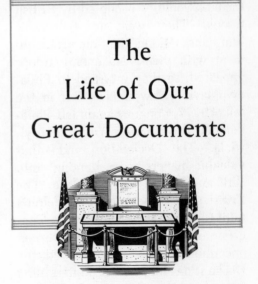

The Life of Our Great Documents

Today, as you have learned at the beginning of this chapter, the original

Declaration of Independence and the Constitution, with its Bill of Rights, are carefully preserved and guarded. But in years past, our great documents had quite a history, including several narrow escapes from fire and destruction.

The Declaration Travels Widely

The older document, the Declaration of Independence, shows the results of much handling in the past. The parchment on which it was written is yellowed and cracked. The bold signature of John Hancock and the other signatures can scarcely be read. When you read its story, you will be surprised that it survived at all.

The British were responsible for a good many of the early adventures of the Declaration. Only a few months after its signing, the members of Congress fled from Philadelphia, fearing the city would be occupied by British troops. They went to Baltimore, Maryland, taking the famous document with them. No enemy troops appeared, so they returned to Philadelphia in a few weeks. But in the fall of 1777, Congress again left Philadelphia, this time for York, Pennsylvania. The Declaration and other valuable papers were bundled into carts and hauled to a safe place. The British actually occupied Philadelphia until the summer of 1778, when Congress and the state papers returned once more. After the war ended, the Declaration followed Congress first to Annapolis, Maryland, then to Trenton, New Jersey, and finally to New York City, the seat of the first government under the Constitution.

More Adventures of the Great Documents

New York served as the home of the new government for a short time only. For ten years, beginning in 1790, the government was located in Philadelphia. Then in 1800, Washington, D. C., became our permanent capital. So from New York to Philadelphia and then on to Washington went the Declaration of Independence and our brand-new Constitution.

The journeys of the famous documents, however, were not over. During the War of 1812 the British advanced on the capital. These important papers were rushed out of Washington just in time before the British forces entered the city. After the War of 1812 the Declaration and the Constitution were put in the Treasury Department. When a fire broke out here, the documents were rescued and taken to the State Department. Later they were housed in the Patent Office for safe keeping.

The Declaration of Independence Goes "Home" for a Visit

In 1876 the Declaration took part in the celebration of the hundredth anniversary of our independence. It was sent by train to Independence Hall in Philadelphia, where it had been adopted and signed a century before. Here the document was unrolled and put into a frame for the first time. On July 4, the grandson of Richard Henry Lee read again the

In a beautiful and dignified setting within the National Archives Building, our Documents of Freedom are safely preserved. Every year, thousands of people come to view the Declaration of Independence, and the Constitution with its Bill of Rights.

immortal words of our Declaration of Independence. Thousands of Americans listened and cheered, as Americans had a hundred years before! On its return to Washington, the Declaration was placed on display with the Constitution in the Library of Congress. In time, however, the old document was so badly faded that it was put away in a dark vault. A copy was shown to the public. But so many Americans wanted to see the original old document that it was put on exhibit again in 1921. This time it was covered with amber glass to protect the precious writing.

Safe at Last!

During World War II, the great documents were sealed in metal cases and shipped to hiding places outside the capital for safekeeping. In 1944 they were returned and again put on display in the Library of Congress. Later they were placed in airtight glass-topped cases filled with helium gas, which will preserve them indefinitely. In December, 1952, the documents were moved to a final resting place in the National Archives Building, as you have learned. In case of war, the documents should not have to be moved, for the safe in which they are kept was designed to resist even enemy bombs. We hope that Americans for centuries to come will be able to view these documents that made us and keep us a free nation.

Our Documents State Our Ideals

Before closing our story of the Declaration of Independence and the Constitution, let us summarize their importance for each one of us. We cherish and safeguard these documents not merely for their age and the glorious incidents in our history which they recall. We honor them for their message today.

Many people speak about our American ideals without knowing exactly what they are or where they are written for all to see. The ideals on which our government was founded are stated in our great documents of freedom.

THE DECLARATION OF INDEPENDENCE

Equality	"All men are created equal."
Liberty	"Life, liberty, and the pursuit of happiness" are rights given to men by the Creator and can never be taken away.
Self-government	Governments get their power from the "consent of the governed," that is, the people.

THE CONSTITUTION (PREAMBLE)

Justice	"To establish justice" is one purpose of the Constitution.
Liberty	"To secure the blessings of liberty" is another purpose of the Constitution.

These splendid ideals are few in number, but all our rights and privileges as Americans have grown out of them. Every American should know these ideals.

CHAPTER 4

Uncle Sam's Government in Washington

Each one of you knows something about our government in Washington. You study about it in school; at home many of you have seen the President and various members of Congress on television. You may have heard your parents discussing a decision of the President or a law passed by Congress. You probably remember the excitement of a Presidential campaign. Yet to many of you, perhaps, Uncle Sam's government — your government in Washington — may seem pretty far removed from your daily life.

Actually, Uncle Sam's government affects your life more than you realize. What goes on in Washington is important to you and your families. The national government calls your brothers and fathers into military service. The national government also decides how much your parents will pay in income taxes this year. It makes the laws for the nation; it runs the post offices and delivers the mail. The national government makes sure the medicines and the canned and packaged foods you buy are pure and safe from harmful ingredients. It does countless other things too numerous to mention. Most of them affect you and your family in some way.

Uncle Sam's government is important to all of us for another reason. It is the government that represents all the people of the United States, for it is through the President and Con-

AMERICA, PRESENT AND PAST: *The stately White House is a well-known symbol of Uncle Sam's government, which has grown hugely since the inauguration of our first President in 1789.*

gress that the American people govern themselves as a nation. As young Americans you will want to know how your government in Washington works. This chapter will help you get acquainted with the work of the President, Congress, and the Supreme Court. Chapter 4 will also give you an idea of the tremendous job it is to govern the U. S. A.

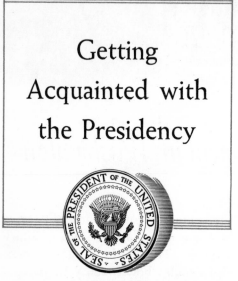

Getting Acquainted with the Presidency

"A President, to be chosen by the people!" How many times these words must have been heard when Americans learned for the first time about their new government under the Constitution. Until 1776 Americans had been ruled by a king. The idea of being governed by an elected president must have seemed strange at first. In fact, there were many citizens who believed that it was dangerous to allow the people to have a say in choosing a president.

But on the whole, "we the people" have done a good job of selecting our Presidents. Although some of them have been average men, many have been outstanding, and some, truly great. For over 170 years the Presidency has passed peacefully from one man to another by the will of the majority of our people. There have been no revolutions against our Presidents like those which have taken place in many countries.

What Does It Mean to Be President?

As you know, the President is the head of the *Executive Branch* of our government. His is the highest office in the nation. To elect a man President is the greatest honor the American people can give any citizen. In fact, the President is often called the "first citizen." The Presidency is not only a position of honor; it is also a position of trust. When we Americans elect a man President, we are, in a way, saying to him, "Mr. President, under our system of representative government we are placing in your hands the leadership of our great nation. We expect you to preserve our democracy and to place the interests of the nation over the interests of any political party or group. You must not only make decisions on the many problems inside our country, but as President of the most powerful free nation in the world, you must be a leader in world affairs. This is a great deal of responsibility, but you were elected because a majority of Americans believe that you can do the job."

Loyal Americans, on the other hand, have a duty toward the President. We owe respect to the office and to the man who holds it. Showing respect for the President does not mean that we must always agree with him or approve of all that he does. But we should remember that the Presidency is a symbol of government by the people. Showing respect for this high office means that we Americans believe in and support our representative government. Failure to show this respect makes it appear that we do not support our form of government and weakens our democracy.

What Are the Qualifications for President?

Many an American boy has dreamed of being President some day. This is not a ridiculous dream. Under our Constitution anyone born in the United States is eligible for the position of President, provided he is at least thirty-five years old, and has lived in the United States for at least fourteen years. Money, social position, religion — these have nothing to do with qualifications for the Presidency. Even a lack of higher education does not bar anyone from this high office.

Of course there are several million citizens who fill the requirements described in the Constitution. But we all know that we cannot entrust the job of running our government to anyone who happens to be eligible. There are certain qualifications not mentioned in the Constitution which we have come to look for in a President. We expect him to be a man of fine character and high ideals, devoted to the service of his country. We expect him to have the wisdom and the ability which the President's job requires. We believe that previous experience in government also helps to prepare him for the task of being President. A President should be able to select capable men to assist and advise him. He should also be a tactful man, because a large part of his job is working with others. And finally, he must not be a man who hesitates to make decisions, but a man who can decide wisely and act firmly on important matters. So you see, while many Americans are *eligible,* fewer are *qualified* for the difficult position of President.

How Is Our President Chosen?

Every four years we hold a Presidential election. Election Day is in November, on the Tuesday following the first Monday. But the business of election begins long before Election Day. The choosing of candidates for

How Many Presidents Have We Had?

Counting our Presidents is a harder job than you may think. Several had two terms in succession, so are counted only once. But Grover Cleveland served two terms with another President between the terms. Shall we count him once or twice? Harry Truman counted Cleveland once, and called himself the 32nd President. But the Republican committee in charge of Eisenhower's inauguration counted Cleveland twice and called Dwight Eisenhower the 34th, not the 33rd, President. By this method of counting, John F. Kennedy became the 35th President in 1961.

Candidate Explains His Views to the Voters.

President and Vice-President is done by the political parties. Our chief parties, as you know, are the Democratic and the Republican. However, other parties may be listed on the ballot and from time to time there have been strong third parties. Leading men of each party announce that they are *candidates* for the office of President. They speak to voters in many parts of the country, explaining their stand on the important political questions of the day. Newspapers, radio, and television keep the people well informed about the candidates.

The next step is the choosing of delegates for the big national conventions held every four years by each party. In many states the delegates to the conventions are chosen by the people in what are called *primary elections.* In other states they are chosen directly by the political parties. During the summer the delegates from each state attend their national party convention, which is held in some big city. Then the excitement begins. The job of the delegates is to nominate (name) one of the party's candidates as its choice for President, and another for Vice-President.

As there are usually many candidates, each convention tries to select the man most likely to win the election. There is much noise, excitement, and suspense while the voting goes on. In 1952, for the first time, the people of the United States were able to see how Presidential candidates are nominated by watching the conventions on television.

After the nominations have been made, each party carries on a campaign to win votes for its candidates. There is no rest for anyone connected with an election campaign. The candidates tour the country by train and plane, accompanied by newspaper men, photographers, and political leaders. They give many speeches explaining how they would solve national problems. Nowadays, radio and television make it much easier for most citizens to get acquainted with the candidates and hear their views on important issues. Perhaps you saw the series of four television debates between candidates John F. Kennedy and Richard Nixon during the 1960 Presidential campaign.

The Election Takes Place

Who will win the election? There are always many guesses, but of course no one really knows until the votes are in. On Election Day, all registered voters may go to the polls to cast their votes. Our system of electing a President and a Vice-President is a little hard to understand. Actually, under the Constitution, the voters do not mark their ballots directly for a President and Vice-President. Instead they vote for a group of people who are called *electors*. These electors in turn vote for their party's candidates.

What really happens in your state at election time is that each political party has a list of electors. The number of electors in each list equals the number of Congressmen from that state (Representatives plus Senators). The political party which wins the largest vote in each state wins *all* the electoral votes of that state. And the Presidential candidate who wins a majority of the electoral votes from all states wins the election.

Later on, the electors of the winning party in each state meet and cast their votes for President and Vice-President. This step is required by the Constitution even though we know soon after the election which persons have been chosen as President and Vice-President. Many Americans believe that we should vote directly for President, just as we do for Congressmen, but the Constitution has not yet been amended to make this possible.

Of course, millions of voters are disappointed when their candidate does not win. But we citizens of a democracy have learned to be good losers. We believe in the rule of the majority, and are loyal to the new President whether we voted for him or not.

How Is the President Installed?

The new President takes office in a ceremony called the *inauguration*. This happens in Washington, D.C., on January 20 of the year after the election. Since the national election always comes in an even-numbered year (1956, 1960, and so on), the inauguration occurs in an odd-numbered year.

There have been many types of Presidential inaugurations since the first one in 1789. At that time George Washington rode to the Federal Hall in New York City in a splendid coach, followed by other coaches carrying prominent officials, foreign ambassadors, and important people. Washington was inaugurated on the balcony of Federal Hall while a large throng of people looked on. Thomas Jefferson, who always believed in doing things very simply, walked to his inauguration at the unfinished Capitol building in Washington, D. C.!

Presidential Inaugurations Today

As time went on, our inaugurations became more and more elaborate. Today the inauguration is a most impressive ceremony. Hundreds of thousands of visitors throng to the capital. Radio and television make it possible for the people of the nation to hear and see this important occasion. Many of you probably watched our last inauguration on television.

The old and new Presidents drive down Pennsylvania Avenue together from the White House to the Capitol. They are followed by cars carrying the old and new Vice-Presidents, family members, and other important people. Huge crowds of spectators watch and cheer as the President's car passes with the Presidential flag flying. The inauguration ceremony takes place about noon outside the Capitol, where a huge platform is built over the steps of the East Front. Assembled on the platform are many important persons. These include the Supreme Court Justices in their black robes, Cabinet members, members of Congress, state governors, foreign ambassadors in formal attire, and military officers in dress uniform. The families of the chief officials are also present.

An inaugural parade is an exciting "Hello" to our new President. Here, parading West Pointers and Kansas cowboys win cheers at a Presidential inaugural.

After the opening ceremonies, the new Vice-President takes the oath of office, as the entire nation watches and listens. Then the Chief Justice of the Supreme Court steps forward to give the oath of office to the new President, as directed in the Constitution. The President stands with his right hand raised and his left on the Bible. He soberly repeats the following words:

> I do solemnly swear (or affirm) that I will faithfully execute the office of the President of the United States, and will, to the best of my ability, preserve, protect, and defend the Constitution of the United States.

It has become customary to add to this oath the words, "So help me God."

The President then gives his inaugural address to the vast throng before him and to the nation. In his

Some Inaugural "Firsts"

1789 First President to be inaugurated was George Washington. The ceremony took place at Federal Hall, New York City.

1801 First President to be inaugurated at Washington, D. C., was Thomas Jefferson, third President of the United States.

1825 First President to wear long trousers at an inauguration was John Quincy Adams. Our first five Presidents wore knee breeches!

1921 First President to ride to his inaugural in an automobile was Warren G. Harding. Horse-drawn carriages were used for 132 years.

1925 First President to have his inaugural address broadcast by radio was Calvin Coolidge.

1953 First President to have his inaugural ceremonies televised on a coast-to-coast network was Dwight D. Eisenhower.

speech he tells the American people what he hopes to accomplish during his term of office. After the inauguration the President returns to the White House, which will be his home for the next four years. During the afternoon there is a huge parade in his honor. Military forces march, many bands play, and every state sends a float, or display on wheels. This is our way of welcoming the new President and wishing him well.

The President Has a Big Job

Once the President is inaugurated, he takes over for four years the biggest job in the world. Many Americans do not realize the very great amount of responsibility and hard work the President's job includes. The Constitution states definitely what his powers and duties are. These have not changed since the Constitution was written; what have changed are the size and importance of our country, and the times we live in. The United States has grown from a few states and a small population to an enormous country with over 180 million people. In the last hundred years it has become a great industrial nation. It has progressed from horse-and-buggy days to the age of jet planes and atomic energy. And from a weak, unimportant nation our country has grown into one of the greatest world powers.

All these changes have tremendously increased the size of the President's job. For instance, the number of laws he must carry out, the number of decisions he must reach, the

Who Succeeds the President?

Congress has decided that in case of the death of the President and Vice-President, the following people should take over the Presidency in the order given.

Speaker of the House of Representatives
President *pro tempore* of the Senate
Secretary of State
Secretary of Treasury
Secretary of Defense
Attorney General
Postmaster General
Secretary of the Interior
Secretary of Agriculture
Secretary of Commerce
Secretary of Labor

Established by an Act of Congress, July 18, 1947.

number of people he must deal with, and the number of reports he must read, have made the President's job what former President Harry Truman called "fantastic."

What Are the President's Powers?

Let us see what the duties and powers of the President are. Here is a list that will give you a better idea of his job:

1. The President is head of the Executive Branch of the government. This means that he has the responsibility of managing the government. As Chief Executive the President must also see that all laws passed by Congress are carried out. He may recommend laws which he thinks Congress should pass. He also sends to Congress the yearly budget of expenses, asking Congress to set aside the money needed to run the government.

2. He is Commander-in-Chief of all the Armed Forces of the United States. All the military services are under his orders, and he may send them to any point of danger. He is responsible for spending the funds voted for these Forces by Congress. The President may ask Congress to declare war and may make decisions on how to carry on the war.

3. The President must sign or *veto* (say "No" to) all bills passed by the Congress. In order to use this important power wisely, the President must study every bill. Since a recent Congress alone passed about 2000 laws, you can see that this one part of his job requires a great amount of time.

4. He appoints, with the advice and consent of the Senate, all judges of the Supreme Court and other United States courts, ambassadors to foreign countries, and Cabinet members, as well as many other officers.

5. He makes treaties with foreign countries with the consent of the Senate. These treaties may have to do with peace or war, with trade, or with any of the many arrangements which nations of the world make with each other.

These are not all the powers and duties of the President, but they are the most important ones. Almost any one of his many duties would be a full-time job.

The President's Cabinet

The President, of course, does not run the Executive Branch of the government alone. There are ten regular departments to handle this enormous job. Each is headed by a Secretary appointed by the President with the consent of the Senate. These Secretaries make up the Cabinet. They not only run their own departments, but they also advise the President on various matters that have to do with the government.

Each department occupies one or more huge buildings in Washington. Each department also has several divisions. Working for each department are hundreds of clerks, secretaries, office heads, and assistants to take care of the enormous amount of business. The chart on this page shows the ten departments of the Cabinet.

In addition to the departments headed by members of the Cabinet, there are many bureaus and commissions connected with the Executive Branch. They have been formed through the years to take over special jobs that needed to be done. The Interstate Commerce Commission, for example, sets the rates charged by railroads and by telephone and telegraph companies which do business in several states. One of the newer commissions which you have heard about is the National Aeronautics and Space Administration. It has charge of the exploration and scientific study of outer space.

The President himself has a personal staff of secretaries and clerks to work in the executive offices at the White House. The President's staff, ten Cabinet departments, many bureaus and commissions — you can easily see how big and complicated the Executive Branch is!

What Are the Symbols of the Presidency?

The position of the President, as we have seen, is one of honor and dignity. Our President, like the head of any nation, has certain symbols of his authority. These are the Presidential coat of arms, seal, and flag.

PICTOGRAPH CORP.

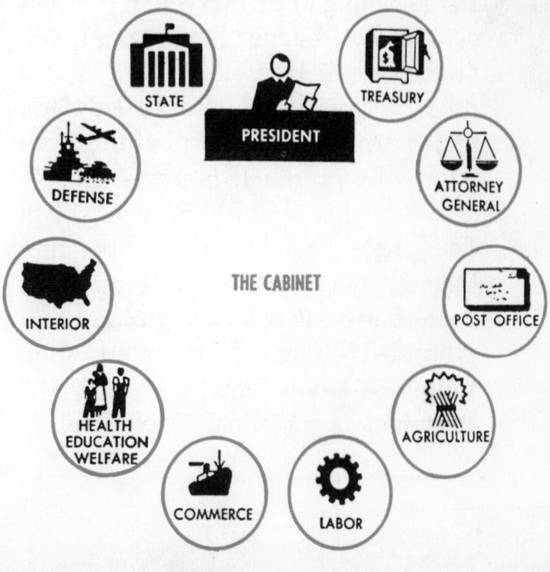

How does the President's seal differ from the Great Seal (page iv)?

1. *The coat of arms and seal.* The President's coat of arms, like the Great Seal, has on it an American eagle and a crest. These are surrounded by a circle of fifty white stars, which represent the states of the Union. The President's seal is the coat of arms encircled by the words, "Seal of the President of the United States." The President's seal appears in the ceiling of his office, and the coat of arms is on the rug in the Green Room of the White House. The seal is also used on letterheads and an enlarged seal is displayed on any platform from which the President makes a speech.

2. *The flag.* The President's flag does not resemble the Stars and Stripes. It consists of the President's coat of arms, in color, on a blue background. The flag is flown on any ship, train, or automobile in which the President is traveling. Of course, no other government official or department may use either the flag or the seal of the President of the United States.

What Personal Sacrifice Must the President Make?

Perhaps you think being President is largely glory and honor. Of course, there is glamour attached to a President's life. Wherever he goes, he is the most important person. He travels in his own plane or railroad car or ship. People crowd to see him.

What many Americans do not realize is that the man who is President must sacrifice a great deal. The minute he is inaugurated his way of living changes. For one thing he must give up much of his private life, and his wife and family must do the same. The reason for this is that the President and his family are very much in the public eye. Can you imagine what it would be like to have millions of people interested in what you do, what you say, what you wear, the kind of food you eat, and so on? Would you like to have to weigh carefully every word you say, realizing that the whole nation will know if you speak tactlessly or unwisely? Would you like to have a Secret Service man always near you even when you take a short walk alone or go with your family to church? If the President has children, they are also in the public eye. When the average young man scrapes fenders with another car in traffic, it is important only to the drivers concerned. But if the President's son does the same, the accident appears on the front page of all the newspapers in the country! If the President's daughter goes out with a young man, that, too, is news.

The President and his family are also expected to follow certain social customs established through the years. They must entertain at many official dinners and receptions. Dinners are given for the Cabinet members and their wives, for the Vice-President, and for the Speaker of the House. The largest reception is the one for foreign diplomats. There are often from two to three thousand invitations sent out. Of course, an invitation from the White House is hardly ever refused. No matter what plans a person has made, he cancels all engagements to accept an invitation from the President of the United States!

Because of the burdens and importance of his position, the President and his wife are cut off from many ordinary friendly visits. For instance, it is not their custom to accept dinner invitations except to formal affairs given by the Vice-President, the Speaker of the House, the Cabinet members, or ambassadors from foreign countries. They seldom make calls except on important people from foreign countries who may be visiting here. While Mr. and Mrs. President are in the White House, they are not free to call on old friends or go to their homes for dinner as you and I do. Even the President's closest friends do not just drop in for a visit. Ordinarily, unless they have received an invitation, they are expected to write to the secretary of either the President or his wife for an appointment! Of course, when the President and his family are on vacation, their life is more informal. But while a man is President, he is not free to live his ordinary life.

As we have seen, the job of being President is not an easy one. It means hard work, sacrifice, and great responsibility. It also means honor and power and fame.

President Kennedy answers newsmen's questions at a televised press conference. What a President says at these news conferences is reported throughout this country and the world.

Getting Acquainted with Congress

As you know, Congress is the *Legislative Branch* of Uncle Sam's government. This means that it has the power to pass laws for the nation. We Americans feel a great interest in Congress because it is through this branch that we have a voice in our government. Our democracy is based on the right of every citizen to vote and to express his opinions on political matters. The members of Congress are our representatives. They are chosen by us in free elections to represent us in making the laws for the country.

How Congress Is Divided

The Constitution states that Congress is to be made up of two houses. The smaller house is the Senate. Each state sends two Senators, and each Senator has one vote. So every state, regardless of its population, has an equal number of votes in the Senate.

The House of Representatives, on the other hand, represents the states according to population. Each state is divided into districts and each district elects a Representative. The number of Representatives in Congress is set at 435, but after each national census the number is redivided among the states.[1] States with large populations have the most Representatives. No matter how small a state's population, however, it has at least one Representative.

How Congressmen Are Chosen

The Constitution gives the states the right to pass laws saying when, where, and how the members of Congress will be elected. All the states have now set the Tuesday following the first Monday in November as national Election Day. Congressional elections take place every two years in even-numbered years. Both Senators and Representatives may run for re-election as many times as they choose. Whether they are re-elected or not depends on how satisfied the voters are with what they have done while in office.

The Constitution wisely states the terms of office and the qualifications for Congressmen just as it does for President. A person does not need to be born in this country to become a Congressman. Naturalized citizens may become members of Congress. The requirements and the terms of office for each house of Congress appear on the next page:

[1]The number of Representatives was raised temporarily to 437 to allow for one Representative each from the new states of Alaska and Hawaii. After 1962 the number goes back to 435.

Senator

1. Must be at least thirty years old.
2. Must have been a citizen for at least nine years.
3. Must be a resident of the state from which elected.

Term — six years.

Representative

1. Must be at least twenty-five years old.
2. Must have been a citizen for at least seven years.
3. Must be a resident of the state from which elected.

Term — two years.

When and Where Congress Meets

According to the Constitution, Congress must meet at least once a year. The meeting begins at noon on January 3. The meetings of Congress are called *sessions.* It was formerly the custom for Congress to meet during the winter and spring months and adjourn for the summer and fall. But in the past few years there have been so many serious and important problems to consider that Congress has been in session for a longer period of time each year. It is interesting to know that each Congress lasts for two years and that each Congress is numbered. For example, the Congress which first met in January, 1961 was the 87th Congress. Both houses of Congress meet in the Capitol Building — the Senate in the Senate Chamber, the House in the Hall of Representatives.

Who Presides over Congress?

The Vice-President serves as the

Each year the President gives a "State of the Union" message. In it he discusses matters important to the nation. Here, President Kennedy gives Congress his message in the Hall of Representatives.

President of the Senate. He is not actually a member, so he does not vote on laws unless there is a tie. Since the Vice-President cannot always attend the sessions, the Senate elects a President *pro tempore* (temporary) to act as chairman in his absence.

Under our system, the Vice-President probably has a less important job than many of our high officials. Thomas Jefferson, our second Vice-President, called the position "honorable and easy." And when Alben Barkley was Vice-President (1949–1953), he used to call himself "the forgotten man." But in recent years, the second highest office in our government has become much more important. Actually, what a Vice-President does depends a good deal on himself and the President. Vice-President Lyndon B. Johnson attends Cabinet meetings, and he and other recent Vice-Presidents have been given important responsibilities. It is also true that seven times during the history of our nation the death of a President has put a Vice-President in the White House. So for this reason alone it is important to choose a capable Vice-President.

The House elects as chairman a man called the *Speaker of the House.* He is the leader of the political party which has the most members in the House. The Speaker is a very important member of Congress. He presides over the meetings and no one may speak unless he is recognized or "given the floor" by the Speaker. The Speaker also swears in the Representatives at each new Congress. All new members rise, raise their right hands, and repeat this oath:

I, ______________, do solemnly swear (or affirm) that I will support and defend the Constitution of the United States against all enemies, foreign and domestic; that I will bear true faith and allegiance to the same; that I take this obligation freely, without any mental reservation or purpose of evasion; and that I will well and faithfully discharge the duties of the office on which I am about to enter. (So help me God.)

The Symbols of Congress

Like the President, Congress has its symbols. If you visit the House of Representatives while it is in session, you will see to the right of the Speaker's table the famous *mace.* The mace is a bundle of black rods, over three feet long, bound together with criss-crossed silver bands. At the top, a silver eagle with outspread wings perches on a silver globe. The present mace is over a hundred years old. It was made to take the place of the original mace which was burned when the British occupied the capital during the War of 1812.

You may be wondering what the mace is used for. It is a symbol of the authority of the House. At every session of the House the Sergeant at Arms carries in the mace and puts it in its place. When the meeting ends, he carries it out again. The mace is used to keep order in the House. Sometimes members get into a violent argument. If they do not pay atten-

Four newly-elected Representatives are sworn in as a new session of Congress begins.

tion to the Speaker's gavel, the Sergeant at Arms may carry the mace toward them. This has been done only a few times, but it has never failed to restore order, because the members of the House respect the authority of the mace.

The Senate has its symbol of authority also. It is an old gavel of ivory and silver used by the President of the Senate. The gavel dates back to 1789, when it was used in our first Congress. It is rather strange-looking, for it is made without a handle. The gavel is so valuable that it is guarded while in use, and is locked up each night in the office of the Senate Sergeant at Arms.

The Capitol Pages

To help the Congressmen carry out their duties, there is a group of about seventy-six teen-age boys, known as pages. They are on hand every day that Congress meets. Before the session starts, they put copies of new bills and other papers at the desk of each Congressman. They run errands, deliver messages, make phone calls, and do other things to save the time of the busy members. One of the jobs of the twenty-six Senate pages is to fill the old inkwells at each desk. Of course the Senators all use fountain or ball-point pens, but the inkwells are a tradition in the Senate. Senators call the pages by a wave of the hand; the Representatives push buttons which light up a board at the page bench, showing in what part of the hall a page is wanted.

The Capitol pages don't miss school; Uncle Sam sees to that! They attend the Capitol Page School together with several pages from the Supreme Court. They study history, languages,

These Capitol pages are studying typing at their school in the Library of Congress. Note the Capitol dome through the window.

mathematics, and other high school subjects. Their school is part of the District of Columbia system, but is paid for by Congress. You would not like the hours, for the boys must be at school from 6:30 A.M. until about 10:30 A.M. After that they go on duty at the Capitol. A page who graduates from the school gets two diplomas. One is a regular diploma from the Board of Education; the other is a special diploma signed by the President of the United States.

Being a page boy has many advantages and is a very interesting job. On the other hand, it means a long day and plenty of work and responsibility. You may be wondering how a page boy gets his job. He applies to the Congressman from his home district, who can recommend him if there is an opening. He must be between fourteen and nineteen years old. A page holds his job as long as the Congressman who appointed him remains in Congress. If the Congressman is not re-elected, the page is out of a job. It is said that no boy can be a Senate page if he is taller than the shortest Senator!

What Congress Can Do

Under the Constitution, Congress is given the power to make laws for the nation as a whole. For example, Congress may: (1) vote taxes, (2) borrow money, (3) coin money, (4) establish post offices, (5) declare war, (6) maintain an army and navy. Congress passes many laws under the powers granted to it in the Constitution, but Congress does not have the right to pass whatever laws it wishes. The Constitution not only lists the things that Congress may do; it also lists some things that it may not do. For a full list of what Congress can or cannot do, see Article I, Sections 8 and 9, pages 232 and 233. Many powers are left to the states. The states make their own constitutions, manage their own government and state elections, and pass laws for the good of the people living within the state. No state, however, may have powers which affect the whole country, such as coining money or making treaties with foreign countries.

How Congress Works

Perhaps you would like to know some of the most important things Congress does. The two houses work together in making our laws. It is interesting to know that every law passed by Congress starts because of some problem which has come up. Passing a law is a long and complicated process. First, a bill or paper stating the exact terms of the law must be introduced by a member of the House or Senate. Both the Senate and the House have committees which study each bill carefully and decide whether it is worth presenting to Congress. If it is presented to the House, for example, the members talk about or "debate" the bill, giving arguments for and against it. Then it is put to a vote, and if the majority of those present votes for the bill, we say it is *passed*.

The bill is then sent to the Senate for debate and the same steps are followed. If the Senate also passes the bill, it is signed by the Speaker and the Clerk of the House, and by the Vice-President and the Secretary of the Senate. It then goes to the President. If the President approves of the bill, he signs it. It is then stamped with the Great Seal of the United States and becomes the law of the land. If the President does not approve of the bill, he refuses to sign it. This is the veto, which you read about earlier in the chapter. The bill is marked "Vetoed by the President" and returned to Congress. The Constitution says that Congress may still pass the law over the President's veto if two thirds of each house votes for it. If the President neither signs nor vetoes the bill, it ordinarily becomes a law within ten days.

Special Powers of Congress

In addition to working with the other house to make laws, each house of Congress has certain special jobs of its own. The Senate has two particular powers which the House of Representatives does not have. You know that the President has the power

An Unusual Power of Congress

It may surprise you to know that our Constitution gives Congress the power to try the President of the United States! If an official of the United States government is suspected of "treason, bribery, or other high crimes," the House of Representatives may accuse, or *impeach,* him. The President, the Vice-President, judges of United States courts, and Cabinet officers, too, may be impeached if they are guilty of serious crimes. The trial is held in the Senate. The accused man may be convicted (judged guilty) or acquitted (judged not guilty). No person may be convicted unless two thirds of the Senate members agree that he should be. The penalty is being removed from office and never being allowed to hold a federal office again.

In the history of the United States twelve men have been impeached by the House of Representatives. Nine of them were judges of federal courts (not the Supreme Court). Of these, four were convicted and removed from office. A senator, a Cabinet member, and a President (Andrew Johnson) have also been impeached. None of them, however, were convicted by the Senate.

How to Address the President and Congressmen in a Letter

Anyone can write to the President. Every year thousands of people write to him and to their Congressmen. Perhaps you may wish to do so some day. Here is the proper way to begin and end such letters.

The President
The President of the United States
or
The President
White House
Washington, D.C.

My dear Mr. President:
or
Dear Mr. President:

Senators
The Honorable (full name)
The United States Senate
or
Senator (full name)
The United States Senate

Sir:
My dear Mr. Senator:
Dear Senator:

Representatives
The Honorable (full name)
House of Representatives

Sir:
My dear Congressman:

Letters to the President and to members of Congress should be signed "Respectfully yours."

to make treaties with foreign countries. The Constitution says that the Senate must approve these treaties. The Senate must also approve important appointments of the President before they can go into effect. Judges of federal courts, Cabinet members, and foreign ambassadors must all be approved by the Senate. Sometimes there is a good deal of discussion by Senators about certain appointments, but usually they are approved.

The House has the special power to start all tax bills and bills voting money for government expenses. Only after the House has passed tax bills and money bills, may the Senate vote on them. The Senate may make changes in the bills, but both Houses of Congress must agree on the bill in its final form. Since our government expenses run into many billions of dollars, Congress has a very great responsibility in voting money.

A Congressman's Job

Like the job of President, the work of a Congressman has grown tremendously since the early days of our nation. The first Congress, meeting in 1789, had twenty-two senators and fifty-nine representatives. It passed thirty-four laws. The 85th Congress, which met in 1957, had 96 senators and 435 representatives. It passed about 1100 laws. This means that every Congressman had to understand and vote on the 1100 bills that were passed and also on those that were defeated! This is an impossible job for any man. Most Congressmen do a great deal of studying on the many bills that come before Congress. However, if they have been unable to study a measure, they usually vote as their party leaders vote.

In addition to keeping informed on the measures before Congress, a Congressman must read and dictate answers to thousands of letters each year. No matter how busy he is, he must see many visitors, most of them people from his home state who like to call on their Congressman when they are in the Capitol. He is often asked to appear on radio or television. He must also attend the important committee meetings of the House or Senate, some of which last long hours. Of course he is expected to be present at the regular daily sessions of Congress. In addition, he and his wife attend many official dinners and other social affairs. The life of a Senator or Representative is indeed a very busy one.

There have been many famous Senators and Representatives. Some of these men have greatly influenced the history of our nation. Some have spent many years of service in Congress. They have become experts in certain fields, such as taxation or foreign affairs. Sometimes we hear grumbling about how slow Congress is. Sometimes we hear people complain because Congress passed a certain law or failed to pass some other one. Let us remember two things. First, much of the criticism may be just politics; that is, it may come from the minority or opposite party. Second, "we the people" elect the members of Congress. If we want an efficient and capable Congress it is up to us to elect efficient and capable men to represent us.

Getting Acquainted with the Supreme Court

The Supreme Court of the United States is the highest court of the *Judicial Branch* of our federal government. It is important because it protects the rights and liberties guaranteed us in the Constitution. When called upon, the Supreme Court also interprets or explains the meaning of powers given to the President or Congress by the Constitution.

What the Supreme Court Is

The Supreme Court is made up of nine men. There are eight Associate Justices and a Chief Justice. They are not elected, but are appointed by the President with the consent of the Senate. Only men of highest character and outstanding ability are chosen to serve on the Supreme Court. Their term is not set for a certain number of years, but for life. These men have a special title — Justice. The name is more than a title; it stands also for the purpose of the Court, to give justice to those who seek its aid. Our democracy was founded on the belief that all men have equal rights in the eyes of the law. This is what our forefathers meant when they wrote in the Declaration of Independence that "all men are created equal." The motto of the Supreme Court expresses the same idea — "Equal Justice under Law."

When a man becomes a member of the Supreme Court, he takes a special oath to be fair to all men, to treat rich and poor equally, and to support the Constitution. Here is the oath:

> I, ____, do solemnly swear (or affirm) that I will administer justice without respect to persons, and do equal right to the poor and to the rich, and that I will faithfully and impartially discharge and perform all the duties incumbent upon me [falling to me] as a Judge, according to the best of my abilities and understanding, agreeably to the Constitution and laws of the United States. (So help me God.)

What Courts Are For

To understand our Supreme Court, you first need to know what courts are for. All governments, as you know, have rules or laws for citizens to live by. Under our national, state, and local governments, the laws are made by representatives elected by the people. Congress makes laws for the good of the nation as a whole; the state legislatures make laws for the people of their own states. We also have local laws made by the county and the town or city governments. What happens if these laws are broken? What happens if dis-

Salaries — Executive, Legislative, Judicial

President	$100,000 a year
Plus $50,000 allowance for expenses; plus $40,000 for travel and official entertainment, tax free	
Vice-President	35,000 a year
Plus $10,000 allowance for expenses	
Supreme Court	
Chief Justice	35,500 a year
Associate Justices	35,000 a year
Congress	
Senators	22,500 a year
Members of House of Representatives	22,500 a year
Speaker of the House	35,000 a year
Plus $10,000 for expenses	

The nine members of the Supreme Court are pledged to preserve "equal justice under law."

putes come up over property or business matters? There has to be some way of settling disputes and of punishing lawbreakers. That is why we have courts. Courts protect people against injustice; they settle disputes and see that lawbreakers are punished. In our country we have many kinds of courts — federal (national) courts, state courts, county and city courts. The Supreme Court is the highest of the many federal courts. In fact, the Supreme Court is the highest court in our land.

What the Supreme Court Does

Perhaps you are wondering what the Supreme Court does, what kind of cases it handles. It is chiefly known as a "court of appeal." This means that it deals mostly with disputes that have already been tried in lower federal courts or in state Supreme Courts. If such cases are of the types mentioned in the Constitution and have not been satisfactorily settled, they may be appealed to the Supreme Court. Here are the kinds of cases the Supreme Court may judge:

1. Cases that have to do with a violation of our Constitution. Perhaps a *state* or *city* has passed a law which the people believe affects their constitutional right to free speech. Such a dispute might reach the Supreme Court, which would give its opinion as to whether the law actually does violate the right to free speech.

Or, if there is a dispute about whether a law of *Congress* violates the Constitution, the Supreme Court might judge the case. It has the power to declare that law "unconstitutional." For example, when Congress first passed an income tax law, the Court declared that the Constitution did not give Congress the power to pass a law taxing incomes. It was necessary to amend the Constitution to give Congress that power before such a law could be passed.

2. Cases that have to do with a violation of a law of Congress. A large company, for instance, that manufac-

tures drugs and medicines might be accused of violating the Pure Food and Drugs Act by using an unsafe drug in cough medicine. This act is a law passed by Congress to protect the people from dangerous drugs, impure food, and so on. A case of this kind might also be appealed to the Supreme Court if not satisfactorily settled in a lower court.

3. Cases between a state and some other party are not tried in a lower court but go directly to the Supreme Court. Cases involving an ambassador or other officials who represent us in foreign countries also go directly to the Supreme Court.

How the Court Opens

The opening of a Court session follows customs as old as the Court itself. The public meetings begin at noon. At twelve o'clock a gavel bangs and the Court crier, dressed in a cutaway coat, calls, "The Honorable Chief Justice and the Associate Justices of the Supreme Court of the United States." Everyone rises as the curtain behind the bench opens and the nine Justices in their black robes enter. The Chief Justice sits first, then the others. After the audience is seated the Court crier calls out, "Oyez! [Hear!] Oyez! Oyez! All persons having business before the honorable, the Supreme Court of the United States, are admonished [warned] to draw near and give their attention, for the court is now sitting. God save the United States and this honorable Court." The business of the Court then follows.

How the Supreme Court Works

When a case is brought to the Court, the lawyers for each side present their arguments before the nine Justices. Each side has just one hour to argue its case. The Chief Justice acts as a chairman. There is no jury and there are no witnesses. The Justices may question the lawyers on any point they wish to know more about. After the hearing, the Court holds a conference to discuss the problem. The Justices may spend a long time, even weeks or months, in studying the case. Then they vote on whether to support the decision of the lower court or not. The case is decided by a majority vote. There cannot be a tie because of the uneven number of judges. The Court then appoints one of the Justices to write a statement giving the reasons for the decision. This "opinion" is read in a session of the Court. Once the decision is made, the President and Congress and all Americans are expected to obey it. It sometimes happens that the Constitution is amended, as in the case of the income tax law. Then, of course, the decision of the Court on that problem is no longer binding.

★ ★ ★ ★ ★ ★ ★ ★

In this chapter you have read about the President, Congress, and the Supreme Court. You have learned how these officials are chosen and what they do. In the next chapter you will learn about Washington, our capital city, where the work of these officials is carried on.

CHAPTER 5

Washington, Capital of Our Nation

What city is in the United States but is not a part of any state? The answer, of course, is the chapter title above. The city of Washington is located in the District of Columbia, which is controlled by the United States. This beautiful city is the home of the United States Government. Perhaps you have not thought about the fact that you, John Jones, or you, Mary Smith, have a share in Uncle Sam's capital at Washington. But you have, for the capital of our nation belongs to every American. It is a part of our heritage. This chapter will help you get acquainted with our capital.

The Birth of Our Capital

Anyone visiting Washington today would find it hard to believe that this

AMERICA, PRESENT AND PAST: *Our nation's capital, over which the Capitol dome rises, began as a little town of muddy streets and open spaces.*

magnificent city was once a handful of buildings near soggy swamps. Washington did not exist when the United States became a nation. It was built, like all of our country, from a wilderness.

How Our Capital City Came to Be

During the Revolution the thirteen states had no capital. The Continental Congress moved from one city to another to escape British troops. When our country became independent, there was still no permanent capital. George Washington, as you know, was inaugurated as our first President in New York and it was here that the first Congress under the Constitution met. But ever since the country had won its independence, Americans had talked about having a "Federal Town" or capital city. This capital was to be located in a territory set aside especially as the seat of the new central government. In 1790 Congress selected Philadelphia as the temporary capital for ten years. During this time a suitable location was to be found and a permanent capital city started.

Many places had been suggested as a location for the capital. The Southerners in Congress wanted the capital somewhere along the Potomac River. The Congressmen from the northern states preferred a site on the Delaware River farther north. How they finally came to an agreement is an interesting story in itself. Alexander Hamilton, our first Secretary of the Treasury, wanted the Federal government to pay the Revolutionary War debts of the thirteen states. He felt that such a move would strengthen the new national government in the eyes of its own citizens and of foreign nations. But some of the prosperous Southern states had already paid off their debts, so they naturally objected to the plan. Finally, Hamilton and Thomas Jefferson worked out a compromise. The Southerners were to vote for Hamilton's plan to take over the state debts; the Northerners in turn were to approve a southern location for the national capital. Both sides agreed to these terms and Congress passed laws to carry out the compromise.

The Capital Is Located

President Washington himself rode on horseback along the Potomac River in search of the best possible location for the new capital city. He finally selected a piece of land lying partly in Maryland and partly in Virginia. He arranged for the United States to buy from the owners the land it needed. The price was $6.66 an acre. Congress named the plot of land the *District of Columbia.* At Thomas Jefferson's suggestion, the capital city-to-be was called *Washington* in honor of the great man who was our first President.

The District of Columbia was originally a square ten miles on each side. Later, Virginia's piece of land was returned to her because Congress believed so much land would not be needed for the capital. So today the District has an area of about seventy square miles instead of the original

L'Enfant Planning the Capital

one hundred. (The map on page 89 shows how the District of Columbia is shaped.) Of this area the United States Government owns about two fifths.

A Magnificent City Is Planned

The next step was to make plans for the capital city. Washington chose a French engineer and architect named Pierre L'Enfant (lahn-fahn') to draw up the plans. L'Enfant, like Lafayette, had come to America during the Revolution, and had fought side by side with American soldiers in the Continental army. He was a man with large ideas and great vision. No one in those days could have foreseen that our little country would become a mighty nation stretching from ocean to ocean. Yet L'Enfant dreamed of a city which he said would be "magnificent enough to grace a great nation." He drew plans for a splendid city with dignified government buildings, beautiful parks, and broad avenues. In those days most city streets were narrow wagon roads, but L'Enfant planned for boulevards one hundred and fifty feet wide.

The Capitol building was to mark the center of the city. It was to be located on a hill facing the wide Potomac. Between the Capitol and the river, L'Enfant planned a monument in honor of George Washington. A broad green park was to stretch from the Capitol down to the monument. L'Enfant located the President's house about a mile and a half northwest of the Capitol on ground sloping down to the river. A broad, tree-lined avenue was to connect the two buildings. The Capitol, the monument, and the President's house were to be the points of a huge triangle in which other government buildings would later be built.

Although not all of L'Enfant's plans for the capital were followed in later years, the idea of the triangle was carried out. One of the most beautiful sights in Washington today is the view looking west from the Capitol across the wide green Mall (park) to the tall shaft of the Washington Monument. The Monument is reflected in a shimmering pool beyond. Still farther west now stands the Lincoln Memorial of gleaming white marble. Both the Capitol and the White House

Pierre L'Enfant, Designer of Our Capital City

L'Enfant's great service to our nation was not realized until long after his death. In 1909 his remains were brought to the Capitol, where they lay in state in the Rotunda. Later his body was buried with military honors in Arlington National Cemetery. In this way our nation expressed its gratitude to the man who planned our beautiful capital city.

In this picture you see the White House as it appeared in President John Adams' time.

can be seen from the Monument, thus completing the lovely view planned by L'Enfant. (See the map, page 89.)

A City Is Born in the Wilderness

The actual building of the city began with the President's house in 1792. A year later George Washington laid the cornerstone of the Capitol building. But the new capital grew slowly. There were many difficulties. L'Enfant, who was not an even-tempered man, got into disputes with some of the landowners and finally resigned. As you know, building requires money, skilled workmen, and materials. Our new nation was poor. It was hard to find good workmen who were willing to go to the new town. Stone and other building materials had to be hauled long distances. The work progressed so slowly that by 1800 neither the Capitol nor the President's house was finished. George Washington did not live to see the city which was named for him, for he died near the close of 1799.

Nevertheless, early in 1800 the government moved from Philadelphia to Washington. The moving was a simple matter. In those days it took only twelve boxes to hold all the government's official papers! All the office furniture was carried in one small sailing ship. There were only fifty-four government officials, counting the President, the Cabinet members, and all the clerks!

President Adams and his wife Abigail moved into their house even though it was not finished. The plaster was still damp and some of the rooms had no floors. Mrs. Adams found it very difficult to keep house, as we may imagine. She wrote in her diary that she used the grand ballroom (now the famous East Room) to hang the washing in!

The President's house seemed a long way from the Capitol. Instead of the tree-lined avenue planned by L'Enfant, there was a muddy road in which carriage wheels sank up to the hubs. There was not a single house along the entire way. No doubt the members of Congress wished they had stayed in Philadelphia. They had to live in hastily built wooden boarding houses near the Capitol. Congress itself met in one wing of the unfinished Capitol. The Senate and the House took turns using the only completed room. Foreign visitors ridiculed the new city. They called Washington the "City of Magnificent Distances," and the "City of Streets without Houses."

From Wilderness to World-Famous Capital

By 1801 Washington had a population of around 3000 people. Gradually the capital grew and conditions improved. A number of comfortable new houses were built near the President's home. Several shops made living less difficult. As years went by, the dirt streets became paved boulevards. Many beautiful houses of the type found in the South were built. Imposing government buildings began to line the streets in the center of the city. Statues and monuments of great Americans added to the beauty of the city.

As our nation grew in size and importance, the capital city grew with it. Today the little town on the banks of the Potomac has become a city of about 760,000 people. It fills the District of Columbia and overflows into Virginia and Maryland. Washington and the overflow areas have a population of about two million. Thanks to its designer, Washington is indeed a city "magnificent enough to grace a great nation." It is famous not only as the seat of our government but as one of the beautiful cities of the world. Washington, D.C., is a capital of which we Americans can be proud.

Getting Acquainted with Our Capital City

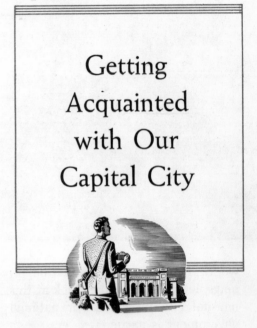

Washington, D.C., is the "most visited" city in the United States. It is filled with tourists the year round, for Americans want to see the city that is the home of our national government. They want to see where the President lives and where Congress meets, and to view the monuments and memorials to great Americans. Washington is the very heart of our democracy. In fact, Washington has become a symbol for the government of the United States, not only to Americans but to people all over the

Population of Washington, D. C.

1800	3,000	1920	437,571
1850	51,687	1930	486,869
1880	147,293	1940	663,091
1900	278,718	1950	802,178
1910	331,069	1960	763,956

The Washington Monument offers a breathtaking view straight down the Mall to the Capitol.

world. Now that we know its beginnings, let us take a closer look at this unusual city in which our national government is located.

Washington Is a Government City

If all the people who work for the Federal government should leave Washington with their families, the capital would seem like a deserted city. The task of governing our nation of over 180 million people is an enormous and complicated one and requires many workers. As you know, the President of the United States, the Vice-President, the Cabinet members, the Congressmen, and the Supreme Court judges all carry on their work in Washington. There are a great many bureaus and agencies connected with the three branches of our government. Most of these also have their headquarters in Washington. Almost one third of the city's population is made up of officials, secretaries, and clerks who work in the hundreds of government offices.

Of course, there are many thousands of people in Washington who do not work directly for the government. Among them are the people who supply living quarters, and run the stores, restaurants, and other businesses needed in the capital. These people depend heavily on government workers to keep their businesses going. In addition there are the visitors who flock to the capital at a rate of about seven million a year. Many come on government business, others to view the interesting city where our government is at work. So you see Washington is truly a "government city."

Who Governs Washington?

As you know, Uncle Sam owns two fifths of Washington — the Capitol, the White House, and all other government buildings and national monuments. All this property is under the control of special government police and the Public Buildings Service. Otherwise, the city of Washington is governed by the Congress of the United States. All laws for the District of Columbia must be passed by Congress and signed by the President! Three Commissioners appointed by the President with the approval of the Senate run the affairs of the city. Citizens of the District of Columbia do not vote on city matters or in national elections. Nor are they represented in Congress.

It may seem strange to you that the Constitution gives Congress the power to make local laws for the national capital. (See Article I, Section 8, of the Constitution.) The makers of the Constitution believed that the seat of the government should be kept free of city or national politics. But most people in Washington do not approve of being governed by Congress. They feel they are deprived of the self-government the rest of us enjoy. In 1960, Congress approved an amendment to the Constitution which would enable citizens of Washington to vote in Presidential elections. The amendment must still be approved by three fourths of the states before it takes effect, but the people of Washington may be able to vote for a President for the first time in 1964.

We Take an Imaginary Airplane Trip over Washington

The most interesting and the most important section of the capital is that part owned by the United States Government. A large number of the government buildings are between the Capitol and the White House, or near them. Let us imagine we are slowly circling over the capital in an airplane. As we approach the Washington Monument, the whole city stretches out before our eyes in all its splendor.

We can get an excellent view of the part of Washington that belongs to Uncle Sam. Looking due east, beyond the Mall we see the Capitol with its massive white dome. Gazing north we discover the White House set in beautiful park-like grounds. Below us to the west of the Washington Monument is the Reflecting Pool, and facing it the Lincoln Memorial with

An air view shows the unusual shape of the huge Pentagon, which has 17½ miles of corridors.

its white columns of gleaming marble. Beyond the Lincoln Memorial the Arlington Memorial Bridge crosses the Potomac to the Arlington National Cemetery. Across the Potomac in Virginia is also the huge Pentagon Building, headquarters for the Armed Services of the nation. As our plane turns south, we can see the beautiful Jefferson Memorial in line with the White House and the Washington Monument.

After taking a second look at these famous landmarks, we are ready to turn our attention to the vast expanse of government buildings lying below us. The map on page 89 will help you locate these various buildings. Like the spokes of a wheel with the Capitol as a hub, several wide diagonal avenues stretch outward cutting through other city streets. At some points where the streets cross avenues, there are circular parks and statues of famous Americans. These broad avenues were part of L'Enfant's plan, and are named after states of the Union. We can see Pennsylvania Avenue, the most famous diagonal avenue, which connects the Capitol and the White House. Now let us locate Constitution Avenue, which is not a diagonal but runs east and west along the Mall. These two broad avenues cross not far from the Capitol. Between them lies a great triangular-shaped section, known as the *Federal Triangle* because so many government buildings are located here.

Not far from the point where Pennsylvania Avenue crosses Constitution Avenue we see the enormous and imposing Archives Building, covering a whole block. Here, you remember, the Declaration of Independence, the Constitution, and other valuable government documents are preserved. In the Triangle are also located four of the Cabinet department buildings. Nearby, we can see the Pan-American Union Building, dedicated to friendship between the United States and the republics of Latin America. It is one of the loveliest places in the capital. Other important buildings lie along the sides of the Mall. On the south side, for example, we see the famous Smithsonian Institution. The Smithsonian has been called "Uncle Sam's Attic" and contains all kinds of fascinating exhibits, from giant dinosaurs to airplanes used in famous flights. This Institution is a center of scientific knowledge and research. North of the Mall, facing Constitution Avenue, is the rose-white marble building called the National Gallery of Art. It holds one of the world's great collections of paintings.

It is not possible to describe here all the buildings which can be seen from our airplane. But beyond the Capitol, looking to the east, are two we cannot miss. One is the majestic marble building where the Supreme Court meets. The other is the Library of Congress, which contains 12 million books and pamphlets. It is used by members of Congress and others for study and research. The school for the Capitol pages is also located in the Library of Congress.

Now that we have a clearer idea of the Federal Triangle and nearby gov-

(Continued on page 90)

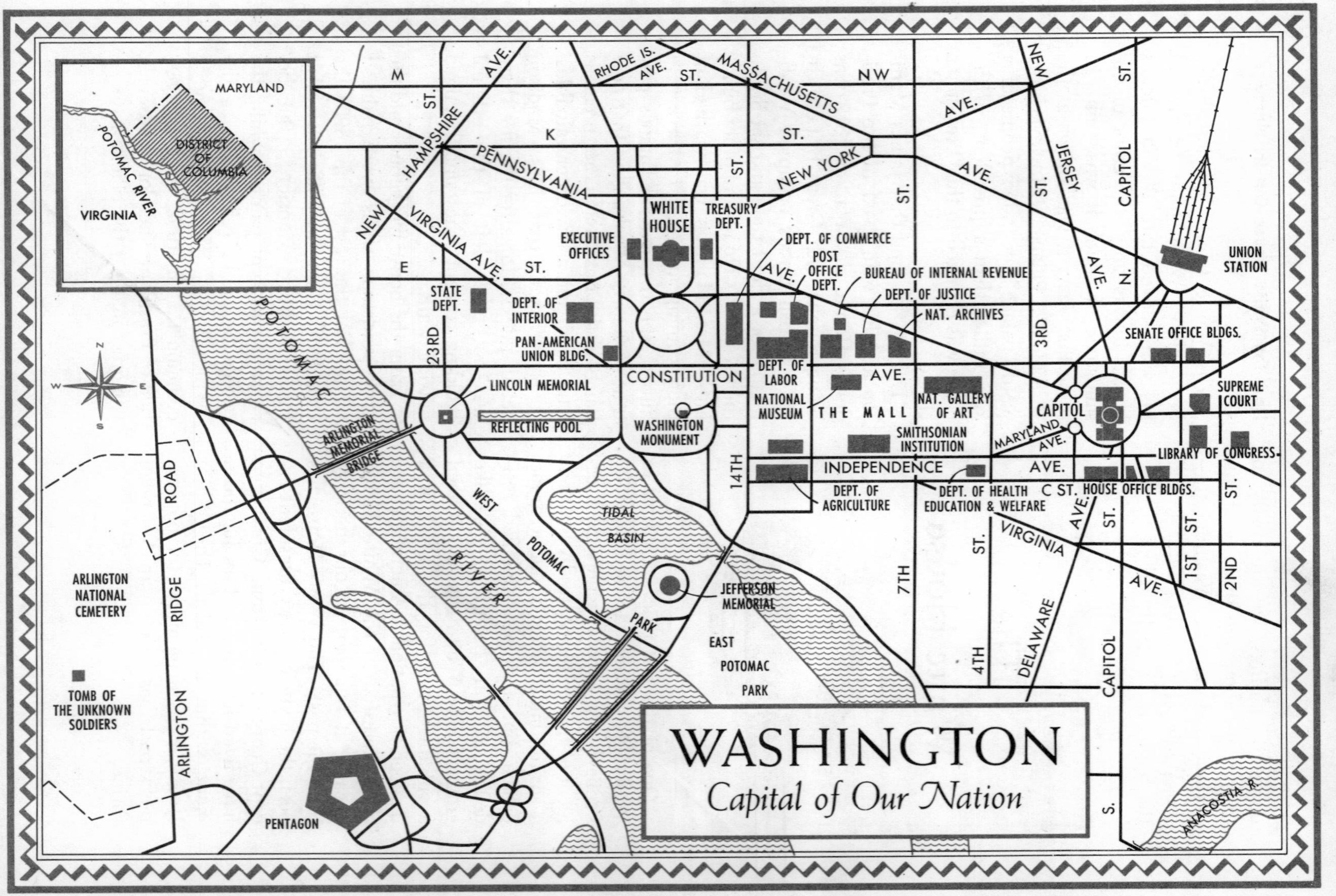
WASHINGTON
Capital of Our Nation
MARYLAND
DISTRICT OF COLUMBIA
VIRGINIA
POTOMAC RIVER
WHITE HOUSE
TREASURY DEPT.
EXECUTIVE OFFICES
STATE DEPT.
DEPT. OF INTERIOR
PAN-AMERICAN UNION BLDG.
LINCOLN MEMORIAL
REFLECTING POOL
CONSTITUTION
WASHINGTON MONUMENT
DEPT. OF COMMERCE
POST OFFICE DEPT.
BUREAU OF INTERNAL REVENUE
DEPT. OF JUSTICE
NAT. ARCHIVES
DEPT. OF LABOR
NATIONAL MUSEUM
THE MALL
NAT. GALLERY OF ART
SMITHSONIAN INSTITUTION
INDEPENDENCE
DEPT. OF AGRICULTURE
DEPT. OF HEALTH EDUCATION & WELFARE
CAPITOL
SENATE OFFICE BLDGS.
SUPREME COURT
LIBRARY OF CONGRESS
HOUSE OFFICE BLDGS.
UNION STATION
TIDAL BASIN
JEFFERSON MEMORIAL
EAST POTOMAC PARK
WEST POTOMAC PARK
POTOMAC RIVER
ARLINGTON MEMORIAL BRIDGE
ARLINGTON RIDGE ROAD
ARLINGTON NATIONAL CEMETERY
TOMB OF THE UNKNOWN SOLDIERS
PENTAGON
ANACOSTIA R.
M ST.
K ST.
E ST.
C ST.
23RD
14TH
7TH
4TH
3RD
1ST ST.
2ND ST.
N. CAPITOL ST.
S. CAPITOL
NEW HAMPSHIRE AVE.
PENNSYLVANIA AVE.
VIRGINIA AVE.
RHODE IS. AVE.
MASSACHUSETTS AVE.
NW
NEW YORK AVE.
NEW JERSEY AVE.
MARYLAND AVE.
DELAWARE
N
E
S
W

ernment buildings, we are ready to learn more about the three most important buildings in Washington — the White House, the Capitol, and the Supreme Court Building.

The White House

One of the first places a visitor to Washington wants to see is 1600 Pennsylvania Avenue, where the President of the United States lives. What a visitor finds there is not a grand palace, but a simple, dignified residence set in beautiful park-like grounds. The White House is indeed a suitable home for the head of a democratic nation. Americans are also interested in the White House because it is a part of our heritage from the past. The White House has been the home of every President except George Washington. Great men have lived here and history has been made within its walls. The White House, rich in memories of our nation's past, has become an American shrine.

How the White House Got Its Name

The White House has not always been white. When John Adams and his wife moved into the President's house, it was grey, the color of the sandstone of which it was built. In these first years it was known as the "President's Palace." However, the word "palace" reminded people of a king rather than a president, so the name was changed to the "President's Home."

During the time that James Madison and his wife lived in the President's Home, the War of 1812 was being fought with Great Britain. In 1814 British troops occupied Washington for a short time and set fire to the President's Home and other buildings. Mrs. Madison was warned of their coming and had to leave in a hurry. She rescued the famous portrait of George Washington that now hangs in the East Room, her precious fruit bowl, and a few other valuables. It is fortunate that Mrs. Madison acted quickly, for after the fire there was not much left of the original building except the smoke-stained outside walls.

Later the house was rebuilt and the grey sandstone walls were painted white. For the rest of the 1800's the President's Home was officially called the "Executive Mansion." But because it was kept painted white, the people began to refer to it as the "White House." The name became so common that in 1902, at the suggestion of President Theodore Roosevelt, Congress made it the official name.

The White House Changes with the Times

It is doubtful whether Abigail Adams would recognize the President's mansion if she could return today. There have been many changes made since the days when she had her washing hung in the huge East Room over one hundred and fifty years ago. In fact there is little left of the plain steep-roofed house which is pictured on page 84. The picture of the White House today on this page shows some of these changes. The familiar *South Portico* (porch) and the great pillared *North Portico,* which faces on Pennsylvania Avenue, were added in the 1820's. You will notice the low, long terraces which join the east and west wings to the main building. The terraces and wings were originally planned by Thomas Jefferson, but have been enlarged and rebuilt many times as more room was needed.

Today the White House includes much more than the four-story main building. The East Terrace, 215 feet long, leads to the East Wing. This building has three stories and is used for offices and also as an entrance to the White House. The West Terrace is shorter than the East Terrace and leads to the Executive Office Building, where the President and his office staff do their work.

There have been as many changes inside the White House as there have been outside. In the early days, of course, there was no gas or electricity or even water in the house. Water was carried from a spring by servants, candles furnished the only light, and fireplaces were used to heat the huge rooms. It is said that one servant did nothing but keep candles lighted throughout the house and replace those that burned out. The first bath tub, made of tin, was introduced in 1814. Water for bathing was poured into it. In 1833 the first water was piped into the kitchen from a private well. But the Presidents and their families did not have a regular bathroom until about twenty years later when the city of Washington put in a water system.

Not until the late 1870's was the first telephone installed. Kerosene lamps had long ago replaced candles, but there was no electric light in the White House until the early 1890's.

This picture shows the White House, home of our Presidents, with its graceful and familiar South Portico.

Why the British Burned Our Capitol and White House

There is more to the burning of our White House and Capitol by the British in 1814 than most Americans know. In the year before, American forces occupied York (now Toronto), the British capital of Upper Canada. Besides setting fire to government buildings, they took the mace from the House of Parliament. Franklin D. Roosevelt ordered the mace returned while he was President, thus ending an incident that occurred over a hundred years before.

It is said that President Benjamin Harrison and his family were afraid to turn the lights on or off for fear of an electric shock! Today, of course, the White House has all the modern conveniences, including air conditioning. The old kitchen, where cooking was once done over a fireplace, has been replaced by three up-to-date modern rooms equipped with the latest electrical appliances.

New Furniture for the White House

The furniture and furnishings of the White House changed a good deal as Presidents and their wives came and went. Each President's wife added furniture to suit her taste. The simple colonial pieces of early days gave way to elegant furnishings from France — gilded chairs with satin seats, ornamented clocks, elaborate crystal chandeliers. Later on, marble-topped tables and horsehair sofas became popular. As time went on, the White House rooms were crowded with many styles of furniture. Soon after he became President, Theodore Roosevelt asked Congress for money to refurnish the White House in a style suited to the beauty and dignity of its architecture. The rooms on the main floor were redecorated. The French style of furniture used in the late 1790's was selected as most suitable to use throughout the house. Since that time the White House has been more beautifully and appropriately furnished.

In 1902 the Executive Office was built. Up to that time the second floor had been used for the President's offices as well as for the family bedrooms. President Theodore Roosevelt had six children. The story goes that there were so few bedrooms, the younger Roosevelts had to sleep crosswise on the nine-foot bed used by President Lincoln! Whether the story is true or not, Congress did, at the request of President Roosevelt, vote money for the new Executive Office Building.

The White House Is Rebuilt

The most complete remodeling of the White House was done while Harry Truman was President. An investigation showed that the historic old mansion was unsafe to live in. Floors and walls were in danger of collapsing. The original walls, now one hundred and fifty years old, had been weakened by the fire in 1814. In the following years, workmen had cut into the walls many times to install plumbing, gas pipes, electric wires, and other modern conveniences. Millions of visitors and sightseers had added to the wear and tear on the building. President Truman asked Congress for about five million dollars to reconstruct the White House completely. The money was voted, and in 1948 the President and his family moved to Blair House across the street.

Engineers and architects found that an entire new interior would have to be built. The simplest way to rebuild the old house would have been to tear it down completely. But Americans did not want the White House with its memories of bygone days destroyed. So the original walls were saved and new walls of steel and concrete built inside them. A deeper foundation was dug and new basements added. Today the White House has a ground floor above the basements, a main floor, and two stories above the main floor.

The plan was to restore the building to the beauty and simplicity of its early years, keeping the original style of furniture and decoration of the 1700's. The workmen carefully removed the wood paneling, the fine old woodwork, and the beautiful chandeliers, so that they could be replaced later. The rebuilding took about four years. In the spring of 1952 President Truman and his family moved back to the White House. The American people were given an opportunity to see the redecorated rooms when the President himself conducted a television tour. He explained the changes made and told bits of White House history. On the first visiting day after the White House was reopened to the public, 5,544 people flocked through it in two hours! On a later day almost 10,000 visited the famous house.

A Visit to the White House

How would you like to have hundreds, even thousands, of tourists passing through your home? That is what happens almost every week in the President's house. The White House, with its furniture, is the property of the nation. Anyone may visit the White House from Tuesday to Saturday between ten and twelve in the morning. The entire White House, of course, is not open to public view. Visitcrs may see some of the rooms on the ground floor, and the formal reception rooms on the main or first floor. Sometimes it is possible to visit the Lincoln Room on the second floor, but the family rooms and the kitchens are closed to the public.

Let us imagine that we are taking a trip through the White House. We do not use the entrance on Pennsylvania Avenue. That is reserved for invited guests. It is with a good deal of awe that we follow one of the official White House guides through the public entrance in the East Wing. The guide takes us along the East Terrace and downstairs to the ground floor. Off the main corridor is the China Room with walls paneled in pine. Here china used by almost every President is displayed in glass cabinets. There are dinner plates used by Washington, and a set of gold plates which belonged to President

The Green Room is used for small gatherings. Over the couch is a portrait of Thomas Jefferson. Note the President's coat of arms in the rug.

Monroe. We see a sugar bowl which was Martha Washington's, and the fruit bowl rescued from the fire by Dolly Madison. There is President Jackson's enormous coffee cup, and salt cellars used by Abigail Adams.

We learn that on the ground floor also is the oval-shaped Diplomatic Reception Room, where foreign ambassadors and diplomats are received. Another room on the ground floor is the library, lined with fine wood paneling many years old. Before we go upstairs, the guide points out the location of the kitchens beneath the State Dining Room. He tells us that the food is sent up from the kitchens on dumb-waiters, or lifts, to a pantry next to the dining room.

The Main Floor

The State Dining Room is located at the west end of the main floor. At the other end is the famous East Room. Between them are three reception rooms called the Red, Blue, and Green Rooms. The State Dining Room is used for the large formal dinners given by the President. It has a long oval table which can be enlarged to seat 102 people. A famous portrait of Lincoln hangs over the fireplace. The walls of this beautiful room are light green, and the draperies are of gold damask (heavy figured satin). We do not see the smaller private dining room next door which is used by the President, his family, and guests.

Next we visit the Red Room, so named because its walls and hangings are of deep red silk. The fireplace is of white marble, and some of the chairs are covered with white damask. Luncheon and dinner guests assemble in the Red Room, and the President's wife also gives teas here.

The Blue Room beyond is just opposite the imposing main entrance to the White House. Through an open window we catch a glimpse of the great front hall, or lobby, with its marble floor and marble columns. The President's Seal in bronze used to be set in the floor near the front door, but has been removed to a more fitting place above the main entrance to the Blue Room. In this room, famous for its oval shape, the President and his wife receive their guests at the formal state receptions. They shake hands with many hundreds of people during an evening. The room is elegant with its rich blue-and-gold hangings and French furniture. Beautiful crystal chandeliers which date back to Jefferson's time hang from the ceiling. In the more homelike Green Room there are portraits of Thomas Jefferson and John Quincy Adams. The walls are of green damask. Woven into the green rug is the President's coat of arms, with its white stars arranged in a circle around the eagle and shield.

We Visit the Famous East Room

The greatest thrill of all on the main floor is the sight of the spacious and magnificent East Room. It is decorated in white and gold. Enormous gold-framed mirrors reflect the elegant furniture and the draperies of gold damask. At each end of the great room stands a concert grand piano. The older of the two is gilded to match the decorations of the room. The guide points out the portrait of Washington saved by Mrs. Madison. Here, we are told, the guests assemble for formal receptions before going into the Blue Room to be presented to the President and his wife. The diplomatic reception for the foreign ambassadors and their staffs is the most colorful reception of the year. Glittering military uniforms of many countries and the beautiful dresses of the women guests make the reception a grand sight indeed.

Pleasant memories of days gone by linger in the East Room. It has seen many gay times. In the days of Dolly Madison it was a ballroom. Ladies in dresses of stiff brocade and gentlemen in knee breeches of satin danced the stately minuet. Later on, the daughters of three Presidents were married here. President Jackson, the hero of the "common man," held an inaugural reception here for all who wished to come. The story goes that many ill-mannered guests broke glassware and stood on satin chairs and sofas with muddy boots to get a better view of

The attractive Red Room is used by the President's wife to receive guests.

the President. Sad memories also linger in the East Room, for seven Presidents lay here in death. The last President to lie in state in this great room was Franklin Roosevelt, who died soon after starting his fourth term as President.

Above the Main Floor

We have now seen as much of the White House as visitors are allowed to see. The guide explains that on the second floor are the private quarters of the President and his family, and the President's study. This room was also Lincoln's study. There is a story that late at night one can hear his ghostly footsteps pacing the floor as he used to do in the anxious war days. The Lincoln Room, where the tall President slept in a nine-foot bed, is also on the second floor. Lincoln's marble-topped table, his desk, and his huge bed are still in the room.

On the second floor also is the Rose Room, or Queen's Room. Here Queen Juliana of Holland and, at another time, Queen Elizabeth II of England slept while visiting at the White House. On the new third floor are thirty-four bedrooms to accommodate White House guests. On the roof a sun parlor enclosed in blue-green glass was built by President Truman. It furnishes a beautiful view of the Washington Monument and the Lincoln and Jefferson Memorials.

As we leave the White House we think of all the memories it holds, memories of the men and women and children who have lived there since our country was young. Some memories are sad, some are happy, but all are part of our country's history.

A Reception in the East Room a Century Ago

Our Capitol

No American can look at our majestic Capitol with its great white dome, without feeling a thrill of pride. The Capitol, where Congress makes our laws, is a building that every one of us has a share in. "We the people" send Congressmen here to represent us. The business done in the Capitol is the people's business. So the Capitol of the United States, more than any other government building, is a symbol of our "government of the people, by the people, for the people."

The Capitol Grew with the Nation

The Capitol stands on a hill. Its west front looks down across the Mall

This picture shows the original Capitol with its wooden dome.

to the Washington Monument, and beyond to the Lincoln Memorial and the broad Potomac. The east front faces the beautiful Supreme Court Building across the street. L'Enfant, as you know, planned that the Capitol would be the center of the new city, but the city has grown to the northwest, so that the Capitol is no longer the geographical center. Yet the Capitol is still the center as far as the government is concerned, because within a mile of it most of the important government buildings are located.

It was a great day when George Washington himself laid the cornerstone of the building in 1793. A band played and a whole ox was barbecued for those who attended the ceremony! When Congress moved to Washington in 1800, the Capitol was only partly completed. The House and Senate took turns meeting in the Senate Chamber until the Hall of Representatives was ready for use in 1807. During the War of 1812 the interior of the Capitol was so badly burned that Congress had to move out while repairs were made. When the building was finally finished in 1829, it was about half the size it is today and was topped by a wooden dome. The picture on this page shows how it looked then.

By the middle of the 1800's the Capitol had already become too small for the rapidly growing Congress, so new wings were started for the House and Senate. During the War Between the States the old wooden dome was replaced with a dome of cast iron painted white. During the war also the huge bronze Statue of Freedom was raised above the dome. A 35-gun salute was sounded on the Capitol grounds, and cannon from nearby forts roared in celebration.

Since that time there has been only one important change in the outside of the Capitol. In 1959–1960 the East Front was extended 32½ feet to make additional space. The beautiful new front is faced with marble. Inside

Within the impressive Capitol, Senators and Representatives carry on our national affairs.

the Capitol many changes have been made to keep up with the times and the needs of Congress. In 1951 the sagging old ceilings of the House and Senate chambers were replaced. Air conditioning and up-to-date lighting were installed. Three office buildings for the House members and two for the Senators have also been built outside the Capitol grounds.

We Visit the Capitol

If you stand facing the east front of the Capitol, you see a massive building with a center section and huge wings on either side. Above the dome towers the Statue of Freedom, in the form of a woman wearing a helmet on which is the head of an eagle. In her right hand she grasps a sword; in her left hand an olive wreath of peace. From her lofty position above the Capitol she appears to be protecting the freedom for which America stands. We see wide stairs leading to each of the three sections of the building. The great center stairs take us up to the East Portico. You remember that Presidential inaugurations are held on a platform built over these stairs (page 64). The steps to the right lead to the Senate Wing; the steps to the left lead to the House Wing.

The Rotunda

We enter the building through the columns of the East Portico and find ourselves in a great circular hall under the dome. Anyone may see the Capitol free of charge but we decide to have a guide take us on the official tour. The guide explains that the hall is called the Rotunda (which means round). We look up at the magnificent domed ceiling, 180 feet above the floor. In the center is a rich painting with many lifelike figures representing George Washington and the thirteen original states. Our guide tells us that this painting, or mural, was done by Constantino Brumidi, an

Italian painter who came to America in 1852. He was hired by Congress to decorate the Capitol, and painted a number of its murals. The ceiling of the Rotunda is his finest work. We wonder what it would be like to work on a scaffold 180 feet above the floor as Brumidi had to do! (See picture on page 100.)

About halfway up to the dome is a circular balcony from which visitors may look down upon the great room below. The guide points out eight huge paintings that encircle the room. They show important events in our history, such as the landing of Columbus and the surrender of the British at Yorktown. On the floor near the wall are statues of great Americans.

Most visitors to the Capitol do not know that on a lower floor directly beneath the Rotunda is a vault holding an empty coffin draped in black. This was built as a tomb for George and Martha Washington. Congress planned to place a marble memorial above the tomb, and open a part of the Rotunda floor so that people could look down upon the last resting place of our great leader. But when Congress asked permission to move the bodies from Mount Vernon to the Capitol, Washington's relatives refused. George Washington had requested to be buried at his beloved home, Mount Vernon, and there he lies to this day. The tomb in the Capitol remains forever empty. The bier (or stand for the coffin) has been used from time to time for great men who have rested in state in the Rotunda. Major L'Enfant, Abraham Lincoln, and the Unknown Soldiers are among the few men held worthy of this honor.

The Old Supreme Court Room

We leave the Rotunda and make our way to the beautiful old room which was the original Senate Chamber. This room is in the shape of a half-circle with columns of black-and-white marble and a half-domed ceiling. It was in this room that the Senate approved the treaty for the purchase of Louisiana in 1803, and the treaties which ended the War of 1812 and the Mexican War. It was here also that Daniel Webster gave his famous speech on the Union in the dark days before the War Between the States. (Turn to page 134.) We can almost hear his deep voice ringing out the glorious words, "Liberty and Union, now and forever, one and inseparable." After the Senate moved into the new wing, the Supreme Court used this room until 1935, when the new Supreme Court Building was completed. The long mahogany table and the nine chairs used by the Justices are still there. The room is now known as the Old Supreme Court Room, and is not in regular use.

The Senate Wing

We now walk through a beautiful corridor into the Senate Wing of the

The Center of the Capitol

The Statue of Freedom atop the Capitol marks the exact center of the building. In the vault below the Rotunda is a marble star which also marks the precise center.

This striking picture of the Capitol Rotunda shows a statue of George Washington, and Brumidi's painting in the ceiling.

Capitol. The guide explains that this wing holds not only the Senate Chamber itself, but many reception rooms, committee rooms and private offices. The Senators have a reception room where they meet visitors, a reading room, and a private lobby outside the Senate chambers for Senators only. On the ground floor are dining rooms and shops of all kinds for the convenience of the Senators. There is also a post office, and ticket and telegraph offices as well. There is even a barber shop! There seem to be miles of corridors in the Senate Wing with beautifully decorated walls and ceilings and floors of colored tile.

Our guide takes us into a magnificent room which seems at first glance to be all of gold. He points out more of Brumidi's work on the beautiful ceiling. The room is decorated in gold, and from the ceiling hangs an enormous golden chandelier. Below it is an old mahogany table used by President Lincoln. This is the President's Room. It was intended for the President's use on his visits to Congress, but since his visits are few, it is used mostly by Senators for meetings with newspapermen.

The Senate Chamber

Next we visit the most important room in the Senate Wing, the Senate Chamber. We notice above the door leading to the Chamber three white and three red lights. The guide explains that the white lights are on when the Senate is in session. For the few meetings when the public is not allowed, the red lights go on as a warning. As we step into the handsome room decorated in red and gold, we see rows of chairs and desks, one set for each Senator, arranged in semicircles. Some of these mahogany desks are more than a hundred years old. The Senators love tradition, so they keep the old desks used by Senators of years gone by. They have other relics of the past also. The guide points out the inkwells of another day, and the sand shakers. These are bottles holding sand, which Senators once used to sprinkle on their papers to dry the ink. As you have already learned, one of the jobs of the Senate pages is to fill the inkwells and the sand shakers on the Senators' desks! The pages also keep two old boxes filled with fresh snuff (powdered tobacco) in memory of the days when Senators used to sniff snuff!

On a raised platform of marble at the front of the room is the carved chair of the Vice-President, who presides over the Senate. There are galleries above on all four sides. From these galleries the public, the newspapermen, and special guests may watch the proceedings.

The guide explains that under the Senate Wing a subway train runs to the Senate Office Buildings. Each Senator has a suite of several rooms in the Office Buildings. Senators save time by riding back and forth between the Capitol and their offices. The subway is an electric railway which can carry as many as 5000 passengers a day. The Senators make a one-way trip in about a minute. This is said to be the shortest electric railway in the world.

The House Wing

Leaving the Senate Wing, we follow a series of corridors over to the House Wing. We find that the House Wing is much simpler than the Senate quarters. The floors are of marble rather than fine tile, and the rooms are not so elaborately decorated. The Representatives do not have subway cars but must walk through an underground passage to their office buildings. As in the Senate Wing, the ground floor has telephone, telegraph, and ticket offices as well as barbershops, places to bank, and restaurants.

The Hall of Representatives is similar in plan to the Senate Chamber, but of course it is much larger. The Representatives do not have individual desks but comfortable black leather chairs arranged in semi-circular rows. The Democrats sit to the right of the Speaker and the Republicans to the left. The Speaker of the House sits at a desk on a marble platform. Behind him is the American Flag and above it a great clock. The guide points out the marble pedestal to the right of the Speaker where the mace stands when Congress is in session. We see the three rows of desks in the balcony of the Hall used by newsmen. The other sections are for the public, for families of members, and for diplomats. Anyone can visit Congress by getting a pass from a Congressman.

We learn that when Congress meets in joint session to hear a message from the President, it meets in the Hall of Representatives. At a joint session, the Senators sit in front, Representatives in back. Cabinet members and important officers sit on chairs in front of the Speaker's desk.

Facts about the Capitol

131 acres of grounds
3½ acres covered by Capitol itself
Over 14 acres of floor area
108 windows in dome
Length .... 751 feet, 4 inches
Height (including statue) .... 287 feet, 5½ inches
Diameter of rotunda .... 97 feet
Largest diameter of dome .... 135 feet, 5 inches

Great events have occurred in this room. Our entrance into World War I was decided here when Congress backed President Wilson by declaring war against Germany on April 6, 1917. Here too, on December 8, 1941, President Franklin Roosevelt in a stirring speech asked Congress to declare war on Japan after its attack on Pearl Harbor. Three times in recent years former Prime Minister Sir Winston Churchill of Great Britain spoke before Congress in joint session. On returning from Korea, General Douglas MacArthur made his home-coming speech to both houses of Congress. President Charles de Gaulle of France also spoke to Congress and the nation during a visit here.

Statuary Hall

On the way back to the Rotunda we stop at Statuary Hall, the old Hall of Representatives. We see the spot where Ex-President John Quincy Adams fell when he suddenly became ill in 1848. He died a short time later in a nearby office. Today the Hall is filled with statues. Each state is allowed to place a statue of one of its great men in this room. We notice Robert Fulton of Pennsylvania, designer of the first steamboat; Ethan Allen of Vermont, hero of the Revolution; and Andrew Jackson of Tennessee, seventh President of the United States.

We have now finished our tour of the Capitol Building, where history has been made in the past and is being made today by the men we elect to Congress. We have yet to visit the building which houses the highest court in the judicial branch of our national government.

Our Supreme Court Building

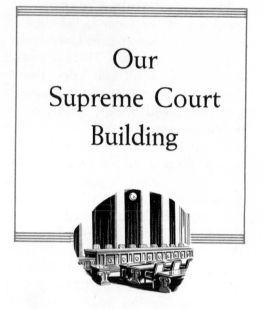

Across the street which runs along the east side of the Capitol grounds is a dignified building of white marble. This is the home of the Supreme Court. It is built in the style of an ancient Greek temple. Enormous columns of marble form a portico at the entrance to the building. Above the portico, carved in large letters for all to read is the motto, "EQUAL JUSTICE UNDER LAW." At either side of the entrance are statues of great lawmakers of the past. Inside are offices for the Justices, a library, a restaurant, and the chamber where the court meets.

The Supreme Court Chamber is a simple and dignified room, suitable for the highest court in the land. Along one side are the long desk and

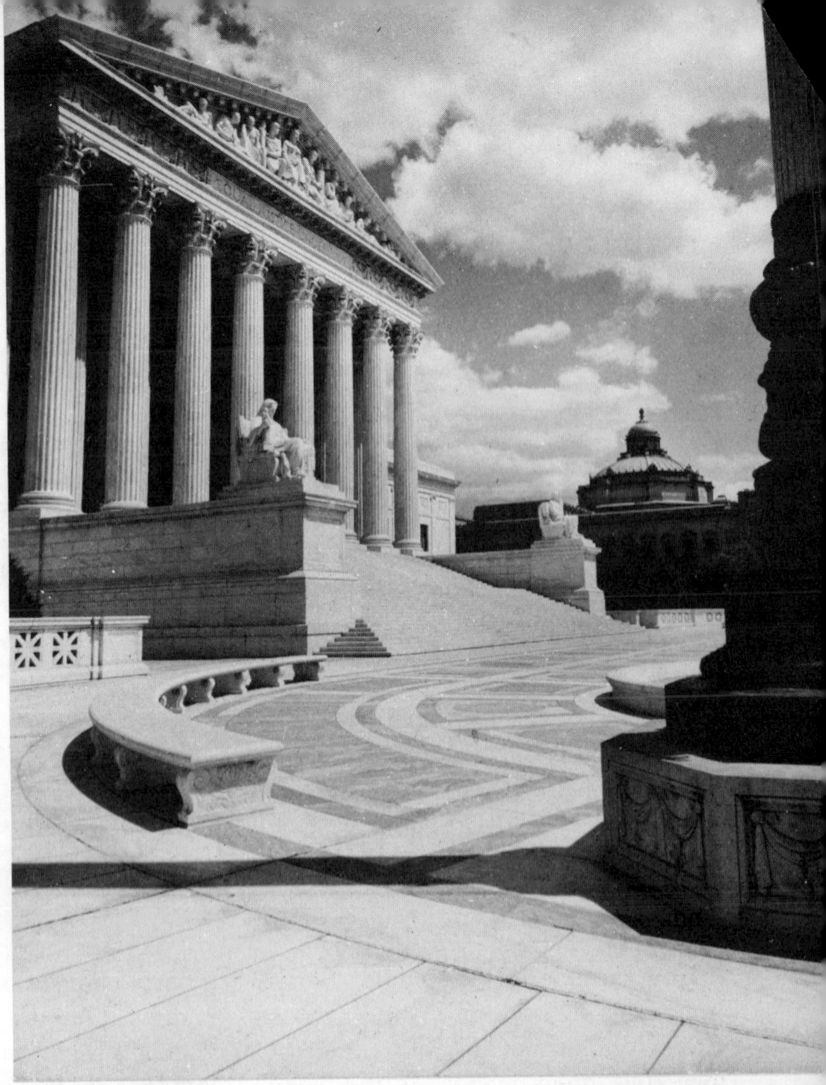

The beautiful and dignified Supreme Court Building is a fitting home for our highest court.

the nine chairs where the Justices sit when court is in session. Behind the chairs is a row of marble columns backed by heavy velvet curtains. In front of the desk are chairs and tables for lawyers and newspapermen. Beyond these are seats for the public. The Supreme Court moved from the Capitol into the new building in 1935. The building was so magnificent that the Chief Justice remarked, "I feel we ought to go in here on nine white elephants!"

The Supreme Court Building is not visited so much by tourists as the White House and the Capitol. One reason may be that it is new, and does not have the historic interest of the other two buildings. Another reason may be that the very work of the Supreme Court sets it apart, as you learned in the previous chapter. But we Americans must not forget that in this building are the guardians and interpreters of our precious Constitution.

CHAPTER 6

Patriotic Landmarks and Monuments Every American Should Know

How wonderful it would be if Americans living today could see on a television or movie screen the great men and great events of the past! Think of being able to watch and hear the debates at the Constitutional Convention, the stirring scenes at Lexington and Concord, or Washington's inauguration as the first President of our country! History being made today is recorded for us by camera, by radio, and by television. We have seen pictures of American troops in recent wars and of important scientific discoveries. We can listen to what famous leaders all over the world have to say. We know what a party convention and a Presidential inauguration are like, for we have watched them on television or in the movies. In fact we can see or hear about the important events of our times only a few hours after they happen.

In the early days of our country's history, however, there were no cameras of any kind, so today we must depend a good deal on paintings — portraits and historic scenes — to help us relive the past. We also have relics from early times which make our country's past more real to us. For example, many historic buildings are still standing. We can visit the very

AMERICA, PRESENT AND PAST: *The Lexington Minuteman is one of many monuments which remind us of daring patriots and stirring events in America's past.*

room where the Declaration of Independence was signed or the house where Washington lived or the log cabin where Lincoln was born. We can see famous battlegrounds of the Revolutionary War and other landmarks dear to Americans. All these have been carefully preserved as part of our American heritage. There are also monuments and memorials built to honor great men and great events.

All parts of our country are rich in history. Very likely you live in or near some spot which is historically famous. In fact, there are so many patriotic landmarks and monuments scattered throughout our broad country that we cannot begin to describe them all in this book. We have selected only a few which are connected with the beginnings of our country or have great significance to us all. Most of them naturally are located in the East because that is where our nation's history began. Some of them, like the Washington Monument, have already been mentioned in the story of our capital city. This chapter will tell you more about a few of our American shrines.

The Washington Monument

Whether you arrive in Washington by plane, by train, or by car you can't miss the Washington Monument. From almost any part of the city you can see its majestic height. At night, lighted by floodlights so that it gleams against the starry sky, the Monument is a beautiful and impressive sight. It is indeed a fitting memorial to the father of our country.

We Visit the Washington Monument

Having read the previous chapter, you already know the general location

The Washington Monument

Height	555 feet, 5⅛ inches
Weight of cap-stone	3,300 pounds
Weight of monument	81,120 tons (including base)
Length of each side at base	55 feet, 1⅛ inches
Length of each side at 500 foot level	34 feet, 5½ inches
Walls	15 feet thick at the base 18 inches thick at the top
Cost	$1,500,000

of the Washington Monument. If we were to draw a line from the White House to the Jefferson Memorial, and another from the Capitol to the Lincoln Memorial, the place where these lines meet would be the site of the Washington Monument. (See the map on page 89.) As you approach the Monument along Constitution Avenue, you notice that it is set on a low grass-covered mound at the end of the Mall. There are no trees or shrubs to distract your attention from the lovely marble shaft as it tapers upward to a height of over 555 feet.

The Monument is built in the shape of an *obelisk,* or four-sided shaft of stone, with a pointed top like an Egyptian pyramid. Over the very top is a tiny pyramid of solid aluminum nine inches high. The outside of the Monument is faced with white marble. As you step onto the big square floor inside, you see that the walls are lined with either bluestone or gray granite.

Of course everyone wants to go to the top level, 500 feet above, for a view of the city and the countryside. You can climb up the 898 steps to the top, or you can take an elevator and be whisked upward in seventy-five seconds. As you can imagine, young people frequently take the stairway while older ones prefer the elevator. In the elevator a loudspeaker gives information about the Monument. You learn, for instance, that its exact height is 555 feet, 5⅛ inches, and that about one million people visit it yearly. Since the tall sides of the building slant toward each other, the top floor is much smaller than the bottom floor. There are twin windows set in each of the four sides of the Monument at the top level. Above the windows are descriptions of the sights to be seen from each.

No matter which way you look there is a breathtaking view. On the east rises the immense dome of the Capitol; to the north a green sloping lawn leads up to the White House. From the west windows you see below you the clear water of the Reflecting Pool and the lovely Lincoln Memorial. Beyond that the Memorial Bridge crosses the Potomac, and still farther can be seen the white columns of Arlington, the former home of Gen-

The Washington Monument, from wherever seen, is an impressive tribute to our first President.

Visitors to the Washington Monument enjoy looking at its many memorial stones. The one pictured here is from the State of Oregon.

eral Robert E. Lee. Looking out the window facing south, you gaze across the blue waters of the Tidal Basin to the Jefferson Memorial with its domed roof and columns of white marble. From this great height people and cars and boats look like toys.

If you came up by elevator, it is a good idea to use the stairs going down. Only by walking can you see the famous memorial stones which are set in the walls at the various stair landings. There are about 188 of these stones, sent from all over the world in tribute to George Washington. There are stones from the states of the Union, from foreign nations, and from many American clubs and organizations. Each one is interesting and quite different from the others. It is fun to read the inscriptions telling who gave the various stones. You see one from Napoleon's tomb in Paris, another from Bunker Hill, and so on. On this page is a photograph of one of the memorial stones.

How the Monument Was Built

Like most of our national monuments, memorials, and landmarks, the Washington Monument is cared for by the National Park Service, which is a part of the Department of the Interior. Although L'Enfant's plans for the capital called for a monument to our first President, the actual building did not start until fifty years after Washington's death. The Monument was begun by a private organization called the Washington National Monument Society, which hoped to build the Monument with money donated by the American people. On July 4, 1848, the cornerstone was laid with the very trowel used by Washington to lay the cornerstone of the Capitol building over a half century before.

The work went very slowly. There were delays in arranging for the necessary land and in raising money. For one period of about twenty-five years no work was done at all. Finally the

United States government took over the building of the monument. It was finished in 1885 and opened to the public three years later. The Washington Monument is noted for being the tallest and one of the most impressive pieces of stonework in the world.

The Lincoln Memorial

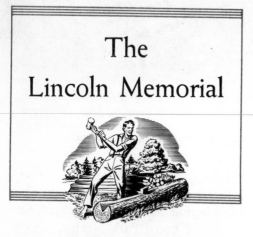

When the Washington Monument casts its reflection in the pool beyond, it seems to point to the memorial of another beloved American — Abraham Lincoln. The Lincoln Memorial, built like a Greek temple, has been called one of the most beautiful buildings in the world. It was not started until almost fifty years after Lincoln's death. The actual work began on Lincoln's birthday in 1914. On Memorial Day, 1922, the building was dedicated.

A Tribute to a Noble American

As we walk up the broad marble steps to the Memorial, we notice that it is enclosed on all four sides by thirty-six enormous columns of white marble. These represent the thirty-six states which belonged to the Union at the time of Lincoln's death. Above each column the name of a state is engraved. But beautiful as the building itself is, our eyes are drawn at once to the inside. Through the entrance we can see a great stone figure of Abraham Lincoln. With hands outstretched on the arms of his chair, he sits looking out toward the pool. At his back is draped his country's flag.

We gaze in silence at the lonely figure with its kind, homely features. We see the sadness in his face. There is strength there, too, and the determination that carried him through the long years of war. The guide tells us that this remarkable statue is the work of Daniel Chester French and is considered the finest of the many Lincoln statues. Behind the statue, these simple but moving words are engraved upon the wall:

IN THIS TEMPLE
AS IN THE HEARTS OF THE PEOPLE
FOR WHOM HE SAVED THE UNION
THE MEMORY OF ABRAHAM LINCOLN
IS ENSHRINED FOREVER.

For a few minutes we have eyes for nothing else in the lofty chamber but the statue of Abraham Lincoln. Later we notice that on each side of the center room there is a smaller room marked off by marble columns. On the wall of one room is engraved Lincoln's Gettysburg Address. In the other room are three tablets which hold his Second Inaugural Address. (You will read further about these

Of the many landmarks in our nation's capital, the Lincoln Memorial is one of the most majestic and inspiring.

two famous speeches in Chapter 7.) There are also murals on the marble walls, showing the great achievements of Lincoln. In one of the murals the Angel of Truth is cutting the chains that bind a slave. We leave the Lincoln Memorial, thinking that it is a perfect tribute to the noble American in whose memory it was built.

It is worth a second trip to see the Capitol, the Monument, and the Lincoln Memorial flood-lighted at night. The great mass of the Monument stretches upward, its upper half shining white. Beyond it the mighty dome of the Capitol gleams against the night sky. And beyond the white columns of the Memorial, the silent figure of Lincoln is bathed in light. No one who has seen this sight will ever forget it.

The Jefferson Memorial

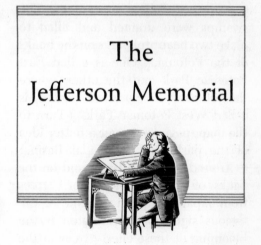

The third and newest memorial in this famous group honors another great American, Thomas Jefferson — author of the Declaration of Independence and third President of the United States. It was dedicated in 1943 by President Franklin Roosevelt.

Framed in the capital's famous cherry blossoms, the Jefferson Memorial makes a striking picture.

The Memorial lies on the shore of the Tidal Basin, a body of water east of the Potomac. The land in this area, including the land where the Lincoln Memorial now stands, was once swampy and full of mosquitoes. The swamps were drained and filled to make two beautiful parks on the banks of the Potomac. One is called East Potomac Park and the other, where the Jefferson Memorial is located, is called West Potomac Park. (Turn to the map, page 89, to get a better idea of the parks and the Tidal Basin.)

Around the Tidal Basin and on the banks of the Potomac, cherry trees from Japan are planted. One of the famous sights of Washington is the blooming of these cherry trees in the spring. It is especially beautiful to drive along the Potomac when the Jefferson Memorial and the cherry blossoms are reflected in the waters of the Tidal Basin.

Some of you may know that Jefferson was not only a writer and a statesman, but one of the great architects of his time. His memorial was designed in the classical style of ancient Greece and Rome that he himself made famous in America. The building is set on a platform (see the picture above), and there are steps leading up to it. It is round in shape and has a high domed roof. Columns over forty feet high and five feet across enclose the building. The portico, supported by eight more columns, is the entrance to the Memorial. The visitor walks through the portico into an enormous circular chamber. More marble columns line the walls of this room. In the center, under the vast domed ceiling, is a large statue of Thomas Jefferson (page 223). Four huge marble panels on the wall contain quotations from the Declaration of Independence and other writings of Jefferson.

Thomas Jefferson Loved Freedom

Inscribed around the wall is a quotation from this famous American, who believed with all his mind and heart in freedom. This quotation probably expresses better than any other what Thomas Jefferson stood for. It reads:

I HAVE SWORN UPON THE ALTAR
OF GOD ETERNAL HOSTILITY
AGAINST EVERY FORM OF
TYRANNY OVER THE MIND OF MAN.

By these words Jefferson meant that he would oppose any man or government or law that forced people to believe or think a certain way. For Jefferson knew that men are not free unless their minds are also free. It is a good thing for us to remember Jefferson's ideas on freedom as expressed in this quotation and in the Declaration of Independence. We know that there are governments today whose purpose is to enslave the minds of men. Under such governments there is no freedom of speech, of the press, or of religion. When we remember Thomas Jefferson, let us be grateful to him for his share in making us a nation of free people.

Arlington and the Tomb of the Unknown Soldier

All Americans have heard of the Tomb of the Unknown Soldier in Arlington National Cemetery. Arlington is not in the District of Columbia, but is located across the Potomac in Virginia about opposite to the Lincoln Memorial. Arlington has been a national cemetery since the days of the War Between the States, when many war dead were buried there. Because it is still used today as a

Huge crowds fill the Amphitheater at Arlington every Memorial Day to pay tribute to our war dead.

Robert E. Lee served his beloved South in peace as well as war. In his last years he was much interested in education.

burying place for our honored dead, Arlington is looked after by the United States Army.

How Arlington Became a National Shrine

Arlington has an interesting history. At one time it was a huge plantation belonging to George Washington Parke Custis, who was the adopted son of George Washington. On a hill overlooking the Potomac he built Arlington House, with white pillars that can be seen across the river. The daughter of Mr. Custis married a young lieutenant in the United States Army whose name is familiar to all Americans — Robert E. Lee. The Lees settled down at Arlington and their children were born there. But when the War Between the States broke out, the Lees left the plantation, never to return. At this time Lee, who was a colonel in the United States Army, resigned that rank to take command of the Confederate Army. He became one of America's most brilliant military leaders.

During the war the house was used by Union forces. Many Union soldiers killed in nearby battles were buried on the grounds of Arlington. After the war, the entire estate was bought by the United States government to be used as a national cemetery. The old house was restored and furnished to look as it did when the Lee family lived there. Visitors find it interesting not only because it was the home of a great American, but also because it gives a good idea of what life in a southern mansion was like in the days before the war.

We Visit Arlington

To reach Arlington from Washington we have only to cross the beautiful Memorial Bridge which spans the Potomac. (See map, page 89.) Several gates open into the grounds and there are many walks and driveways leading through the cemetery. Shade trees, flower beds, shrubbery, and green lawns make it a beautiful resting place for the thousands who lie buried here. Elaborate monuments mark some of the graves; others have simple stone markers. We learn that many famous Americans, civilians as well as soldiers, are buried at Arlington. We see the tombs of Pierre L'Enfant; Robert E. Peary, discoverer of the North Pole; William H. Taft, former President of the United States; General John J. Pershing of World War I; General George C. Marshall of World War II; and many others.

There are two places in Arlington we shall always remember. One is the Memorial Amphitheater, which was built to seat the crowds that throng to Arlington for the Memorial Day exercises. As the picture on page 111 shows, the amphitheater consists of a huge circle of white marble benches, surrounded by a circular gallery made by a double row of white marble columns. In its setting of green, the amphitheater is a beautiful sight.

The other place we shall never forget is nearby — the Tomb of the Unknown Soldier. It is set on a marble terrace facing the Potomac and the city of Washington. No one knows who lies beneath the great block of marble that forms the tomb. We know only that he is one of the unidentified soldiers killed in World War I. The inscription on the tomb says simply:

HERE RESTS IN HONORED GLORY
AN AMERICAN SOLDIER
KNOWN BUT TO GOD.

Men remove their hats and tears fill the eyes of many of us as we look upon the lonely tomb of a man we do not know. We realize that the Unknown Soldier is a symbol of all the brave Americans who have died for our country. Day and night, through rain or sun, there is a sentry on guard. He paces back and forth keeping vigil at the tomb. Thus does our nation pay honor to its soldier dead.

The Unknown Soldiers

To honor American servicemen who died in recent wars, two more soldiers were buried beside the first Unknown Soldier in 1958. Under matching slabs of marble lie unknown soldiers who died in World War II and the Korean War. One tomb bears the simple inscription *1941–1945;* the other, *1950–1953.*

Mount Vernon

Every year over a half million Americans visit the home of George Washington at Mt. Vernon. Mt. Vernon is more than two hundred years old. The house was built a quarter of a century before the Revolutionary War by George Washington's half-brother Lawrence. When Lawrence died, he left the house and the plantation grounds to George Washington, who lived here with his wife Martha from 1759 until his death in 1799. Washington loved Mt. Vernon and enjoyed the life of a southern farmer.

Overlooking the Potomac, Mt. Vernon is as peaceful and stately today as in Washington's time.

He was far ahead of his time in trying new methods of improving the soil and his livestock.

As we know, Washington left the plantation many times to serve his country. During these trying years he often longed for the peace and quiet of Mt. Vernon. When at last in 1797 Washington returned to his beloved home, he had only two years there before he died at the age of 67. The whole nation mourned the death of George Washington. Flags flew at half-mast and memorial services were held in his honor. Many words were spoken in praise of the great patriot. The finest tribute and one that we all know was given by Harry Lee, who had been a member of Washington's military staff during the Revolution. In a speech before Congress, Lee described Washington as "first in war, first in peace, and first in the hearts of his countrymen."

Mount Vernon Today

After Washington's death the plantation was held by his nephew's family for a good many years. In 1855 it was offered for sale. It may seem strange that neither the state of Virginia nor the federal government took steps to preserve the home and property of the greatest American of his day. Instead, it was due to the patriotic efforts of Miss Ann Pamela Cunningham of South Carolina that Mt. Vernon was saved for the people of America. Miss Cunningham organized the *Mt. Vernon Ladies' Association of the Union,* and began seeking contributions to purchase the property. With the help of the American people and especially the children, enough money was raised to buy the house and two hundred acres of the property.

The old house itself, the workshops, and other buildings near the house have been restored so that they appear today much as they did in the days of George Washington. The Association still has charge of Mt. Vernon. A small admission fee pays for the upkeep of the house and grounds. There is a tearoom for visitors, and also a museum on the grounds.

Mt. Vernon is on the Virginia side of the Potomac River about sixteen miles below Washington, D. C. It is open every day to the public and can be reached by boat or by sight-seeing bus or in one's own car. The house stands on a rise of land overlooking the Potomac. It is built of wood painted white to look like stonework. A grassy lawn slopes down to the water. There is a veranda running the length of the house and supported by eight large pillars. A guide takes visitors through the house, showing the rooms and telling about the interesting pieces of furniture, the paintings on the walls, and so on. He points out the formal parlors and the great banquet room with a carved marble mantel sent as a gift from Italy. There is a story that the ship carrying the mantelpiece was seized by pirates. When they heard that the ship was carrying an important gift for George Washington, they released it and sent it on its way! Whether true or not, the story suggests the high regard felt for Washington, not only in his own country but throughout the world.

In the library we see old newspapers printed in the 1790's. We see Washington's bedroom with its enormous square bed, and the room where Lafayette slept when he visited Mt. Vernon. As was true of most southern mansions, the kitchen is not a part of the house but is a separate building in the back. We look at the open fireplace with its iron crane, where the family cooking was done. Some of the kettles and utensils were used by Washington and his family. We see the wash house and the coach house and the quarters for the slaves who worked in the house and on the plan-

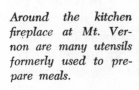

Around the kitchen fireplace at Mt. Vernon are many utensils formerly used to prepare meals.

Homes of Our Presidents

Mt. Vernon and Monticello are not the only homes of our Presidents which are open to the public. Near Nashville, Tennessee is the home of Andrew Jackson, which is called the Hermitage. At Hyde Park, New York, is the home of Franklin Roosevelt. The only house Lincoln ever owned can be seen at Springfield, Illinois. Sagamore Hill, the summer place of Theodore Roosevelt on Long Island, is also open to visitors. The frame house in Abilene, Kansas, where Dwight Eisenhower lived as a boy, has been made a national shrine.

tation. Although Washington kept slaves like every southern planter, he did not believe in slavery. He left a will freeing all his slaves after his death.

We follow a sloping path at one side of the house to the burial place of George and Martha Washington. You remember it was finally decided that Washington and his wife would not be buried under the Capitol building but at Mt. Vernon where he wished to be (page 99). A good many years after his death a simple tomb was erected at Mt. Vernon and the coffins of the great American and his wife were placed in it. On each side of the entrance to the tomb hangs an American flag. On a plaque above the tomb we read these simple words:

WITHIN THIS ENCLOSURE
REST
THE REMAINS OF
GEN. GEORGE WASHINGTON

Although Mt. Vernon is on land fought over by both sides in the War Between the States, the grounds were not invaded by either side. Both the Union and Confederate Armies respected Washington's home. Today, in tribute to the great man buried there, ships of the United States Navy in the Potomac lower their flags to halfmast while passing Mt. Vernon.

Monticello

Jefferson's home is a beautiful southern mansion near Charlottesville, Virginia. It is called Monticello, which in Italian means "Little Hill." Jefferson had inherited from his father a large plantation in what was then a frontier section of Virginia. The original family home was on low land, but from his boyhood days Jefferson had dreamed of building a home on top of a wooded hill on the estate. When he took over the plantation he set about planning his home. He designed it in the classical Roman style which he admired, with columns and a domed roof. There was to be a driveway wide enough for a coach and six horses to turn around in. The lawns and gardens and shrubbery were to cover the entire hillside. In those days the beauty of southern mansions was often spoiled by the sheds and the slave quarters placed at the back. Jefferson planned for large terraces of stone to be built on two sides of the house. Under these were to be the servants' quarters and the kitchen.

The house took about thirty years to complete, for Jefferson had to be away a good deal. Lumber was cut and sawed on the estate; even the nails were made right there. Slaves were trained to be carpenters, bricklayers, cabinetmakers, and so on. Elegant furniture was imported from Italy and France. When Monticello was at last completed in 1800, it was the finest home in the United States. It was also one of the most unusual, for among the many talents of Thomas Jefferson was a genius for invention. In almost every room was some clever device of his making.

Here at Monticello, Thomas Jefferson entertained many distinguished people of his time.

Monticello Reflects Jefferson's Interests

Let us take a closer look at Monticello as it appears now. The red brick house trimmed in white is set among huge trees. Above the center section is a domed roof. As we step onto the porch with its large white columns, we see in the ceiling a dial that points the direction of the wind. The dial is worked by a weather vane on the roof. In the great entrance hall we see above the doorway another of Jefferson's inventions. This is a large double-faced clock that not only tells the time of day, but also the day of the week. Below, leaning against the wall, is a folding ladder for use in winding the clock. At the other end of the hall are hinged glass doors which open like the doors of a bus or a streetcar. In the dining room we see a dumb-waiter, which carried food up from the kitchen below. Jefferson himself had a combination study and bedroom. He had rigged his bed with rope pulleys so that it could be lifted up out of the way during the day.

These ideas may not be unusual to us, but we must remember that they were most unusual in Jefferson's day. If Jefferson had not been so busy as a statesman, he might have been a great inventor. Even while he was Vice-President, he made a study of the steam engine with the idea of pumping water into houses! It seems strange that Jefferson never took out a patent on any of his inventions.

Jefferson's Last Years

Jefferson, like Washington, hoped to be able to settle down on his plan-

Over the door at Monticello is the clock Jefferson invented. The cannon balls, moving down, mark the days of the week on the wall.

tation as a farmer. But again and again he was called to serve his country — in writing the Declaration of Independence, as ambassador to France, as Secretary of State under Washington, as Vice-President under Adams, and finally as President for two terms. At last he was able to retire to Monticello, but not to rest. His home was always open to the many visitors who wanted to see and talk to the famous man. He did a good deal of writing and corresponded frequently with his many friends. He was often asked for advice on government matters. Jefferson, in fact, became known as the Sage (wise man) of Monticello.

Jefferson had always believed that education was necessary in a democracy. It had been his hope to found a university in Charlottesville. When he retired to Monticello, Jefferson set about interesting people in a university and raising funds to finance it. This took many years. Jefferson was an old man in his late seventies when he actually designed the plans and supervised the building of the University of Virginia. He also planned the course of study and engaged the finest instructors to be had. When the university finally opened in 1825, Jefferson was eighty-two years old!

The next year was his last one. Jefferson knew his time was short but hoped he could live until Independence Day. And strange as it may seem, he died on July 4, 1826, the fiftieth anniversary of the famous Declaration he had written! He was buried in Monticello near the grave of his wife. Jefferson left directions for a simple obelisk to mark his grave and an epitaph (a saying chiseled on a tombstone) which he had written for himself. This brilliant man of many achievements was content to mention only three:

HERE WAS BURIED THOMAS JEFFERSON, AUTHOR OF THE DECLARATION OF AMERICAN INDEPENDENCE, OF THE STATUTE FOR RELIGIOUS FREEDOM, AND FATHER OF THE UNIVERSITY OF VIRGINIA.

Plymouth Rock

So far you have read about famous historic monuments located in our nation's capital or in its neighborhood. In the rest of this chapter you will learn of other memorials connected with our country's early history. Let us turn first to Plymouth Rock.

On the water front in the little town of Plymouth, Massachusetts is a large boulder. It is protected by a portico of New England granite. There is an iron fence around it to prevent souvenir hunters from chipping pieces off the rock. Engraved on the rock in large figures is the date 1620 — nothing else. Yet few Americans would need to be told that this is Plymouth Rock. The story goes that the Pilgrims stepped on this rock when they first landed from the *Mayflower.* Whether this is true or not, the rock does mark the place where this little company of courageous people landed to begin new lives in America.

They were mostly humble farmers, these Pilgrim Fathers. You all know the story of how they happened to come to the New World. They belonged to a religious group in England called *Separatists.* They were persecuted because they had separated from the Church of England to which most Englishmen belonged. Some of the Separatists finally decided to go to America where they could worship as they pleased. In the fall of 1620 the first group left Plymouth, England, in a little ship called the *Mayflower.* Two months of stormy sailing brought them to the wild shores of what is now Massachusetts. After a few weeks of exploring the coastline, the Pilgrims finally anchored in a small bay and set about building shelters to protect them from the cold New England winter. They called their settlement Plymouth, after the port in England from which they had sailed.

Historic Plymouth Rock is one of our oldest and best-known national shrines.

During that first hard winter about half the little group died of hunger and sickness. The Pilgrims buried their dead at night and leveled off the ground so that the Indians wouldn't know how few of them remained alive. Somehow they managed to survive until spring came. Their life gradually improved as they learned from some friendly Indians how to plant corn, to hunt, and to fish. As more colonists came to Plymouth, the little Separatist colony became firmly established.

The Pilgrims Stand for Freedom

Why are the Pilgrims important to us? The Pilgrims came to America so that they could worship as they wished. Not only did they find freedom to worship in America, but they also gave that freedom to those in the colony who were not of their faith. In doing so, they laid the foundations of the religious freedom we enjoy today. Although the idea of religious freedom grew slowly in the colonies, the first seeds were planted by that brave band of Englishmen over three hundred years ago. Plymouth Rock is their memorial. It is a monument to their courage and determination and belief in freedom. These lines from a well-known poem (page 161) express the spirit of the Pilgrims:

Aye, call it holy ground,
  The soil where first they trod!
They left unstained what there they
    found —
  Freedom to worship God!

Lexington and Concord Memorials

April 19, 1775 is a famous day in American history. On this day the "minutemen" of Massachusetts faced the British "regulars" and fired the shots that changed the course of history in the American colonies. Thus began the Revolutionary War which ended in the birth of a new and independent nation, the United States of America.

Let us look back at the events of that long-ago spring in 1775. The Boston Tea Party had taken place, Massachusetts was under military rule, and the First Continental Congress was meeting to see what could be done about the quarrel with England. These events you read about in Chapter 3. The men of Massachusetts had organized the "minutemen," so called because they had to be ready to fight at a minute's notice. John Hancock and Samuel Adams, who were leaders against the British in Massachusetts, had been declared dangerous rebels. The British commander in Boston, General Gage, had been ordered to arrest them and return them to England to be tried for treason. General Gage had heard that Hancock and Adams were hiding in the nearby town of Lexington. He also knew that the patriots had guns and ammunition stored in Concord, a few miles farther on. So he ordered British troops to march at night, take the two men by surprise, and destroy the supplies.

The Minutemen at Lexington

Young Dr. Joseph Warren of Boston learned of Gage's plans and took steps to warn the people. He arranged to signal from the tower of the Old North Church what route the troops would take. What happened that night, the 18th of April, and the day that followed has been told in many a story and poem. Paul Revere and William Dawes rode through the countryside calling to the patriots, "The regulars are coming!"

When the British troops arrived at dawn in Lexington, they found about fifty minutemen under Captain John Parker, armed and ready. We do not know exactly what happened, but apparently the "rebels" were ordered to put down their arms and go home. There were a few scattered shots, then a volley from British guns. Eight patriots were killed and ten wounded, but the British did not capture Adams and Hancock.

The place where Captain Parker and his minutemen took their stand on that historic morning is marked by

Statues of minutemen at Concord (above) and Lexington (page 104) mark the scenes where early blows for freedom were struck.

a large boulder. On it are carved the now famous words which he is reported to have said to his men:

STAND YOUR GROUND.
DON'T FIRE UNLESS FIRED UPON
BUT IF THEY MEAN TO HAVE A WAR
LET IT BEGIN HERE.

The Battle at Concord Bridge

From Lexington, the British troops marched on to Concord about six miles away. Here they burned the courthouse and destroyed some of the supplies held by the patriots. At the edge of town the British met a large group of determined minutemen who had gathered at a bridge over the Concord River. Again shots were fired by both sides. But this battle did not end at the bridge. Angry minutemen from the whole countryside shot at the redcoats as they retreated to Boston. All day long the American patriots fired on the enemy from behind stone fences and hedges and barns. Altogether the British lost almost three hundred men killed or wounded. In this first test of their courage and determination the patriots had shown King George that they could and would fight to defend their liberty.

The old wooden bridge has been copied in concrete to mark the battle in Concord. At one end is a bronze statue of a minuteman by Daniel Chester French. Gun in hand, he stands beside his plow. On the monument is inscribed the first verse of a familiar poem by the famous American writer, Ralph Waldo Emerson. You will find the entire poem on page 166.

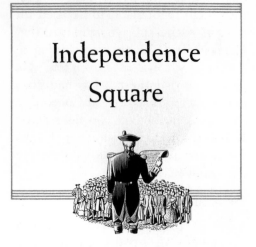

Independence Square

Visiting Independence Square in Philadelphia is like stepping back into the 1700's. This historic square with its three old red brick buildings is part of our heritage from our nation's past. It was used in early days as a meeting place. Chapter 2 described the reading of the Declaration of Independence to the people of Philadelphia in the statehouse yard. Since that time the yard has become known as Independence Square.

Here is Independence Square, with Independence Hall (center), Congress Hall (left), and Old City Hall (right). The artist has shown how the new Mall will appear when completed.

The oldest and best-known of the buildings on the square has been mentioned in our book many times — Independence Hall. The other two are Congress Hall and Old City Hall. All three buildings date back to the 1700's. They are built of red brick with white doors and woodwork, and are beautiful examples of colonial architecture. Anyone may visit Independence Square and its historic buildings free of charge.

The United States government has set aside the old square and other nearby historic buildings as the Independence National Historical Park. A vast project is under way to rebuild the entire area. Unwanted buildings are being torn down and colonial buildings will be restored to complete this memorial of our nation's past.

The Buildings in Independence Square Witnessed Stirring Events

Independence Hall. Most Americans remember Independence Hall as the home of the Liberty Bell, but even if the famous old Bell were not there, a visit to the building would be worthwhile. This ancient Hall has seen many great events in our nation's history. It was used as early as 1735 for the colonial government of Pennsylvania. The Continental Congress met here before and during the Revolution. It was in this Hall that George Washington was given command of the Continental Army. Here, also, the Declaration of Independence was adopted and the Constitution drawn up and signed.

If you visit Independence Hall, you see a two-story building topped by a white tower. Wings at each side are connected to the building by covered passageways. To the left as you enter is the Declaration Chamber. You see a copy of the Declaration on the wall and a picture of George Washington above the entrance. The silver inkwell used by the signers is there, and the old tables and chairs of long ago. Near the rear entrance of the building you see the grand old Liberty Bell, the crack in its side held together with bands of steel.

The rest of Independence Hall is now a museum, holding relics of colonial days. In the wings there are exhibits of furniture, clothes, firearms, and other interesting things used by the colonists. As you wander through the old hall, it might not surprise you much to see a gentleman in knee breeches, ruffled shirt, and powdered wig. It is easy to imagine old Dr. Franklin here, leaning on his cane, or stout John Adams on his way to a meeting of the Continental Congress.

Congress Hall. When the new government of the United States moved from New York to Philadelphia in 1790, the Congress met in a new building on Independence Square called Congress Hall. Here you see the room on the first floor where the House of Representatives held its sessions, and the Senate room on the second floor. You learn that Washington gave his Second Inaugural Address and his Farewell Address from Congress Hall. Today this hall, too, is set aside as a museum. Among the things you see are a chair used by Lafayette, a card table belonging to Thomas Jefferson, and a pair of George Washington's spectacles.

Old City Hall. Built in 1791, Old City Hall is much like Congress Hall, but smaller. You learn that the United States Supreme Court met in this building until the government moved to the new capital in 1800. It was later used by the city government of Philadelphia, which is the reason for its name. Old City Hall today is set aside as an historic building, like Independence Hall and Congress Hall.

The visitor leaving this old Square truly feels that he has been close to the great men and the stirring events of our early history.

Old Ironsides

Do you know that among the ships of the United States Navy is a 44-gun frigate? If you go to the Boston Navy Yard, you can see among the modern steel fighting ships an old sailing warship made of wood — the *Constitution.* She is trim and shipshape as befits a Navy ship. The *Constitution* was a great fighter in her day. She was saved from destruction in memory of her gallant past. Young Americans are always interested in her story.

The *Constitution* is a frigate, as the last of the smaller, faster sailing warships were called. Frigates were common in the navies of the early 1800's just before the days of steamships. They were three-masted vessels built for speed and easy handling, with two gundecks carrying from twenty-four to fifty guns. The *Constitution* is a 44-gun frigate, but she usually carried more than forty-four guns. She was built in the Boston shipyards. Oak planks twenty-one inches thick made her sturdy sides; her decks and topsides were of red cedar. The long iron bolts which held her together were made in the shop of Paul Revere. Launched in 1797, she was a trim fighting ship, 204 feet long. Her guns had a range of 1200 yards or roughly about two-thirds of a mile. She was proudly christened the *Constitution* and commissioned in the United States Navy.

Old Ironsides Has a Proud History

The new ship was first sent to sea in 1798 against the French, who were capturing American merchant ships. Later she took part in our war against the pirates from North Africa who were preying on our ships in the Mediterranean. But it was not until our War of 1812 against Britain that the *Constitution* won fame as a fighting ship. Her most famous sea battle was with the British ship *Guerrière* (gair-ee-air′). Like most men of the great English navy, the captain of the *Guer-*

The Constitution *may seem small to us today, but her battle record fills American hearts with pride.*

rière had little respect for American ships and seamanship. When he sighted the *Constitution* off the North Atlantic coast late one afternoon in 1812, he closed in for action. But the battle, which lasted about an hour and a half, turned out to be a brilliant victory for the *Constitution.* In the words of the commander of the *Constitution,* Captain Isaac Hull, the *Guerrière* was left "without a spar standing." The British lost seventy men, the Americans only seven.

The sturdy *Constitution* won other victories in the war. One was over the British frigate *Java,* which was so badly damaged it could not be towed to port but had to be blown up. It was in this battle that the *Constitution* won her nickname. The story goes that an American seaman saw a heavy shot bounce off her oaken hull. He proudly shouted, "Huzza, her sides are made of iron!" From then on she was known as *Old Ironsides.* Throughout the war her victories won respect for American ships and seamen.

Old Ironsides Becomes a Memorial

In 1830 *Old Ironsides* was discovered to be unseaworthy and the Navy ordered her to be broken up. The gallant ship would have been destroyed if it had not been for the poet, Oliver Wendell Holmes, who believed she deserved a kinder fate. In a poem called *Old Ironsides* he protested against the destruction of the ship. He referred to her long service:

Ay, tear her tattered ensign down!
Long has it waved on high,

He also recalled her many battles:

Her deck, once red with heroes' blood,
Where knelt the vanquished foe,

He pleaded that she be sunk in the sea rather than broken up on shore:

Her thunders shook the mighty deep,
And there should be her grave.

If you wish to read the entire poem, turn to page 167. The American people were so stirred by the poem that *Old Ironsides* was rebuilt and put back into service. During the War Between the States she was used as a training ship. Later the old ship was repaired so that she could be kept as a memorial. In 1930 American school children gave their pennies so that *Old Ironsides* could be put into shape for an actual voyage. From 1931 to 1934 the historic ship entered many United States ports on the Atlantic and Pacific coasts. Everywhere she went, people flocked to see her. When she returned she had covered 22,000 miles. Today she is a "floating monument" of our past which thousands visit every year.

Lincoln's Tomb

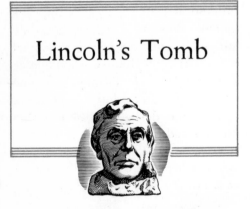

The final resting place of Abraham Lincoln is not in Washington, D. C., but in Springfield, Illinois, where he lived for many years. He is buried in Oakridge Cemetery with his wife and three sons. A few years after Lincoln's death the state of Illinois erected a beautiful monument above his grave. Americans all over the nation sent subscriptions to help with the expense. The monument is a simple square building in a setting of oak and elm trees. From the top of the marble building rises an obelisk one hundred feet high. Lincoln's tomb and monument are open daily, and visitors from all over the country come to pay their respects to the great American whom it honors.

There are two stairways leading to the entrance of the monument. (See opposite page.) High above, at the foot of the obelisk, is a standing statue of Abraham Lincoln. As we enter, we see a small copy of the Seated Lincoln which is found in the Lincoln Memorial in Washington, D. C. Opposite the entrance is a semi-circular room with marble walls. Here we see the sarcophagus (sar-cof′a-gus), or casket of stone, which covers the coffin of Lincoln. On it is the simple inscription:

ABRAHAM LINCOLN
1809–1865

Carved on a black marble panel on the wall are the words spoken by Secretary of War Edwin M. Stanton when Lincoln died: "Now he belongs to the ages." The simple tomb and beautiful shaft are a fitting memorial to this great American.

No one can visit the tomb of Lincoln without recalling his tragic and unexpected death at the hands of the crazed actor, John Wilkes Booth. Lincoln was only fifty-six years old when he was shot. You may remember that he was attending the Ford Theater in Washington, D. C., on the night of April 14, 1865, a few days after the end of the long War Between the States. After the shooting, he was carried across the street to a private home, where his life slowly ebbed away during the long night. He died in the early morning.

The nation was shocked and saddened at the news. Newspapers announcing his death were bordered in black. People wept unashamedly on the streets. Lincoln's coffin was placed in the East Room of the White House, where funeral services were held. Later he lay in state in the Capitol Rotunda, and thousands of sorrowing Americans passed by his coffin. Buildings, shops, and homes in Washington were draped with black for a period of two weeks after Lincoln's death. The funeral train which carried his body back to Springfield followed the same route that Lincoln had taken when he traveled to Washington to become President. Many stops were made along the way so that Americans could pay a last tribute to this great American. Millions waited at the stations to get a glimpse of the black-draped train and the coffin, and wept as it passed by. Few men have ever been more deeply mourned than Abraham Lincoln.

Early in May, about three weeks after his death, Abraham Lincoln was buried at Springfield. At his grave were read the words of his Second Inaugural Address which he had given only two months before. (You will find part of this Address on page 138.)

Here is Lincoln's Tomb at Springfield, Illinois. In front, is a bronze head of Lincoln by the famous sculptor, Gutzon Borglum.

As people listened to Lincoln's noble words, they knew that a man of true greatness and goodness had been lost to the world. A great man who has served humanity is loved and honored not only by his own countrymen, but by all people everywhere. Abraham Lincoln was such a man. Edwin Stanton must have had this thought in mind when he said of Lincoln, "Now he belongs to the ages."

(Continued on page 130)

Other Patriotic Monuments

Atop this monument at Gettysburg burns an eternal flame, honoring those who died at that famous battle.

This monument at Yorktown recalls the victory that ended the Revolutionary War.

The Alamo remains as a tribute to the heroic men who fought to free Texas from Mexico.

A statue of George Rogers Clark at Vincennes, Indiana, honors the Revolutionary War hero of the frontier region.

This memorial arch is located at Valley Forge, where Washington's men endured severe winter hardships.

Federal Hall Memorial in New York City marks the site of old Federal Hall.

In Portland, Oregon, stands a statue of Sacagawea, Indian woman who guided Lewis and Clark through the Rockies.

Mount Rushmore

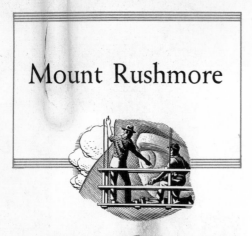

Although most of our patriotic landmarks and memorials are in the eastern United States, there are many historically famous spots in other parts of our country, too. For instance, one of our outstanding national memorials is in the Black Hills region of South Dakota. From the highway northeast of the town of Custer, travelers can see four gigantic heads carved in the granite side of Mount Rushmore. This is the famous Mount Rushmore Memorial honoring George Washington, Thomas Jefferson, Abraham Lincoln, and Theodore Roosevelt. The enormous sculpture can be seen sixty miles away. The heads are carved to the scale of men 465 feet tall! The head of George Washington is 60 feet from the chin up, and the eye of Jefferson is large enough to hold a man standing up!

Among the most unusual of our patriotic monuments is the Mt. Rushmore Memorial. Try to identify the heads.

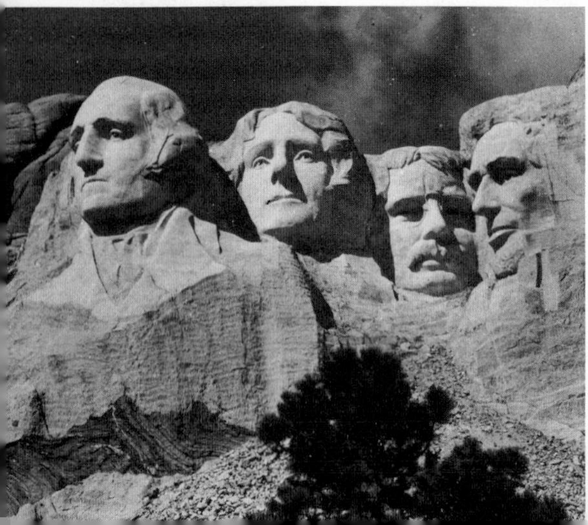

Of course, everyone wonders how these gigantic heads could have been carved 500 feet high on a mountainside. The carving on Mount Rushmore was designed and supervised by Gutzon Borglum, who did the head of Lincoln in the Oakridge Monument (page 127). The rock was first blasted with dynamite, so that the part to be carved stood out from the side of the mountain. The sculptor outlined in red the parts to be cut away. Workmen were then lowered in seats from the top of the mountain by means of cables. They cut into the rock with compressed air drills. The finer work was done with chisels, following the pattern marked by Borglum. As you can imagine, this was an enormous undertaking. Gutzon Borglum worked on it about eleven years until his death in 1941. The Mount Rushmore Memorial was finally completed by his son the following year. Since then it has been visited by thousands of Americans.

* * * * * * * *

The landmarks and monuments included in this chapter are but a few of the many memorials to our nation's past. It is good for us to know about them. It is better yet to see them if we can, for they are part of our heritage as Americans.

CHAPTER 7

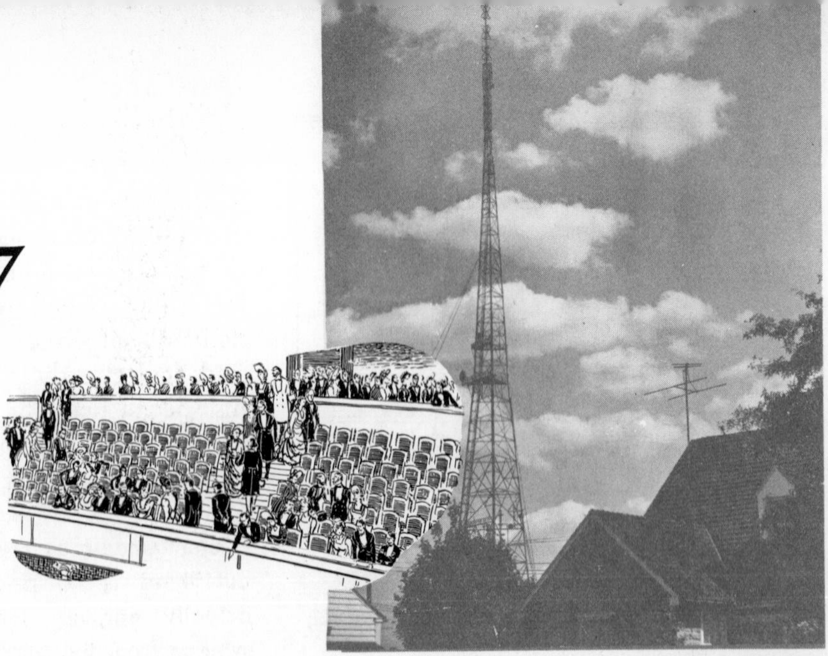

Great Americans Express the Spirit of Our Nation

We Americans have a priceless heritage in the inspiring words left us by our great men. They are words of freedom, of patriotism, of belief in democracy. They are words that express the very spirit of America, and because this is so, they live on through the years. Some are stirring speeches that have aroused men to action at a time of crisis. Some are writings of patriotic men who believe in our democracy and all it stands for. Some are the words of heroes — short, dramatic phrases spoken in a fateful moment. These words of great patriots bring home to us, as nothing else can, the deep love of liberty and democracy that has always existed in the hearts of Americans.

From many hundreds of patriotic sayings and writings we have selected for this chapter some that all Americans should know. Not all the selections are easy to understand. For this reason an explanation has been added in brackets wherever the meaning of a word is important in order to understand a thought. But the main thing is to get the feeling and the challenge in the words of great Americans. So read and enjoy these patriotic selections!

AMERICA, PRESENT AND PAST: *Years ago, only people within speaking distance could listen to famous Americans. Today, radio and television reach millions of listeners in their homes.*

Famous Speeches

1

Liberty or Death

Patrick Henry

How it came to be spoken. We have all heard of Patrick Henry, the hot-tempered and patriotic Virginian who believed that the American colonies must fight for their liberty. His fiery speeches helped to persuade the people of Virginia and the other colonies that war must come. Patrick Henry's most famous speech is the one which is known as "Liberty or Death."

In March, 1775, the battles of Lexington and Concord had not yet taken place. But the men of Massachusetts and other colonies were already preparing for war with the British. In Virginia a convention was being held to decide what steps that colony should take. Many men hesitated to prepare for war because they hoped that actual fighting could still be avoided. In the midst of all the talk and delay, Patrick Henry arose and made a speech that roused the convention to take action. He argued that peace was no longer possible unless they wished to give in to the demands of Great Britain. War, he said, had already begun. He finished his speech with the dramatic call for liberty that still has the power to move the hearts of all who read it.

Gentlemen may cry, Peace, Peace — but there is no peace. The war is actually begun! The next gale that sweeps from the north will bring to our ears the clash of resounding arms! Our brethren are already in the field! Why stand we here idle? What is it that gentlemen wish? What would they have? Is life so dear, or peace so sweet, as to be purchased at the price of chains and slavery? Forbid it, Almighty God! I know not what course others may take; but as for me, give me liberty, or give me death!

Patrick Henry served the cause of liberty by his eloquent speeches urging defiance of England.

2

Message to American Troops Before the Battle of Long Island

George Washington

How it came to be spoken. As you well know, Americans did decide to risk death to preserve their liberty. Patriots from the different colonies flocked to join the Continental forces under the command of George Washington.

In August, 1776, General Washington and his Continental Army were on Long Island, awaiting an attack by the British troops. It was very important to prevent General Howe and his forces from capturing New York City, for if New York fell to the British, all of New England might be cut off from the rest of the colonies. It must have been a discouraging time for General Washington. No one knew better than he that his poorly trained army was only half the size of Howe's force of seasoned British redcoats. But Washington refused to be discouraged. His steadiness and confidence inspired his men.

The words in the next column are from a message Washington gave his troops before the Battle of Long Island. In it he reminded them how much Americans had at stake in the war and how much depended on the patriot army. He made it very clear that the choice was to conquer or to die. Unfortunately, that particular battle turned out to be a decisive victory for the British. But although the British took New York City and held it throughout the war, Washington's army managed to escape under cover of darkness and fog to fight on other battlefields. Washington's words before the Battle of Long Island remain an inspiration to Americans of later generations.

The time is now near at hand which must probably determine whether Americans are to be freemen or slaves; whether they are to have any property they can call their own; whether their houses and farms are to be pillaged [robbed] and destroyed, and themselves consigned [given over] to a state of wretchedness from which no human efforts will deliver them. The fate of unborn millions will now depend, under God, on the courage and conduct of this army. Our cruel and unrelenting enemy leaves us only the choice of a brave resistance, or the most abject [shameful] submission. We have, therefore, to resolve to conquer or to die.

3

Liberty and Union

Daniel Webster

How it came to be spoken. After America won its independence and the Constitution was adopted, President George Washington's firm and wise hands guided the new republic through its first years of trial. As na-

Daniel Webster Calls for Liberty and Union.

tions go, ours was still young when Senator Daniel Webster rose in 1830 to give his now famous speech on the Union (see page 99). Webster had been a Senator from Massachusetts for many years. He was also known as one of the great orators of his time. He had a deep, booming voice and a gift for expressing himself in unusually eloquent phrases. Webster was a short, dark man with a large head and deep, glowing eyes. On the days he made his speeches he liked to wear an old-fashioned, long-tailed blue coat with brass buttons. When people knew he was going to speak, they crowded to the Senate Chamber to hear him.

Although Webster is famous for several great speeches, his oration on "Liberty and Union" is probably the best known and most often quoted. Most of us today would find it hard to listen to the entire speech, for it lasted four hours! This famous address was part of a debate which took place in the Senate between Webster and a brilliant young orator from South Carolina, Robert Hayne. Mr. Hayne made a speech in which he declared that any state had the right to set aside a law of Congress which it did not like. Daniel Webster, who believed that the Union must be more powerful than the states, attacked this idea of "states' rights."

So exciting did the debate become that the members of the House of Representatives left their chamber to crowd into the Senate! On the day of Webster's final speech the crowds were so great there was not even standing room. Webster stated his view that if the idea of states' rights was followed, it would mean the breaking up of the Union, and possibly war. He finished with a dramatic call for liberty and union. The speech is full of the flowery phrases and long sentences that were used by speakers of that day. You may need to read this selection from it more than once to get the full meaning, but these thrilling and patriotic words are well worth reading twice!

While the Union lasts we have high, exciting, gratifying prospects spread out before us, for us and our children. . . . When my eyes shall be turned to behold for the last time the sun in heaven, may I not see him shining on the broken and dishonored fragments of a once glorious Union; on States dissevered [separated], discordant [disagreeing], belligerent [warlike]; on a land rent with civil feuds [quarrels between countrymen], or drenched, it may be, in fraternal [brothers'] blood! Let their last feeble and lingering glance rather behold the gorgeous ensign [flag] of the Republic, now known and honored throughout the earth, . . . not a stripe erased or polluted [soiled], nor a single star obscured [hidden], bearing for its motto no such miserable interrogatory [question] as, "What is all this worth?" nor those other words of delusion [falseness] and folly, "Liberty first and Union afterward"; but everywhere, spread all over in characters of living light, blazing on all its ample folds, as they float over the sea and over the land, and in every wind under the whole heavens, that other sentiment dear to every true American heart — "Liberty **and** Union, now and forever, one and inseparable!"

4

The Gettysburg Address

Abraham Lincoln

How it came to be spoken. Webster did not live to see the War Between the States which he had feared might come. From 1861 until 1865, the North and South fought over the right of states to leave the Union. In July, 1863, near the little town of Gettysburg in Pennsylvania, General Robert E. Lee and his Confederate forces met the Union army in a desperate battle. After a gallant attack on the Union lines, the Confederates were driven back. Gettysburg marked the turning point in the War Between the States, for never again was the South able to invade the North. Since thousands of dead were left on the field, it was decided to bury them there and make Gettysburg a national cemetery for both the Blue and the Gray. The dedication ceremony was to take place on November 19. Edward Everett, a famous orator, was asked to be the chief speaker of the day. The President of the United States was merely requested to make "a few appropriate remarks."

Many of us have read the story that Lincoln borrowed a pencil on the train to Gettysburg and wrote his speech on the back of an envelope. But like several other legends in our history, it probably isn't true. Lincoln had already prepared the first draft of his speech before he left for Gettysburg. Historians believe that he worked on it again, probably on the morning of the dedication. On page 136 is a picture of part of the actual copy which Lincoln held in his hand as he gave his speech. It is now in the Library of Congress.

Lincoln rode to the cemetery on horseback with other important guests and took his place on a platform overlooking the battlefield. Edward Everett, as chief speaker, was called on before Lincoln. He spoke for two hours and was given great applause by the huge crowds gathered there. Then the President rose. He spoke only 267 words and it took him less than five minutes to say them. But though Edward Everett's polished

Four score and seven years ago our fathers brought forth, upon this continent, a new nation, con-ceived in Liberty, and dedicated to the proposition that all men are created equal.

Now we are engaged in a great civil war, test-ing whether ... n, so conceived, and so ded ... We are met here on a g ... war. We ~~are~~ have come ~~here~~ to ded ... final rest-ing place ~~of~~ f ... their lives that that natio ... gether fitting and proper ... is.

But in a ... not dedicate— we can not consecrate— we can not hallow this ground. The brave men, living and dead, who strug-gled here, have consecrated it far above our poor power to add or detract. The world will little note, nor long remember, what we say here, but can never forget what they did here. It is for us, the living, rather to be dedicated phrases have been forgotten, Lincoln's words will live forever. Lincoln expressed his ideas so simply, so eloquently, and so beautifully that the Gettysburg Address has become one of the world's great speeches.

After you have read the Address slowly and thoughtfully, perhaps your teacher will read it aloud so that you can appreciate the deep feeling and the beautiful phrases.

Fourscore and seven years ago our fathers brought forth upon this continent a new nation, conceived in liberty, and dedicated to the proposition that all men are created equal.

Now we are engaged in a great civil war, testing whether that nation, or any nation so conceived and so dedicated, can long endure. We are met on a great battlefield of that war. We have come to dedicate a portion of that field as a final resting place for those who here gave their lives that that nation might live. It is altogether fitting and proper that we should do this.

But, in a larger sense, we cannot dedicate — we cannot consecrate — we cannot hallow — this ground. The brave men, living and dead, who struggled here, have consecrated it far above our poor power to add or detract. The world will little note nor long remember what we say here, but it can never forget what they did here. It is for us, the living, rather, to be dedicated here to the unfinished work which they who fought here have thus far so nobly advanced. It is rather for us to be here dedicated to the great task remaining before us — that from these honored dead we take increased devotion to that cause for which they gave the last full measure of devotion; that we here highly resolve that these dead shall not have died in vain; that this nation, under God, shall have a new birth of freedom; and that government of the people, by the people, for the people, shall not perish from the earth.

Lincoln's Message to Americans

Now that you have heard the Gettysburg Address, let us try to understand better the *ideas* which Lincoln so beautifully expressed. This speech ranks with the Declaration of Independence and the Constitution as a document on democracy. Let us remember that in Lincoln's day the United States was the only large country in the world founded on the idea of "government of the people, by the people, for the people." Our government was still considered an experiment by other nations of the world. Lincoln, with his keen understanding, realized that if the Union were not saved it might mean the end of democracy not only for Americans, but for other men in the world who yearned for liberty. So in his first sentence he reminds us of the ideals on which our nation was founded, saying that it was "conceived [planned] in liberty and dedicated to the proposition [idea] that all men are created equal." In his second sentence Lincoln states that the war is a test of whether a democratic government such as ours can endure. After a tender tribute to the men who gave their lives in the war, Lincoln ends

◀ *In the background of this famous statue of Abraham Lincoln is part of the Gettysburg Address in his own handwriting.*

with a plea to "the living" to save the Union so that our form of government "shall not perish from the earth."

No one has ever stated the ideals and the purpose of democracy more clearly than Lincoln did in the Gettysburg Address. If he were alive today, he might well speak those same words to us. For *we* are now "the living," and our democracy is always in danger from men who do not believe in liberty and equality for all mankind. They are men who would crush democracy unless we who believe in it keep it safe. Let us remember the message that Lincoln left to us in the Gettysburg Address. "It is for us, the living" to see that "government of the people, by the people, and for the people" does not "perish from the earth."

5

Second Inaugural Address

Abraham Lincoln

How it came to be spoken. Lincoln was elected President a second time in 1864. The war was not over, but both North and South knew that it was only a matter of time before the Confederate Army must surrender. In his Second Inaugural Address (March 4, 1865) Lincoln told the people how he hoped to unite the nation once more after the war had ended. There was no room in his heart for hatred or revenge toward those who had fought so valiantly in the Southern cause. His tragic death at the hands of a madman was a blow to the South as well as to the North, for the President who followed Lincoln did not have his greatness of spirit. Abraham Lincoln's own words in this Second Inaugural Address show his compassion toward the South and his hopes for peace.

With malice [ill will] toward none; with charity [good will] for all; with firmness in the right, as God gives us to see the right, let us strive on to finish the work we are in; to bind up the nation's wounds; to care for him who shall have borne the battle, and for his widow and his orphan — to do all which may achieve and cherish a just and lasting peace among ourselves and with all nations.

6

War Message to Congress

Woodrow Wilson

How it came to be spoken. The half-century following the War Between the States saw our nation become stronger and more united. Pioneers settled the broad western plains. America became a land of great farms and cattle ranches, booming cities and busy factories. America also became a world power. Then came World War I and the fateful year of 1917.

On the evening of April 2, 1917,

Woodrow Wilson (far right) chats with the English, Italian, and French leaders during the peace talks after World War I.

Woodrow Wilson, President of the United States, stood before a joint session of Congress. He was speaking at this unusual hour to make an unusual request. Woodrow Wilson that night asked the Congress to declare war on Germany. For three years France, England, and other Allied nations had been fighting a desperate war against a group of European nations called the Central Powers, and headed by Germany. From the beginning Wilson had done all he could to keep our country out of the war, although most Americans sympathized with France and England. Germany had an undemocratic government which believed that might makes right.

Because our government believed that neutral nations had the right to continue trade with other countries at war, we became involved in the conflict. Germany had set up a submarine blockade around the British Isles and all ships in this zone were sunk without warning. President Wilson had protested this "reckless and lawless" warfare. In the early months of 1917 Germany had sunk several American merchant ships and many American lives had been lost. In his War Message, Wilson told Congress there was no safety for democratic nations while such governments as Germany's existed in the world, and stated that "the world must be made safe for democracy."

Congress declared war and Germany was defeated, but among the millions who lost their lives were thousands of young Americans. After the war, it became Wilson's dream to keep peace in the world through an international organization. He even went to Europe to help organize such a body. Wilson was deeply disappointed when his own country failed to join the League of Nations. He died a few years later, some say of a broken heart. The words we quote here from Wilson's War Message show his belief in democracy and his hope for peace in the world.

It is a fearful thing to lead this great peaceful people into war, into the most terrible and disastrous of all wars, civilization itself seeming to be in the balance. But the right is more precious than peace, and we shall fight for the things which we have always carried nearest our hearts — for democracy, for the right of those who submit to authority to have a voice in their own governments, for the rights and liberties of small nations . . . To such a task we can dedicate our lives and our fortunes, everything that we are and everything that we have, with the pride of those who know that the day has come when America is privileged to spend her blood and her might for the principles that gave her birth and happiness and the peace which she has treasured. God helping her, she can do no other.

7

The Speech That Was Never Given

Franklin Delano Roosevelt

How it came to be written. Only twenty-three years after World War I ended, our nation was forced to take part in another great conflict, World War II. Our President at this time was Franklin Delano Roosevelt. (Roosevelt was elected President four times and served from 1933 to 1945.)

All of you know that after the Japanese attack on Pearl Harbor in 1941, our country declared war on Japan and on Hitler's Germany. For almost four years we, along with England and our other allies, fought in a great world war against Germany, Italy, and Japan. During the war, President Roosevelt was our confident and inspiring leader. His sudden death in 1945 prevented him from seeing the surrender of Germany and Japan and the end of World War II.

Two reasons for which Franklin Delano Roosevelt will be remembered are: (1) he was the man who led our nation successfully in World War II, and (2) more than any other person, he was responsible for the United Nations organization for world peace. From the beginning of the war, Roosevelt, like Wilson some twenty years earlier, had been planning to establish a great organization of the nations to keep peace. He died in the very month in which the United Nations was to meet for the first time in San Francisco. The United Nations today is a memorial to the man who helped found it — Franklin D. Roosevelt.

President Roosevelt made many speeches during his years as President. He was scheduled to speak at a Jefferson Day Dinner on April 13, 1945, the birthday of Thomas Jefferson. But the speech he had written was never given, for the President died on April 10. He had planned to speak about

Franklin D. Roosevelt stands at salute on a ship of the United States Navy. During World War I, Roosevelt was Assistant Secretary of the Navy, and all his life he loved ships and the sea.

the subject closest to his heart — peace. Of course, Roosevelt could not know that the peace he so earnestly desired would not last long after the end of the war, but his words are as true today as they were then. He pointed out that war is not the way to settle disputes between nations, and that we must find a way to keep war from starting if we are to have peace in the world. Today we are working with other nations to carry out the ideas that Franklin Roosevelt expressed in his last message.

We seek peace — enduring peace. More than an end to war, we want an end to the beginnings of all wars — yes, an end to this brutal, inhuman, and thoroughly impractical method of settling the differences between governments. . . .

Today, science has brought all the different quarters of the globe so close together that it is impossible to isolate them one from another.

Today we are faced with the . . . fact that, if civilization is to survive, we must cultivate the science of human relationships — the ability of all people, of all kinds, to live together and work together, in the same world, at peace.

"The Speech That Was Never Given," by Franklin D. Roosevelt, reprinted in part from *The Public Papers and Addresses of Franklin D. Roosevelt,* edited by Samuel I. Rosenman. Copyright, 1950, by Samuel I. Rosenman. Published by Harper & Brothers.

Here, Dwight D. Eisenhower is being inaugurated President in 1953. Behind the late Chief Justice Vinson, who is administering the oath of office, are former Presidents Truman and Hoover. At the right is Richard Nixon, who served as Vice-President under Eisenhower.

8

First Inaugural Address

Dwight D. Eisenhower

How it came to be spoken. No American needs an introduction to Dwight Eisenhower. As you know, General Eisenhower served as Supreme Commander of the Allied Forces in Europe during World War II. A few years after the war he returned to Europe as head of NATO (North Atlantic Treaty Organization). It was his job then to work with nations of western Europe to build up a strong defense against Communist powers. In 1952 Eisenhower ran for President as the candidate of the Republican Party, and was elected by a large majority. He was elected for a second Presidential term in 1956.

In his First Inaugural Address, Eisenhower spoke confidently of what he hoped to accomplish in the next four years. He called on all Americans to renew their faith in our American ideals. In the part of his speech given below, he emphasized our democratic way of life and our belief in the dignity and equality of all men. He made it clear that Americans in all walks of life, from the farmer to the statesman, can and do serve their country.

At such a time in history, we who are free must proclaim anew our faith.

This faith is the abiding creed of our fathers. It is our faith in the deathless dignity of man, governed by eternal moral and natural laws.

This faith defines our full view of life. It establishes, beyond debate, those gifts of the Creator that are man's inalienable rights, and that make all men equal in His sight.

In the light of this equality, we know that the virtues most cherished by free people — love of truth, pride of work, devotion to country — all are treasures equally precious in the lives of the most humble and of the most exalted.

The men who mine coal and fire furnaces, and balance ledgers, and turn lathes, and pick cotton, and heal the sick and plant corn — all serve as proudly and as profitably for America as the statesmen who draft treaties and the legislators who enact laws.

This faith rules our whole way of life. It decrees that we, the people, elect leaders not to rule but to serve. It asserts that we have the right to choice of our own work and to the reward of our own toil.

. . . And it warns that any man who seeks to deny equality among all his brothers betrays the spirit of the free and invites the mockery of the tyrant.

Thoughts of Great Americans on Liberty and Democracy

Where liberty dwells, there is my country.

BENJAMIN FRANKLIN, 1706–1790.
Statesman, scientist, and writer

God grants liberty only to those who love it, and are always ready to guard and defend it.

DANIEL WEBSTER, 1782–1852. Senator, statesman, brilliant orator

Democracy means not, "I'm as good as you are," but, "You're as good as I am."

THEODORE PARKER, 1810–1860. Minister, reformer, grandson of Captain John Parker (see page 121).

What is liberty? Liberty is an elusive thing. It isn't a thing you can lock up in the safe, turn the key on and go away, and expect to find there when you come back. Eternal vigilance alone is the price that you pay.

ALFRED E. SMITH, 1873–1944. Political leader and former governor of New York State

Liberty is one thing *you* can't have unless you give it to others.

WILLIAM ALLEN WHITE, 1868–1944.
Newspaper editor and writer

Other Patriotic Selections

All of you know the Pledge of Allegiance to our Flag and have repeated it many times. But there are other patriotic pledges and creeds that are also well worth knowing and learning. (A pledge, you remember, is a promise. A creed is a statement of what you believe in.) They are brief and simple statements of American ideals and liberties. Rising with your class at school and repeating one of the pledges or creeds helps you to remember all that America stands for, and your duty as a loyal citizen.

In this section you will find some patriotic pledges and creeds, as well as a few patriotic quotations by prominent Americans.

Addition to the Pledge

Until 1954 the Pledge of Allegiance did not include the words "under God." These words were added in that year by a resolution of Congress, signed by the President.

1

The Pledge of Allegiance

Francis Bellamy

How it came to be written. The importance and meaning of the well-known and widely used Pledge of Allegiance have already been given in Chapter 2. The story of how it came to be written is an interesting one. Back in 1892 a man named Francis Bellamy worked for a young people's magazine called "The Youth's Companion." Some of your grandparents may remember reading that magazine when they were young. Bellamy was interested in patriotism. He wrote the Pledge of Allegiance, and it was then printed in "The Youth's Companion."

The Pledge was considered so fine that it was sent in leaflet form to schools throughout the country for use in celebrating National Public Schools Week. Millions of children in every state in the Union repeated the Pledge in school programs. Gradually it became the custom to have an American Flag in every schoolroom so that pupils could begin their day with the Pledge of Allegiance. The Pledge is repeated below.

I pledge allegiance to the Flag of the United States of America and to the republic for which it stands; one nation under God, indivisible, with liberty and justice for all.

2

The Freedom Pledge

What it means to us. The pledge given below expresses better than any other what it means to be an American. It was composed by a group of prominent citizens and has been widely used in schools, churches, and public meetings. When you repeat it, you are naming proudly the freedoms that are part of your American heritage. You are promising not only to preserve these freedoms but to believe in them for all men everywhere.

I am an American. A free American.
Free to speak — without fear
Free to worship God in my own way
Free to stand for what I think right
Free to oppose what I believe wrong
Free to choose those who govern my country.
This heritage of Freedom I pledge to uphold
For myself and all mankind.

3

The American's Creed

William Tyler Page

How it came into use. You will recognize many phrases in the American's Creed, by William Tyler Page, because they were taken from American documents and speeches. This creed won a contest for a national creed which would express briefly the ideals of American democracy. The American's Creed was so well liked that the House of Representatives officially accepted it for the people of America on April 3, 1918. This creed says that as Americans we believe in our kind of government, in our Union of states, and in the ideals of our country. It ends by stating five important duties of an American citizen.

I believe in the United States of America as a Government of the people, by the people, for the people; whose just powers are derived from the consent of the governed; a democracy in a Republic; a sovereign Nation of many

A new arrival in the United States (next to the teacher) joins his classmates in the Pledge of Allegiance.

The Freedom Pledge is reprinted by courtesy of The American Heritage Foundation.

sovereign States; a perfect Union, one and inseparable; established upon those principles of freedom, equality, justice, and humanity for which American patriots sacrificed their lives and fortunes.

I therefore believe it is my duty to my country to love it; to support its Constitution; to obey its laws; to respect its flag; and to defend it against all enemies.

4

Credo (I Believe)

Elias Lieberman

What this creed expresses. The lines below are part of another creed that expresses simply and clearly your belief in your country and your duties toward her. The author, Elias Lieberman, was born in Russia and was brought to this country by his parents when he was seven years old. He became a teacher in the city schools of New York, and is well known as a poet, editor, and playwright. *Credo* expresses Lieberman's intense love of America.

I believe
In my country and her destiny,
In the great dream of her founders,
In her place among nations,
In her ideals;

I believe
That her democracy must be protected,
Her privileges cherished,
Her freedom defended.

Credo, by Elias Lieberman, copyright by the author and reprinted, in part, by his permission.

5

Your Country

Edward Everett Hale

From "The Man Without a Country"

What this quotation points out. The story of Philip Nolan, the "man without a country," was told on page 9. In the selection quoted here Nolan is talking to a member of the crew of a ship he sailed on several times. He is urging the young man to be loyal even though he should be treated unfairly by an officer of the government. Nolan points out that serving our country and Flag is the job of patriotic Americans at all times.

"And for your country, boy, and for that flag, never dream a dream but of serving her as she bids you, though the service carry you through a thousand hells. No matter what happens to you, no matter who flatters you or who abuses you, never look at another flag, never let a night pass but you pray God to bless that flag. Remember, boy, that behind all these men you have to do with, behind officers and Government and people even, there is the Country Herself, your Country, and that you belong to Her as you belong to your own mother. Stand by Her, boy, as you would stand by your mother!"

6

What Is an American?

Harold L. Ickes

How it came to be spoken. Here is a description of an American that is worth reading and remembering. It is by Harold Ickes, who was Secretary of the Interior under President Franklin Roosevelt. Ickes was a loyal American who did not hesitate to speak out bluntly for what he believed to be right. The words below are from a speech which he gave on "I Am an American Day" in 1941. Notice the things that Ickes says do *not* make an American — neither race nor religion nor family nor money, nor even being a citizen of the United States makes us true Americans. According to Icks, only by believing in our ideals and being willing to fight for them can we be true Americans.

What constitutes [goes to make] an American? Not color, nor race, nor religion. Not the pedigree of his family [the importance of his ancestors] nor the place of his birth. Not the coincidence [accident] of his citizenship. Not his social status nor his bank account. Not his trade nor his profession. An American is one who loves justice and believes in the dignity of man. An American is one who will sacrifice property, ease, and security in order that he and his children may retain the rights of free men. An American is one in whose heart is engraved the immortal second sentence of the Declaration of Independence.

7

The Making of an American

Jacob Riis

How it came to be written. Jacob Riis came to America from Denmark in 1870 when he was a young man, and worked his way up until he was famous as a journalist and author. He became interested in improving the terrible slum conditions that existed among the foreign-born people of New York City in the late 1800's. Much of his life was spent in making conditions better for the poor people of the city. Jacob Riis was one of the

Young Jacob Riis Arriving in New York

many foreign-born Americans who have served our country and made it a better place to live in. *The Making of an American* is the story of his life. Below is a touching incident from the book, telling how the sight of the Stars and Stripes in a foreign land helped a naturalized American to realize that he had become a true American at last.

I have told the story of the making of an American. There remains to tell how I found out that he was made and finished at last. It was when I went back (to Denmark) to see my mother once more . . . There I fell ill of a fever and lay many weeks in the house of a friend . . . One day when the fever left me, they rolled my bed into a room overlooking the sea . . . Ships passed under full sail . . . But the sunshine and the peaceful day bore no message to me. I lay . . . sick and discouraged and sore — I hardly knew why myself. Until all at once there sailed past, close inshore, a ship flying at the top the Flag of Freedom, blown out on the breeze till every star in it shone bright and clear. That moment I knew.

. . . I sat up in bed and shouted, laughed and cried by turns, waving my handkerchief to the Flag out there . . . I knew then that it was **my** Flag; . . . that I also had become an American in truth. And I thanked God, and . . . rose from my bed and went home healed.

This vivid painting of the Battle of Lexington is one of Brumidi's murals in the Capitol.

Famous Slogans from Our Past

1

"If they mean to have a war, let it begin here!"

Spoken by Captain John Parker at Lexington, Massachusetts April 19, 1775

How it came to be said. The story of the battle between the British redcoats and the minutemen of Lexington was told in Chapter 6. What courage it must have taken for a handful of untrained patriots to face three companies of British regulars on that long-ago April morning! Doubtless these brave words spoken by their captain gave them confidence: "Stand your ground. Don't fire unless fired upon; but if they mean to have a war, let it begin here!" As we know, the shots fired in Lexington did indeed begin a war, a war that ended in independence for the American colonies.

2

"Don't fire until you see the whites of their eyes."

Spoken by Captain Israel Putnam at the Battle of Bunker Hill, Massachusetts June 17, 1775

How it came to be said. After the battles of Lexington and Concord, patriot forces had been recruited in large numbers. They were for the most part without training, without uniforms, and armed only with the rifles they used for hunting. On the night of June 16, hoping to force the British to leave Boston, patriot troops occupied Bunker Hill and Breed's Hill overlooking Boston harbor. You can imagine the surprise of the British next morning when they found the colonial troops in possession of the hills. The colonial forces fortified themselves on Breed's Hill, and so the redcoats were sent to teach the bold Americans a lesson.

Almost three thousand strong the British advanced up the hill in perfect formation, with flags flying and drums sounding. Captain Israel Putnam of Connecticut knew better than to let his troops fire too soon. He walked among his men, giving the order that has now become famous: "Don't fire until you see the whites of their eyes." The volleys of the British did little harm to the patriots, who were protected by breastworks. The British continued to advance with bayonets fixed. At last, when they got about fifty feet from the top of the hill, the Americans fired. Many redcoats fell; the rest retreated down the hill. Once more the British advanced. Once more the Americans waited until they could see the whites of their eyes, then poured on a deadly fire. Again the redcoats were forced to fall back, leaving the hillside strewn with dead and wounded.

At this point the Americans had to withdraw from their position because their supplies of powder and ammunition were gone. So the battle ended in victory for the British. But it was a costly victory; over 1500 men, more than half the British force, lay dead or wounded on the hill. Because of a mix-up in names, the battle on Breed's Hill has always been called the Battle of Bunker Hill.

On the campus at Yale University is this statue of Nathan Hale, one of Yale's most famous graduates.

3

"I only regret that I have but one life to lose for my country."

Spoken by Nathan Hale in New York
September 22, 1776

How it came to be said. The fall of 1776 was a discouraging time for the American patriots. As you learned on page 133, General Howe and his army had badly defeated Washington's troops in the Battle of Long Island, and had taken possession of New York City. The American army was in a desperate situation. It was vitally important for Washington to know where and when the British forces planned to attack again. So he asked for volunteers to go through the British lines and bring back the necessary information. Such a job required more than courage. It meant being a spy, which is a job any honorable man naturally dislikes. It also meant death if captured.

The man who was chosen for this dangerous assignment was Nathan Hale, a young schoolteacher from Connecticut. Hale managed to reach New York City in disguise and secure the needed information. He had almost reached safety when he was

Thoughts of Great Americans on Patriotism

These are the times that try (test) men's souls. The summer soldier and the sunshine patriot will, in this crisis, shrink from the service of their country; but he that stands it now deserves the love and thanks of man and woman.

THOMAS PAINE, 1737–1809. Writer of Revolutionary days

There are no days of special patriotism. There are no days when you should be more patriotic than on other days, and I ask you to wear every day in your heart our Flag of the Union.

WOODROW WILSON, 1856–1924. 28th President of the United States

Gold is good in its place, but living, brave, patriotic men are better than gold.

ABRAHAM LINCOLN, 1809–1865. 16th President of the United States

Our country, right or wrong. When right, to be kept right; when wrong, to be put right.

CARL SCHURZ, 1829–1906. Famous writer, speaker, political leader

Ask not what your country can do for you — ask what you can do for your country.

JOHN F. KENNEDY, 1917– 35th President of the United States

seized and taken to General Howe's headquarters. Hale made no attempt to deceive the British. He told them who he was and what he was doing. He was condemned to be hanged as a spy. Life must have seemed very dear to the young patriot who faced death on that autumn day. But Nathan Hale's last words, uttered as he faced the hangman's noose, will live forever in the hearts of Americans: "I only regret that I have but one life to lose for my country."

4

"I have not yet begun to fight!"

Spoken by John Paul Jones
of the American Navy
September 23, 1779

How it came to be said. On a September day during the Revolutionary War, Captain John Paul Jones was cruising off the coast of England looking for British ships. Jones was a

John Paul Jones Attacking the *Serapis*

former Scottish seaman who had joined the tiny American Navy at the beginning of the war. He was then in command of an old merchant ship that had been bought from France and converted into a warship. It was called *Bonhomme Richard* (boh-nom' ree-shard') in honor of Benjamin Franklin. ("Bonhomme Richard" is the French way of saying Poor Richard, who was a character in *Poor Richard's Almanac,* written by the famous Ben Franklin.)

When Jones spotted a fleet of British merchant ships guarded by two men-of-war, he "crowded every possible sail" to attack the largest warship. This was the *Serapis,* a fine new 44-gun fighting ship. Jones ran his old and clumsy vessel alongside the enemy ship at seven o'clock that night. The *Bonhomme Richard* fired a broadside at the *Serapis,* and the famous battle began. The heavy guns of the British tore great gaping holes in the sides of the American ship, and blew up her biggest gun battery. Two more guns of the *Bonhomme Richard* exploded when they were fired, killing many Americans. But Jones lashed the two ships together and kept his remaining guns firing at the *Serapis.*

There was fierce hand-to-hand fighting with swords and pistols on deck and in the rigging. The guns roared; wrecked masts and sails fell upon the dead and wounded lying on the decks. After almost three hours of desperate battle, the captain of the *Serapis* called to Jones, "Have you lowered your flag?" Although his own ship appeared to be sinking and both ships were afire, Jones shouted back his courageous answer, "Sir, I have not yet begun to fight!" Jones kept on firing until at ten-thirty the mainmast of the *Serapis* was shot away and the British flag was lowered in surrender.

The next day Jones sailed the captured *Serapis* toward Holland, but the sinking *Bonhomme Richard* could not follow. As Jones and his crew watched from the *Serapis,* the old ship with its dead slipped slowly into the sea. The heroic bravery and fine seamanship of John Paul Jones won honor for the new American Navy in the eyes of the world. The gallant commander who refused to recognize defeat, is now buried at Annapolis as a naval hero.

5

"Don't give up the ship!"

Spoken by Captain James Lawrence
in the War of 1812
June 1, 1813

How it came to be said. In 1812, as you know, our country went to war a second time with Great Britain. At that time the British Navy was the largest and most powerful in the world. The American Navy was small, but ship for ship, it was a match for the British. Although we won many a battle against the enemy on the sea, this is the story of a gallant defeat.

The battle took place between the American frigate, *Chesapeake,* commanded by Captain James Lawrence, and the British ship, *Shannon,* whose captain was Philip Broke. While Lawrence was in Boston Harbor trying to recruit experienced seamen, Broke challenged him to battle. Lawrence accepted the challenge and sailed out to meet the *Shannon.* It was a brave but foolhardy thing to do, for Captain Broke was known to have one of the finest crews in the British Navy and half of Lawrence's crew were untrained seamen. In a fifteen-minute battle the *Chesapeake* was badly damaged and Lawrence mortally wounded. As his crew prepared to lower the flag in surrender, it is said that the dying captain begged the men over and over again, "Don't give up the ship! Don't give up the ship!" Although Lawrence died and his ship was captured by the British, his heroic words have become an American slogan.

6

"We have met the enemy and they are ours."

Sent by Commodore Oliver Hazard Perry
after the Battle of Lake Erie
September 10, 1813

How it came to be sent. One of the famous naval victories of the War of 1812 took place on Lake Erie. When the war began, the lake was controlled by a British fleet from Canada. Since

In this old painting, Commodore Perry leaves his crippled flagship to carry on the Battle of Lake Erie.

there was no way to sail ships into this inland lake, the Americans were forced to build ships on its shore. Trees from the forests were cut for lumber; nails and other necessary metal were carted overland. By the fall of 1813 a fleet of small vessels had actually been built. Commodore Oliver Hazard Perry commanded the fleet. Many of his crew were boys who had never before set foot on a ship. It was not much of a fleet to challenge a British squadron, but when Perry sighted the enemy he gave orders to attack.

Perry's flagship was named the *Lawrence* in honor of the gallant commander of the *Chesapeake*. Before the American ships could get close enough to fire their guns, the *Lawrence* was crippled by the British guns, which had a longer range. Perry was rowed to another ship and continued the attack. In the meantime the two largest ships of the British fleet had collided; their sails and rigging were hopelessly tangled. Perry battered the two ships with his heavy guns while his other ships bore down on the rest of the fleet. The British were forced to "strike their colors" in surrender. While the smoke of the battle still hung thick over the water, Perry sent this brief message to General William H. Harrison, leader of the American forces in the west:

We have met the enemy and they are ours, two ships, two brigs, one schooner and one sloop.

Yours with great respect and esteem,
O. H. Perry.

7

"Our Federal Union: it must be preserved!"

Spoken by President Andrew Jackson
at Washington, D. C.
April 30, 1830

How it came to be said. Andrew Jackson become President of the United States at a difficult time. In 1829 the North and South were quarreling over the question of the tariff (tax on imported goods). The North had many factories and wanted to protect its industries by placing a high tariff on manufactured goods from Europe. The South, which grew large quantities of cotton and exchanged it for European goods, was against the high tariff. In fact, John Calhoun of South Carolina, who was then Vice-President of the United States, took the stand that any state had the right

Before becoming President, Andrew Jackson had been an Indian fighter, a soldier, and a frontier lawyer.

to set aside a tariff law passed by Congress. Naturally everyone wanted to know which side the President was on, but he kept still.

In 1830, President Andrew Jackson was guest of honor at a dinner in celebration of Jefferson's birthday. People were hoping that he would have something to say on the tariff question. Not a sound was heard as the President rose to his feet to propose a toast. Looking directly at Mr. Calhoun, he said in his rough soldier's voice: "The Federal Union: it must be preserved." The old soldier had given his answer. He had made it clear that his loyalty was to the Union which he had sworn to "preserve, protect, and defend," and not to any section of the country.

The San Jacinto Memorial near Houston, Texas, commemorates the battle that finally won Texas independence from Mexico.

8

"Remember the Alamo!"

Battlecry of Colonel Sidney Sherman in the war for Texan Independence April 21, 1836

How it came to be said. Some of you may remember the story of the Alamo and the heroes who died defending it. Texas, as you know, was at one time a part of Mexico. The Americans who had settled there were unhappy under Mexican rule and in 1836 they fought to gain their independence. Three thousand Mexican troops led by General Santa Anna besieged the town of San Antonio. There were fewer than two hundred Texan soldiers there, so they withdrew to a small adobe (a-do′ bee) mission called the Alamo and prepared to hold out against the Mexican army. Santa Anna called on them to surrender, threatening death for all if they refused. But Colonel Travis sent out this message: "I shall never surrender or retreat." The Mexicans shelled the mission, until at last they broke through its heavy walls and rushed in to kill the defenders, who had refused to surrender. The Texans fought on against overwhelming odds until not one man of them remained alive.

The deaths of the brave defenders of the Alamo aroused the people of Texas. Their men fought harder than ever. To gain time against the larger Mexican forces, General Sam Houston retreated to the San Jacinto River.

Here, on April 21, 1836, about eight hundred Texans launched a surprise attack on Santa Anna's army. Led by Colonel Sherman, they attacked the enemy shouting, "Remember the Alamo!" It was a complete victory for the Texans. Santa Anna was captured; his army destroyed. The Battle of San Jacinto ended the war and Texas became an independent republic. Nine years later it entered the Union as the twenty-eighth state.

9

"Lafayette, we are here."

Credited to General John J. Pershing at the tomb of Lafayette in Paris July 4, 1917

How it came to be spoken. We Americans honor the memory of the Marquis de Lafayette, the gallant young French nobleman who offered his services and his wealth in the cause of American liberty and independence. Lafayette was only twenty-one years old when he joined the American army. He served as one of Washington's trusted officers throughout the war and was among the men who helped to trap General Cornwallis at Yorktown. When Lafayette returned to the United States in 1824, he was welcomed everywhere with great honor and respect. To show the gratitude of the American people for his service to the nation, Congress made him a gift of $200,000 and 24,000 acres of rich land.

About 135 years after the Revolutionary War, American troops arrived in France to fight in World War I against the Germans. Frenchmen cheered as the lines of husky, confident Americans marched through the streets of Paris on July 4, 1917. After the parade a ceremony was held at the tomb of the Marquis de Lafayette. American officers and troops as well as many important Frenchmen were there. The Americans placed a wreath of roses on Lafayette's tomb, and one of the officers spoke. Although the record is not clear, it is believed the speaker was General John Pershing, commander of the American Expeditionary Force. He acknowledged the debt our country owed to Lafayette

General Pershing leads American troops under the Arch of Triumph in Paris.

Thoughts of Great Americans on Citizenship

The first requisite of a good citizen in this Republic of ours is that he shall be willing and able to pull his weight.

THEODORE ROOSEVELT, 1858–1919. 26th President of the United States

If you will help run our government in the American way, then there will never be danger of our government running America in the wrong way.

OMAR N. BRADLEY, 1893– . General and former Chief of Staff of the Army

In too many countries — including our own — too many people are too willing to put party loyalty and personal privilege above the needs of their nation.

PAUL HOFFMAN, 1891– . Industrialist and government official

Our American heritage is threatened as much by our own indifference as by the most unscrupulous (dishonest) office or by the most powerful foreign threat. The future of this republic is in the hands of the American voter.

DWIGHT D. EISENHOWER, 1890– General of the Army and 34th President of the United States

and to France for their help in the Revolution so many years before, and ended with this dramatic sentence: "Lafayette, we are here."

10

"Sighted sub — sank same."

Radio message from Donald Francis Mason of the United States Navy, January 8, 1942

How it came to be sent. The author of the message above was a man of few words. He told a story and announced a victory in four words. This is probably the shortest message of victory ever sent. When the United States entered World War II after Pearl Harbor, the Germans sent large numbers of submarines to prey on our ships off the Atlantic Coast. Every day brought news of ships torpedoed and crews left to drown. The safety of our ships depended on spotting the submarines as they closed in for action. Army and Navy planes and small craft of all kinds were constantly patrolling the Atlantic for submarines. On January 8, 1942, Aviation Machinist's Mate Donald Mason was piloting a Navy bomber when the periscope of a submarine appeared below. Two depth bombs were dropped on the target, sending up huge columns of water. A submarine rose from the depths, turned on its side, then sank below the surface. When several large spots of oil on the water showed that he had destroyed the submarine, Mason radioed back this welcome news: "Sighted sub — sank same."

* * * * * * * *

In these pages patriotic and liberty-loving Americans have spoken to us out of the past. Their words hold a message for us today, a strong clear message of courage and of faith in our country and its future.

CHAPTER 8

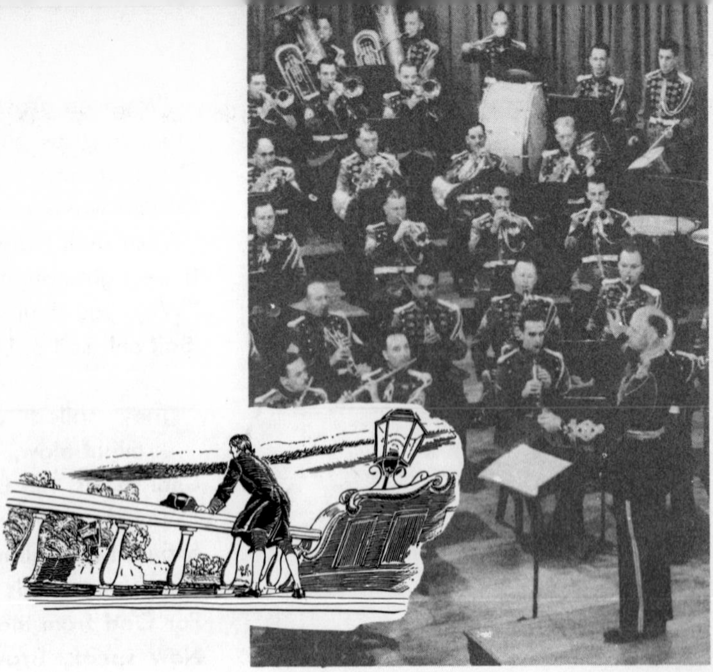

Patriotic Poems and Songs for Americans

A beautiful song or a stirring poem has a way of reaching our hearts as nothing else can. It has the power to arouse in us noble thoughts and deep emotions. We Americans have many patriotic poems and songs that are dear to us because they express our love for our country. We have songs that Americans have sung together since our nation was young, and poems that have been known and loved for many years. Some of the poems and songs written in times when our nation was in danger are filled with fiery patriotism. Others express the deep pride felt by Americans in our country or in the great men who helped to build it.

In this chapter you will find a number of America's best-loved patriotic poems and songs. If some of the words of the songs and poems seem strange to you, it may be because they were written long ago. Then, too, poets often use unusual words to make rhymes or to arouse deeper feelings than commonplace words do. But the thoughts and emotions of the writers are quite clear. You will find that these poems express the spirit that has made America the great and free nation she is today.

AMERICA, PRESENT AND PAST: *Great moments in our history, such as the bombardment of Fort McHenry, have inspired many of our patriotic songs and poems.*

Patriotic Poems

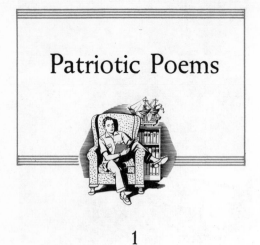

1

Columbus

Joaquin Miller

What this poem is about. Joaquin Miller (1839–1913) grew up in pioneer times in Oregon, and later mined gold in California. He loved the West, and wrote many poems and plays about it. This particular poem, however, is about an earlier pioneer. It is a tribute to the man who reached the Western Hemisphere and to the determination that drove him to sail on across "shoreless seas" and find a new world.

Behind him lay the gray Azores,
Behind the Gates of Hercules;
Before him not the ghost of shores;
Before him only shoreless seas.
The good mate said: "Now must we pray,
For lo! the very stars are gone.
Brave Adm'r'l, speak; what shall I say?"
"Why, say: 'Sail on! sail on! and on!' "

Columbus, by Joaquin Miller, reprinted by permission of Juanita J. Miller.

"My men grow mutinous day by day;
My men grow ghastly, wan and weak."
The stout mate thought of home; a spray
Of salt wave washed his swarthy cheek.
"What shall I say, brave Adm'r'l, say,
If we sight naught but seas at dawn?"
"Why, you shall say at break of day:
'Sail on! sail on! sail on! and on!' "

They sailed and sailed, as winds might blow,
Until at last the blanched mate said:
"Why, now not even God would know
Should I and all my men fall dead.
These very winds forget their way,
For God from these dread seas is gone.
Now speak, brave Adm'r'l, speak and say —"
He said: "Sail on! sail on! and on!"

Christopher Columbus claims the New World for Spain.

They sailed. They sailed. Then spake the mate:
"This mad sea shows his teeth to-night.
He curls his lip, he lies in wait,
With lifted teeth, as if to bite!
Brave Adm'r'l, say but one good word:
What shall we do when hope is gone?"
The words leapt like a leaping sword:
"Sail on! sail on! sail on! and on!"

Then, pale and worn, he kept his deck,
And peered through darkness. Ah, that night
Of all dark nights! And then a speck—
A light! A light! At last a light!
It grew, a starlit flag unfurled!
It grew to be Time's burst of dawn.
He gained a world; he gave that world
Its grandest lesson: "On! sail on!"

2

The Landing of the Pilgrim Fathers

Felicia Dorothea Hemans

What this poem is about. The poem that follows describes the courageous Pilgrims who landed on a "wild New England shore" in November, 1620. They had braved many dangers in their search for freedom in an unknown land. Oddly enough, this poem was written by an English poet. It has been a favorite of Americans for over a hundred years. Here are six of the ten verses.

After the first hard winter in Plymouth, the Pilgrims were greeted by Samoset, a friendly Indian.

The breaking waves dashed high
On the stern and rock-bound coast,
And the woods, against a stormy sky,
Their giant branches tossed;

And the heavy night hung dark
The hills and waters o'er,
When a band of exiles moored their bark
On the wild New England shore.

. . . .

There were men with hoary hair
Amidst that pilgrim band;
Why have they come to wither there,
Away from their childhood's land?

There was woman's fearless eye,
Lit by her deep love's truth;
There was manhood's brow, serenely high,
And the fiery heart of youth.

What sought they thus afar?
Bright jewels of the mine?
The wealth of seas, the spoils of war? —
They sought a faith's pure shrine!

Aye, call it holy ground,
The soil where first they trod!
They left unstained what there they found —
Freedom to worship God!

3

Paul Revere's Ride

Henry Wadsworth Longfellow

What this poem is about. All American schoolchildren know some of Longfellow's most famous poems, such as *The Village Blacksmith, The Children's Hour, Hiawatha,* and *Paul Revere's Ride.* Henry Wadsworth Longfellow, who lived from 1807 to 1882, was a descendant of John and Priscilla Alden of Plymouth Colony. He wrote many of his poems in Cambridge, Massachusetts, when he was a professor at Harvard College.

Many a former schoolboy has recited the exciting verses of *Paul Revere's Ride.* This poem, as most of you know, tells the story of Paul Revere's gallop through the countryside to warn the people of Massachusetts that the British were advancing on Lexington. As poets sometimes do, Longfellow changed the facts slightly to make a good poem. Paul Revere was actually captured by the British after he reached Lexington; he really never reached Concord. It was another rider who got through and gave the alarm. But Longfellow gives us a thrilling picture of this famous ride.

Listen, my children, and you shall hear
Of the midnight ride of Paul Revere,
On the eighteenth of April, in Seventy-five;
Hardly a man is now alive
Who remembers that famous day and year.

He said to his friend, "If the British march
By land or sea from the town tonight,
Hang a lantern aloft in the belfry arch
Of the North Church tower as a signal light —
One, if by land, and two, if by sea;
And I on the opposite shore will be,
Ready to ride and spread the alarm
Through every Middlesex village and farm,
For the country folk to be up and to arm."

. . . .

Meanwhile, his friend, through alley and street,
Wanders and watches, with eager ears,
Till in the silence around him he hears
The muster of men at the barrack door,
The sound of arms, and the tramp of feet,
And the measured tread of the grenadiers,
Marching down to their boats on the shore.

Then he climbed the tower of the Old North Church,
By the wooden stairs, with stealthy tread,
To the belfry-chamber overhead,
And startled the pigeons from their perch
On the somber rafters, that round him made
Masses and moving shapes of shade —
By the trembling ladder, steep and tall,
To the highest window in the wall,
Where he paused to listen and look down
A moment on the roofs of the town,
And the moonlight flowing over all.

. . . .

Meanwhile, impatient to mount and ride,
Booted and spurred, with a heavy stride
On the opposite shore walked Paul Revere.
Now he patted his horse's side,
Now gazed at the landscape far and near,
Then, impetuous, stamped the earth,
And turned and tightened his saddle girth;
But mostly he watched with eager search
The belfry-tower of the Old North Church,
As it rose above the graves on the hill,
Lonely and spectral and somber and still.

Henry Wadsworth Longfellow was the most popular American poet of his time. Paul Revere's Ride, *like many of Longfellow's poems, shows his patriotic feeling and his interest in New England history.*

And lo! as he looks, on the belfry's height
A glimmer, and then a gleam of light!
He springs to the saddle, the bridle he turns,
But lingers and gazes, till full on his sight
A second lamp in the belfry burns!

A hurry of hoofs in a village street,
A shape in the moonlight, a bulk in the dark,
And beneath, from the pebbles, in passing, a spark
Struck out by a steed flying fearless and fleet:
That was all! And yet, through the gloom and the light,
The fate of a nation was riding that night;
And the spark struck out by that steed, in his flight,
Kindled the land into flame with its heat.

. . . .

It was twelve by the village clock,
When he crossed the bridge into Medford Town.
He heard the crowing of the cock,
And the barking of the farmer's dog,
And felt the damp of the river fog,
That rises after the sun goes down.

It was one by the village clock,
When he galloped into Lexington.
He saw the gilded weathercock
Swim in the moonlight as he passed,
And the meeting-house windows, blank and bare,
Gaze at him with a spectral glare,
As if they already stood aghast
At the bloody work they would look upon.

It was two by the village clock,
When he came to the bridge in Concord Town.
He heard the bleating of the flock,
And the twitter of birds among the trees,
And felt the breath of the morning breeze
Blowing over the meadows brown.
And one was safe and asleep in his bed
Who at the bridge would be first to fall,
Who that day would be lying dead,
Pierced by a British musket-ball.

Behind this statue of Paul Revere is Boston's Old North Church. Twice since the signal lanterns were hung there, the tower has been destroyed and has had to be rebuilt.

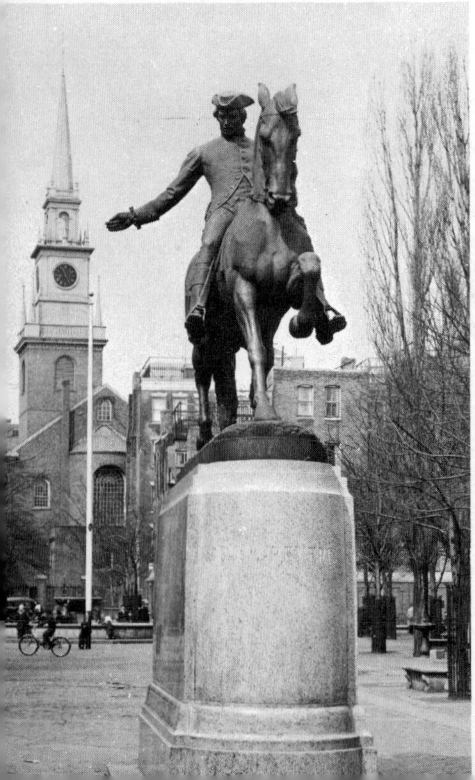

You know the rest. In the books you have read
How the British Regulars fired and fled —
How the farmers gave them ball for ball,
From behind each fence and farm-yard wall,
Chasing the red-coats down the lane,
Then crossing the fields to emerge again
Under the trees at the turn of the road,
And only pausing to fire and load.

So through the night rode Paul Revere;
And so through the night went his cry of alarm
To every Middlesex village and farm —
A cry of defiance and not of fear,
A voice in the darkness, a knock at the door,
And a word that shall echo forevermore!
For, borne on the nightwind of the Past,
Through all our history, to the last,
In the hour of darkness and peril and need,
The people will waken and listen to hear
The hurrying hoof-beats of that steed,
And the midnight message of Paul Revere.

4

What's in a Name?

Helen F. More

What this poem is about. Longfellow's poem and our history books have made Americans familiar with Paul Revere's ride. But we seldom give a thought to William Dawes, who also rode that night. He was sent from Boston by one route, Paul Revere by another, to give the alarm. In the poem below, the forgotten Dawes says, "Me, too." It is not, of course, a great poem but you will enjoy the three stanzas given here.

'Tis all very well for children to hear,
Of the midnight ride of Paul Revere;
But why should my name be quite forgot,
Who rode as boldly but no fame got?
Why should I ask? The reason is clear —
My name was Dawes and his Revere.

When the lights from the Old North
 Church flashed out,
Paul Revere was waiting about,
But I was already on my way.
The shadows of night fell cold and gray
As I rode, with never a break or pause;
But what was the use, when my name
 was Dawes?

History rings with his silvery name;
Closed to me are the portals of fame.
Had he been Dawes and I Revere,
No one had heard of him, I fear.
No one has heard of me because
He was Revere and I was Dawes.

5

The Concord Hymn

Ralph Waldo Emerson

How it came to be written. Ralph Waldo Emerson is another writer who lived about the same time as Longfellow. Emerson's home was in Concord for many years, not far from the famous bridge where the minutemen fired on the British on April 19, 1775. In 1836, ceremonies to honor the minutemen were held in Concord, and Emerson wrote the following poem, which was sung as a hymn at the ceremonies. Many years later, when the famous monument to the minutemen was erected in Concord (page 122), the first stanza of Emerson's poem was carved on its base.

Here at Concord Bridge, calm and peaceful now, valiant minutemen "fired the shot heard round the world."

GALLOWAY

By the rude bridge that arched the flood,
 Their flag to April's breeze unfurled,
Here once the embattled farmers stood
 And fired the shot heard round the world.

The foe long since in silence slept;
 Alike the conqueror silent sleeps;
And Time the ruined bridge has swept
 Down the dark stream which seaward creeps.

On this green bank, by this soft stream,
 We set to-day a votive stone;
That memory may their deed redeem,
 When, like our sires, our sons are gone.

Spirit, that made those heroes dare
 To die, and leave their children free,
Bid Time and Nature gently spare
 The shaft we raise to them and thee.

6

Old Ironsides

Oliver Wendell Holmes

How it came to be written. You have already read a little about this poem

This view from the stern shows part of Old Ironsides' *rigging.*

in Chapter 6. Its author, Oliver Wendell Holmes, was studying law at Harvard in 1830 when he read in the paper that the Navy planned to break up the frigate *Constitution.* He sat down and wrote a poem to protest against the destroying of *Old Ironsides.* When his poem was printed in the newspaper, it aroused the American public and the ship was saved. Oliver Wendell Holmes later became a well-known author of the 1800's. But it is as the writer of this patriotic poem that most of us know him today.

Ay, tear her tattered ensign down!
  Long has it waved on high,
And many an eye has danced to see
  That banner in the sky;
Beneath it rung the battle shout,
  And burst the cannon's roar; —
The meteor of the ocean air
  Shall sweep the clouds no more!

Her deck, once red with heroes' blood,
  Where knelt the vanquished foe,
When winds were hurrying o'er the flood,
  And waves were white below,
No more shall feel the victor's tread,
  Or know the conquered knee; —
The harpies of the shore shall pluck
  The eagle of the sea!

Oh, better that her shattered hulk
  Should sink beneath the wave;
Her thunders shook the mighty deep,
  And there should be her grave;
Nail to the mast her holy flag,
  Set every threadbare sail,
And give her to the god of storms,
  The lightning and the gale!

7

O Captain! My Captain!

Walt Whitman

This painting of Walt Whitman shows the poet hiking across the land he loved so well.

How it came to be written. Walt Whitman is one of America's great poets. He was born in 1819 and lived almost to the end of the 1800's. As a young newspaper writer he traveled widely about the United States and came to know it and its people well. During the War Between the States, he helped to take care of wounded soldiers in the military hospitals near Washington. When Abraham Lincoln was shot, Whitman put into the moving words of the following poem the deep sense of loss which millions of Americans felt.

O Captain! my Captain! our fearful trip is done;
The ship has weather'd every rack, the prize we sought is won,
The port is near, the bells I hear, the people all exulting,
While follow eyes the steady keel, the vessel grim and daring;
But O heart! heart! heart!
O the bleeding drops of red,
Where on the deck my Captain lies,
Fallen cold and dead.

O Captain! my Captain! rise up and hear the bells;
Rise up — for you the flag is flung — for you the bugle trills,
For you bouquets and ribbon'd wreaths — for you the shores a-crowding,
For you they call, the swaying mass, their eager faces turning:
Here Captain! dear father!
This arm beneath your head!
It is some dream that on the deck,
You've fallen cold and dead.

My Captain does not answer, his lips are pale and still,
My father does not feel my arm, he has no pulse nor will,
The ship is anchor'd safe and sound, its voyage closed and done,
From fearful trip, the victor ship comes in with object won;
Exult O shores, and ring O bells!
But I, with mournful tread,
Walk the deck my Captain lies,
Fallen cold and dead.

8

Your Flag and My Flag

Wilbur D. Nesbit

Poems about our Flag. Many inspiring poems have been written about our country's Flag. We have selected two which we think you will like. The first poem by Wilbur D. Nesbit expresses the pride and love we feel for our Flag. The second one is about an American who flew for France in World War I, until our country entered the war. Read about his feeling as he paints the Stars and Stripes on his battle plane. You may also want to find and read other poems written about our Flag.

Your Flag and my Flag!
And how it flies to-day
In your land and my land
And half a world away!
Rose-red and blood-red,
The stripes forever gleam,
Snow-white and soul-white —
The good forefather's dream.
Sky-blue and true-blue,
And stars to gleam aright,
The gloried guidon of the day,
A shelter through the night!

Your Flag and my Flag,
And O, how much it holds —
Your land and my land
Secure within its folds;
Your heart and my heart
Beat quicker at the sight
Sun-kissed and wind-tossed,
The red and blue and white.
The one Flag, the great Flag,
The Flag for me and you —
Glorified all else beside,
The red and white and blue.

Our Flag flies over the Capitol in Washington, D.C.

GALLOWAY

Your Flag and my Flag!
   To every star and stripe
The drum beats as hearts beat,
   And fifers shrilly pipe!
Your Flag and my Flag —
   A blessing in the sky;
Your hope and my hope —
   It never hid a lie!
Home land, and far land
   And half the world around,
Old Glory hears our glad salute
   And ripples to the sound!

9

A Battle Plane in France

O. C. Child

My driver came this morning on the run.
High above his head he waved a paint brush,
And in his other hand there were some small cans.
He wore a new coat, a spickity-span coat,
A coat of brownish yellow. It was khaki!
Bronze buttons it had, with an eagle on each —
A fierce beaked eagle!
Very carefully he laid the coat down,
Tenderly, like something precious,
Then he opened the cans, and, as he worked,
He whistled "Yankee Doodle" and "Dixie."
His eyes were all alight with something splendid,
Like the eyes of one who loves greatly.
He sighed just a little as he painted
The insignia of France from my wings.
He has flown far, and high, and well, for France!
Then, smiling, he dashed blood-red stripes on my wings,
Until there were seven,
And white stripes he painted,
And a field of dark blue, and many small stars.
Standing erect, he gazed at it a while, and said:
"Dear God! It's wonderful — that flag!"

Getting Ready to Fly for America

10

It Is Your Democracy

Walt Whitman

What this poem is about. Walt Whitman was a man who believed deeply in America. He loved our land; he loved our people; he loved our democracy. This poem by Whitman makes the American citizen feel important. It should also make those who read it feel responsible for the democracy he describes. Unlike *O Captain! My Captain!*, most of Whitman's poetry is written in what we call *free verse,* without the rhythm and the rhyme that some poems have. The following lines about our democracy are an example of free verse.

The sum of all known reverence I add up in you whoever you are.
The President is there in the White House for you, it is not you who are here for him.
The Secretaries act in their bureaus for you, not you here for them,
The Congress convenes every Twelfth-month for you,
Laws, courts, the forming of states, the charters of cities, the going and coming of commerce and mails, are all for you.

11

"What Makes a Nation?"

Wilbur D. Nesbit

The words of the poem below answer the question raised by its title. First, read the poem carefully and then see if you can put into your own words the answer which the poet has given in verse.

What makes a nation? Bounding lines that lead from shore to shore,
That trace its girth on silent hills or on the prairie floor,
That hold the rivers and the lakes and all the fields between —
The lines that stand about the land, a barrier unseen?

Or is it guns that hold the coast, or ships that sweep the seas,
The flag that flaunts its glory in the racing of the breeze;
The chants of peace, or battle hymn, or dirge, or victor's song,
Or parchment screed, or storied deed, that makes a nation strong?

What makes a nation? Is it ships or states or flags or guns?
Or is it that great common heart which beats in all her sons —
That deeper faith, that truer faith, the trust in one for all
Which sets the goal for every soul that hears his country's call?

This makes a nation great and strong and certain to endure,
This subtle inner voice that thrills a man and makes him sure;
Which makes him know there is no north or south or east or west,
But that his land must ever stand the bravest and the best.

12

I Am an American

Elias Lieberman

What this poem is about. Elias Lieberman, whose *Credo* you read in Chapter 7, wrote this poem to picture two Americans. One is native-born and can trace his family back to the Revolution. The other is Russian-born and tells how little human dignity his people had until they came to the United States. Their backgrounds are different, but both are Americans.

I am an American.
My father belongs to the Sons of the Revolution;
My mother, to the Colonial Dames.
One of my ancestors pitched tea overboard in Boston Harbor;
Another stood his ground with Warren;
Another hungered with Washington at Valley Forge.
My forefathers were America in the making:
They spoke in her council halls;
They died on her battle-fields;
They commanded her ships;
They cleared her forests.
Dawns reddened and paled.
Stanch hearts of mine beat fast at each new star
In the nation's flag.

Keen eyes of mine foresaw her greater glory:
The sweep of her seas,
The plenty of her plains,
The man-hives in her billion-wired cities.
Every drop of blood in me holds a heritage of patriotism.
I am proud of my past.
I am an American.

I am an American.
My father was an atom of dust,
My mother a straw in the wind,
To his serene majesty.
One of my ancestors died in the mines of Siberia;
Another was crippled for life by twenty blows of the *knout*.
Another was killed defending his home during the massacres.
The history of my ancestors is a trail of blood
To the palace-gate of the Great White Czar.
But then the dream came —
The dream of America.
In the light of the Liberty torch
The atom of dust became a man
And the straw in the wind became a woman
For the first time.
"See," said my father, pointing to the flag that fluttered near,
"That flag of stars and stripes is yours;
It is the emblem of the promised land.
It means, my son, the hope of humanity.
Live for it — die for it!"
Under the open sky of my new country I swore to do so;
And every drop of blood in me will keep that vow.
I am proud of my future.
I am an American.

★ ★ ★ ★ ★ ★ ★ ★ ★

Patriotic Songs

1

The Star-Spangled Banner

Words by Francis Scott Key

How it came to be written. The strains of *The Star-Spangled Banner* bring a thrill of pride to American hearts. This stirring song is our National Anthem, and, like the Flag, is a symbol of patriotism to all of us. We Americans stand when *The Star-Spangled Banner* is played or sung, just as we rise to honor the Flag. The National Anthem is one of our oldest patriotic songs. It was written during the War of 1812 by a young lawyer named Francis Scott Key. To understand what the words of *The Star-Spangled Banner* mean, we should know how it came to be written.

You remember that British troops had actually captured Washington, D.C., in August, 1814. In September of the same year the British were planning another attack, this time on Baltimore, Maryland. Several British warships were anchored in Chesapeake Bay opposite Fort McHenry, which guarded the city. Aboard one of these ships was a Maryland doctor, William Beanes, who had been taken prisoner by the British because he interfered with their troops.

On September 13, Francis Scott Key and a friend set out in a small government boat to try to have the doctor set free. They boarded the British ship with a letter from President Madison. The letter asked for the release of Dr. Beanes on the grounds that he was a civilian, not a soldier. The British admiral agreed to let the doctor go free, but since the British fleet was then ready to bombard Fort McHenry, he could not let the three Americans return with such news. So Mr. Key and the others were ordered to return to their own boat and remain there during the bombardment.

At sunset the men could still see the Flag of the United States flying over the fort. But would the fort hold out during the night? We can imagine how anxiously they watched and listened that night to the "bombs bursting in air," and how they watched for the Flag by the "rockets' red glare." When dawn came at last, they were overjoyed to see that the Flag was still flying. The British had failed to take the fort, and Baltimore was safe! On seeing the Flag, Francis Scott Key cried out, "O say, can you see?" In his relief and joy he took out an envelope and wrote down the stanza of a poem beginning with these words. On the way back to shore he completed his poem about the "perilous fight."

The next day Key showed a copy to a friend who was so enthusiastic that he had the poem printed on sheets of paper and distributed through Baltimore. Then it was found that the words would fit a British tune which Americans knew. The tune had been written by an Englishman named John Stafford Smith and was just right for Key's words. This is the way *The Star-Spangled Banner* was born. Its fiery phrases and deep patriotic feeling caught the public enthusiasm. Newspapers in the cities printed the words, and soon Americans all over the nation were singing the new song.

First Printing of *The Star-Spangled Banner*

In spite of its great popularity, *The Star-Spangled Banner* was not officially made the National Anthem until March 3, 1931. In tribute to its author an American Flag flies over his grave. The flag which flew over Fort McHenry during the bombardment can be seen in the National Museum in Washington. Old and frayed, one of its stars shot out by a bullet, it is the "Star-Spangled Banner" of our National Anthem. Here are three verses.

O say, can you see, by the dawn's early light,
What so proudly we hailed at the twilight's last gleaming?
Whose broad stripes and bright stars, through the perilous fight,
O'er the ramparts we watched were so gallantly streaming!
And the rocket's red glare, the bombs bursting in air,
Gave proof through the night that our flag was still there:
O say, does that star-spangled banner yet wave
O'er the land of the free and the home of the brave?

On the shore, dimly seen through the mists of the deep,
Where the foe's haughty host in dread silence reposes,
What is that which the breeze, o'er the towering steep,
As it fitfully blows, now conceals, now discloses?
Now it catches the gleam of the morning's first beam,
In full glory reflected now shines on the stream:
'Tis the star-spangled banner! O long may it wave
O'er the land of the free and the home of the brave!

. . . .

O thus be it ever, when freemen shall stand
Between their loved homes and the war's desolation!
Blest with victory and peace, may the heaven-rescued land
Praise the Power that hath made and preserved us a nation.
Then conquer we must, when our cause it is just,
And this be our motto: "In God is our trust,"
And the star-spangled banner in triumph shall wave
O'er the land of the free and the home of the brave!

2

Yankee Doodle

How it came to be sung. Although *The Star-Spangled Banner* is our National Anthem, the lively little song called *Yankee Doodle* is our first patriotic song. It goes way back to the days of the French and Indian War in the 1760's. In fact, the song was first sung by the British to poke fun at the American backwoodsmen who were helping them fight the French and Indians. The Americans must have seemed an odd-looking lot to the British soldiers. Many of them wore coon-skin caps on their long, uncombed hair. There were some who had long coats flapping about their legs and others who wore no coats at all. The uniformed British soldiers laughed at these men in their strange clothes who didn't even know how to march.

According to an old story, a British army doctor and poet wrote some stanzas to an old English tune, mocking the "Yankee Doodles." The word "Yankee," as we know, was a nickname for the Americans (see page 33), and "Doodle" was an English word of that day which meant "silly" or "do-nothing." But when the Americans heard the British singing the song to ridicule them, they liked the catchy rhythm and soon they were singing it, too! They marched to the lively tune, singing or whistling it as they went along, not minding the English soldiers' laughter.

In the Revolution several years later, *Yankee Doodle* became the favorite song of the American troops. They sang it as they marched into battle against the redcoats. When the British surrendered at Yorktown in 1781, the Continental band played "Yankee Doodle"! Some of the British might well have thought that their joking had back-fired.

Through the years *Yankee Doodle* has remained a favorite with Americans. It is an excellent marching tune and Americans like to sing its funny, lively words written so long ago. *Yankee Doodle* is the kind of song that easily picks up new verses as it is sung. Many stanzas have been handed down to us, but the ones given below are some of those which are supposed to have been written by the British doctor about two hundred years ago. Today these verses give us a good picture of the countrified backwoodsman of America in those early times. Of course you all know the tune!

Father and I went down to camp,
Along with Captain Goodwin,
And there we saw the men and boys,
As thick as hasty puddin'!

(chorus)
Yankee Doodle, keep it up,
Yankee Doodle dandy,
Mind the music and the step
And with the girls be handy!

And there we see a thousand men,
As rich as Squire David;
And what they wasted ev'ry day,
I wish it could be saved.

And there I see a swamping gun,
Large as a log of maple,
Upon a deuced little cart,
A load for father's cattle.

And every time they shoot it off,
It takes a horn of powder,
And makes a noise like father's gun,
Only a nation louder.

We saw a little barrel, too,
The heads were made of leather;
They knocked upon it with little clubs,
And called the folks together.

3

America

Words by Samuel Francis Smith

How it came to be written. *America* is not a song connected with war. Its words are not a triumphant cry of victory like those of our National Anthem. It is instead a hymn which expresses our love for our country, our love of liberty, and our faith in God.

No one knows who wrote the music of *America.* The melody was sung in several countries of Europe. England's national anthem, *God Save the Queen,* and Austria's, too, use the old tune we know as *America.* But the words of *America* were written in 1832 by a young man named Samuel Francis Smith, while he was studying to be a minister. He came across the old melody in a German songbook, and, as he hummed the tune, he wrote down some verses in praise of the country he loved. It took him

Americay

Do you recognize this word? The name of our country used to be pronounced Americay! In the early days the Presidents all used this pronunciation. Even in songs and poetry America was rhymed with words ending in *ay*.

less than a half hour to compose the four stanzas of the song he called *My Country, 'Tis of Thee* but which we know as *America.* It never entered his head that he was writing a patriotic hymn that would be sung by many generations of Americans.

America was sung in many public places and was later put in hymnbooks, but it was not until the War Between the States that the song became popular. Americans began to sing it then, and it has been one of our great national songs from that time on.

My country, 'tis of thee,
Sweet land of liberty,
  Of thee I sing;
Land where my fathers died,
Land of the pilgrims' pride,
From every mountain-side
  Let freedom ring.

My native country, thee,
Land of the noble free,
  Thy name I love;
I love thy rocks and rills,
Thy woods and templed hills;
My heart with rapture thrills
  Like that above.

Let music swell the breeze,
And ring from all the trees
  Sweet freedom's song;
Let mortal tongues awake,
Let all that breathe partake,
Let rocks their silence break —
  The sound prolong.

Our fathers' God, to Thee,
Author of liberty,
  To Thee we sing;
Long may our land be bright
With freedom's holy light;
Protect us by Thy might,
  Great God, our King.

GALLOWAY

The beauty of America — her "rocks and rills," her "templed hills" — is a constant inspiration to poets and composers.

American hearts beat faster when bands, such as the United States Army Band shown here, play our favorite national songs.

4

Songs of the Armed Forces

What these songs are about. Songs have always been important to fighting men. Songs have furnished encouragement during long marches or dreary hours of duty. They also help to build up patriotic feeling and pride in the various branches of the armed services. Small wonder that the songs of various branches of our Armed Forces rank high among our popular patriotic songs.

All of us know *The Marines' Hymn,* the famous song which men of the United States Marine Corps have sung for over a hundred years. Many of us know the Navy's *Anchors Aweigh,* and the song of the U.S. Air Force. Since the Army has no official song, *The Caissons Go Rolling Along* has been chosen to represent it. A verse from each of these service songs follows.

Words and music to *The U. S. Air Force* by Major Robert M. Crawford. Copyright 1939 by Carl Fischer, Inc., New York. Reprinted by permission.

The Marines' Hymn

From the Halls of Montezuma
To the shores of Tripoli;
We fight our country's battles
In the air, on land and sea;
First to fight for right and freedom
And to keep our honor clean;
We are proud to claim the title
Of United States Marine.

The U. S. Air Force

Off we go into the wild blue yonder,
Climbing high into the sun;
Here they come, zooming to meet our thunder,
At 'em, boys,
Give 'er the gun!
(Give 'er the gun now!)
Down we dive, spouting our flame from under,
Off on one terrible course!
We live in fame
Or go down in flame,
(Shout!)
Nothing'll stop the U. S. Air Force!

The Marines' Hymn reprinted through the courtesy of the United States Marine Corps.

Anchors Aweigh

Blue of the Seven Seas,
Gold of God's great sun —
Let these our colors be
Till all our time be done.
By Severn's shore we learn
Navy's stern call:
Faith, courage, service true
With honor over, honor over all.

The Caissons Go Rolling Along

Over hill, over dale,
We have hit the dusty trail,
And those caissons go rolling along.
"Counter march! Right about!"
Hear those wagon soldiers shout,
While those caissons go rolling along:

(chorus)
For it's Hi! Hi! Hee!
In the field artillery,
Call off your numbers loud and strong.
And where'er we go
You will always know
That those caissons are rolling along,
That those caissons are rolling along.

5

Dixie

Words and Music by
Daniel Decatur Emmett

How it came to be written. The story of *Dixie* is a curious one. Although written by a Northerner, it is a song about the South which became a Confederate war song. This is the story.

In the 1800's minstrel shows were a favorite kind of entertainment all over the United States. Actors with hands and faces blacked would amuse their audience by dancing, telling stories and jokes, playing the banjo, and singing. When the audience liked the songs they shouted, "Hooray!" A famous minstrel and song-writer was Daniel Emmett.

One cold night in the winter of 1858 Dan Emmett was in New York City. As he walked along to his hotel, he was trying to compose a new song. He began to think of the warm Southland far away from cold northern winters. "I wish I was in Dixie," he said to himself. These words gave him the idea he needed. He began humming a tune as he hurried to his hotel. There he wrote down the music and some words to go with it, and *Dixie* was born.

The song made a hit in the minstrel show, and soon its catchy tune was being sung everywhere. It became especially popular in the South. During the War Between the States the words were changed, and *Dixie* became the Confederate battle song.

After the war the tune was played and sung all over the United States. Today it is one of our favorite American songs. Below are three verses and the chorus of *Dixie*:

I wish I was in the land of cotton,
Old times there are not forgotten;
  Look away, look away, look away,
    Dixie land!
In Dixie land where I was born in,
Early on one frosty mornin',
  Look away, look away, look away,
    Dixie land!

(chorus)
  Then I wish I was in Dixie! Hooray!
    Hooray!
  In Dixie's land we'll take our stand,
    to live and die in Dixie,
  Away, away, away down south in
    Dixie!
  Away, away, away down south in
    Dixie!

This world was made in just six days,
And finished up in various ways.
  Look away! look away! look away!
    Dixie land!
They then made Dixie trim and nice,
And Adam called it "Paradise."
  Look away! look away! look away!
    Dixie land!

There's buckwheat cakes and Injun batter,
Makes you fat or a little fatter;
  Look away, look away, look away,
    Dixie land!
Then hoe it down and scratch your
    gravel,
To Dixie's land I'm bound to travel;
  Look away, look away, look away,
    Dixie land!

6

The Battle-Hymn of the Republic

Words by Julia Ward Howe

How it came to be written. While the Southerners were singing *Dixie* during the war, the people of the North had a battle song called *The Battle-Hymn of the Republic.* It was not a gay, lively tune like *Dixie,* but a strong and moving hymn. Like many great songs, it grew out of the spirit of the times. Mrs. Julia Ward Howe, the wife of a newspaper editor, went to Washington at the beginning of the war. Everywhere she saw soldiers marching and training, and heard talk of battles to come. The troops at that time were singing and marching to the tune of a hymn with a chorus that began "Glory! Glory, Hallelujah!" The verses had been made up by the soldiers.

A friend suggested to Mrs. Howe that she write new words for the fine old tune by William Steffe. Mrs. Howe had done a good deal of writing. She tells us that the words for *The Battle-Hymn of the Republic* came to her one night as she lay in bed. She got up and wrote down the five stanzas so that she would not forget them.

The poem was printed in a magazine in 1862 and later, newspapers carried the old hymn tune with Mrs. Howe's stanzas. Her stirring and religious words appealed to the people.

The Union soldiers were soon marching to the *Battle-Hymn* and singing the new words, "As He died to make men holy, let us die to make men free." It is said that when Lincoln heard the new song, he was moved to tears.

The Battle-Hymn of the Republic is perhaps not so well-known by young people of today as some of our other patriotic songs, but it should be remembered as a great hymn of freedom. Below are four stanzas and the chorus:

Mine eyes have seen the glory of the coming of the Lord;
He is trampling out the vintage where the grapes of wrath are stored;
He hath loosed the fateful lightning of His terrible swift sword;
His truth is marching on.

(chorus)
Glory, glory, hallelujah! Glory, glory, hallelujah!
Glory, glory, hallelujah! His truth is marching on.

I have seen Him in the watch-fires of a hundred circling camps;
They have builded Him an altar in the evening dews and damps;
I can read His righteous sentence by the dim and flaring lamps;
His day is marching on.

. . . .

He has sounded forth the trumpet that shall never call retreat;
He is sifting out the hearts of men before His judgment-seat:
Oh, be swift, my soul, to answer Him! be jubilant, my feet!
Our God is marching on.

In the beauty of the lilies Christ was born across the sea,
With a glory in His bosom that transfigures you and me;
As He died to make men holy, let us die to make men free,
While God is marching on.

7

America the Beautiful

Words by Katharine Lee Bates

How it came to be written. It is good to sing or to hear a song like *America the Beautiful*, for it is a song of faith and hope. It gives us pride in our land and our past; it reminds us of our ideals of liberty and equality. The words were written as a poem by Miss Katharine Lee Bates, a teacher of English at Wellesley College. In 1893 Miss Bates took a trip to the top of Pike's Peak in Colorado. As she stood looking at the great mountains and valleys spread out before her, the first line of the poem came to her mind, "O beautiful for spacious skies." When she returned to her hotel she finished the verses.

When her poem later appeared in a magazine, many Americans read it and liked it, for *America the Beautiful* seems to express what we feel about our country. The words were later set to an old hymn tune by Samuel A. Ward, to make a national song. People liked the hymn so well that many believed it should be

This picture of snow-capped Pike's Peak shows the grandeur and spaciousness which caused Katharine Lee Bates to write America the Beautiful.

chosen as the national anthem instead of *The Star-Spangled Banner*. Today, *America the Beautiful* is one of our most beautiful and best loved songs.

O beautiful for spacious skies,
For amber waves of grain,
For purple mountain majesties
Above the fruited plain!
America! America!
God shed His grace on thee
And crown thy good with brotherhood
From sea to shining sea!

O beautiful for pilgrim feet,
Whose stern, impassioned stress
A thoroughfare for freedom beat
Across the wilderness!
America! America!
God mend thine every flaw,
Confirm thy soul in self-control,
Thy liberty in law!

O beautiful for heroes proved
In liberating strife,
Who more than self their country loved,
And mercy more than life!
America! America!
May God thy gold refine
Till all success be nobleness
And every gain divine!

O beautiful for patriot dream
That sees beyond the years
Thine alabaster cities gleam
Undimmed by human tears!
America! America!
God shed His grace on thee
And crown thy good with brotherhood
From sea to shining sea!

8
God Bless America

Words and Music by Irving Berlin

How it came to be written. We all know of Irving Berlin, America's famous writer of popular songs. He was born in Russia and came to America with his family as a boy. One of his earliest and best-known tunes is *Alexander's Ragtime Band. White Christmas* is another Berlin song that we all know and love.

God Bless America was part of a musical comedy which Berlin wrote and produced for the Armed Forces during World War I. It was first introduced over the radio by Kate Smith. During World War II the song became very popular. When General MacArthur marched into Manila after recapturing the Philippines from the Japanese, the Filipino children sang *God Bless America.* It is interesting to know that Irving Berlin assigned this song and all profits from it to worthy causes, particularly the Boy and Girl Scouts of America.

Irving Berlin plays the piano while a group of American soldiers sing.

God bless America!
Land that I love,
Stand beside her and guide her
Through the night with a light from above.
From the mountains to the prairies,
To the ocean white with foam,
God bless America, my home sweet home,
God bless America, my home sweet home.

* * * * * * * *

We hope you have enjoyed these poems and songs about America and Americans. Perhaps you will want to learn one of the poems or some of the less familiar verses of the songs. An inspiring poem or song, you know, is worth learning and worth remembering for the rest of your life.

CHAPTER 9

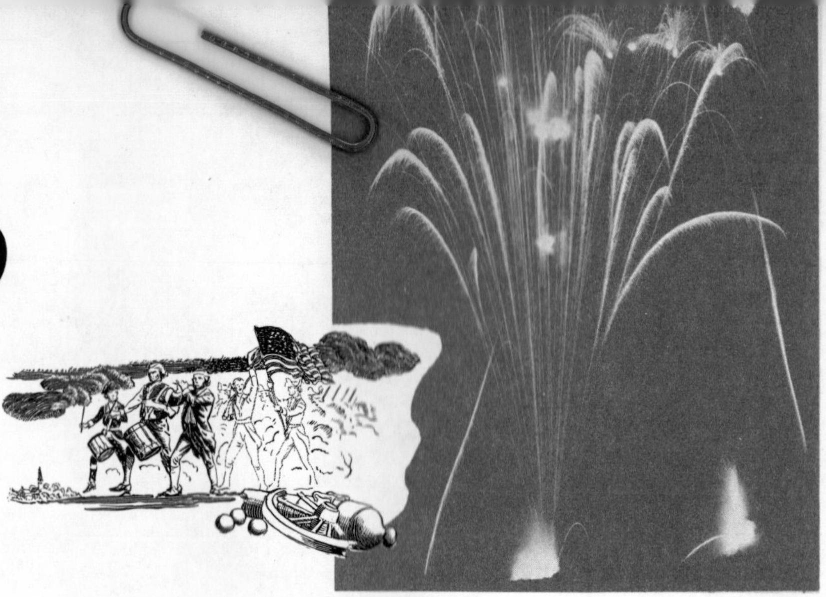

AMERICA, PRESENT AND PAST: *On our national holidays, we Americans recall with fireworks or other celebrations the patriotic spirit which built America.*

Patriotic Holidays that Americans Celebrate

We Americans share many holidays such as Easter, Christmas, and New Year's Day with the rest of the world, but most of our patriotic holidays are celebrated by Americans only. Everybody looks forward to holidays, but all too often we welcome them as days off from school or work, and nothing more. Our patriotic holidays deserve the attention of all good Americans, for they have grown out of our life as a nation. Every patriotic holiday has a meaning. If we do not stop to think of what the particular day stands for, it will lose its meaning and we in turn will lose something very valuable — a pride in the great men and events in our history.

This chapter tells about a number of our patriotic holidays and why we observe them. Except for Independence Day, the chief holidays are arranged as they occur during the year. We hope that reading about these holidays will help you to appreciate their importance as part of our American heritage. We hope that you will want to do your part as American citizens to preserve the true meaning of our patriotic holidays.

Independence Day

July 4 (1776)

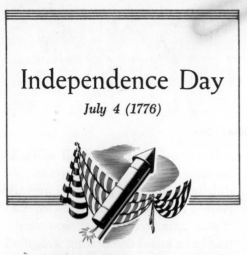

On July 4, as every American knows, we celebrate the "birthday" of our nation. Independence Day is our greatest patriotic holiday and a day for all Americans to remember. The thrilling story of American independence has been told in Chapter 3, so we will not repeat it here. Instead let us find out how Independence Day has been celebrated at different times in our history.

The First Independence Celebrations

In all the colonies of that long-ago July, 1776, independence was celebrated as the Declaration was posted in the cities and towns. In Philadelphia, for example, the great bell in the statehouse rang out its message of liberty. Even though the bell had been cast years before, it seemed as though the words which were engraved on it had been intended for this great event: "Proclaim liberty throughout all the land unto all the inhabitants thereof." The other bells of the city joined in. That night bonfires and torches lighted the sky, and cannon boomed as the people of Philadelphia celebrated independence. In other colonies men and women paraded to the sound of beating drums, and there were bonfires and fireworks to celebrate the news.

The people showed their approval of independence in other ways. They turned their pictures of King George to the walls of their homes. In Philadelphia the King's coat of arms was torn from the statehouse door. In Baltimore a figure representing the King was burned while hundreds cheered at the "just reward of a tyrant." When George Washington's troops heard the Declaration, some of them showed their enthusiasm by "beheading" a statue of King George. Many statues of the King ended up in a melting pot and were made into bullets for the patriots. The many "King Streets" throughout the colonies were given the new name of "State Street."

Later Celebrations of Independence Day

In the war years that followed there were also independence celebrations. In 1783, when Great Britain had at last been defeated and independence was certain, July 4 was celebrated in all the states with deep thanksgiving. George Washington himself was guest of honor at a great celebration in Philadelphia. And so Independence Day became our first patriotic holiday. Special ceremonies were held for the hundredth anniversary of our independence in 1876, and for the hundred and fiftieth anniversary in 1926.

Celebrating the First Independence Day

July 4 is a legal holiday in all the states and possessions of the United States. (A legal holiday must be declared by the states, either by an act of the legislature, or a proclamation of the governor. Banks and businesses are usually closed.) Except for the date, we Americans have carried out the wishes of John Adams for observing Independence Day. He wrote to his wife after July 2, when Congress had voted for independence: "I am apt to believe that it (July 2) will be celebrated by succeeding generations as the great anniversary Festival. It ought to be commemorated, as the day of deliverance, by solemn acts of devotion to God Almighty. It ought to be solemnized with pomp and parade, with shows, games, sports, guns, bells, bonfires, and illuminations, from one end of this continent to the other, from this time forward, forevermore."

A Safe and Sane Fourth of July

As years went by, the shooting of fireworks made the Fourth of July a dangerous holiday for the children of America. Boys and girls used to save their money to buy firecrackers, cannon crackers, rockets, and other fireworks to shoot off on the Fourth. Many a child was badly burned or had a finger or hand blown off when he became careless with fireworks. Nor did the injuries stop there. Fireworks caused the loss of many lives. By 1900 it was estimated that as many people had been killed celebrating independence as had been killed fighting for it in the Revolution! Today we believe in a "safe and sane Fourth of July." Over half our states have laws regulating the sale of fireworks. In a large number of cities no fireworks may be sold at all. It is becoming the custom in many communities to have a display of evening fireworks which everyone can enjoy in safety.

An Independence Day Story

There is an unusual story connected with the fiftieth anniversary of Independence Day in 1826. It concerns two great patriots, John Adams and Thomas Jefferson. Jefferson, you recall, wrote the Declaration; Adams helped get it adopted.

Both men lived for a half-century after the first Independence Day. Many years of their lives had been devoted to the service of their country. John Adams had been our second President, Jefferson, our third. In 1826 both were old men nearing the end of their long and useful lives. On July 4 both lay near death, Jefferson at

Monticello and Adams at his home in Quincy, Massachusetts. The thoughts of John Adams must have wandered back to that long-ago July in 1776, for his last words before he died were, "Jefferson still lives." Adams did not know that Thomas Jefferson had died a few hours before him. It is remarkable that both men died on the fiftieth anniversary of the day they had helped to make famous.

★ ★ ★ ★ ★ ★ ★ ★

As we celebrate July Fourth, let us pause to remember the Americans of long ago who risked their lives and fortunes in the cause of freedom. Let us be grateful for the liberty they passed on to us, and give thanks that we are still free citizens of a free nation. Let us fly our Flag at home to show that the Star-Spangled Banner still waves over the land of the free.

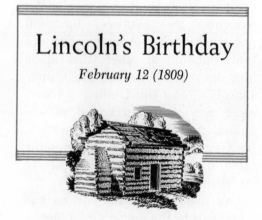

Lincoln's Birthday

February 12 (1809)

Each year on February 12, we observe the birthday of a man who was not only a great American, but one of the great men of all time — Abraham Lincoln. To honor his memory thirty-two states have declared the day of his birth a legal holiday, and other states observe the day with celebrations. Our public schools hold special programs in his memory. Newspapers over the nation carry Lincoln's picture and publish editorials and stories about him. Flags are flown from public buildings and from homes in his honor. Truly, Abraham Lincoln holds a special place in our hearts.

From Log Cabin to White House

Although every schoolboy has some knowledge of Abraham Lincoln, it will be worth while here to recall a few of the important facts of his life. He was born in a one-room log cabin in Kentucky in 1809. His pioneer parents moved on to Indiana when Abraham was seven years old and his mother died there two years later. Lincoln had to work hard and had little time for schooling. Altogether he had less than a year of school, but he managed to teach himself by studying at night from borrowed books. When the family moved to Illinois, Lincoln set out to earn his own way. He worked at many jobs, studied law, and became a lawyer in Springfield, Illinois. In 1842 he married Mary Todd of Kentucky. People liked Lincoln for his honesty, his friendliness, and his gift for telling humorous stories.

Lincoln was elected to the Illinois legislature and later to the United States Congress. In 1858 he ran for Senator against Stephen A. Douglas. As part of their campaign Lincoln and Douglas held a series of debates. People traveled long distances to hear the two men speak. Although Douglas won the Senate election, Lincoln gained national fame. The debates showed his ability to speak convincingly and his firm belief that slavery must not be allowed to spread into the western territories that had not yet become states. In 1860 Lincoln was nominated for President by the Republican Party and was elected.

As President, Lincoln Carried Heavy Burdens

Even before Lincoln was inaugurated President, several Southern states seceded from the Union because of Lincoln's well-known stand against the spread of slavery. But Lincoln was determined to save the Union no matter what it cost. In the four-year war that followed, the Union was saved; soon after, the slaves were freed. It is a tragedy of history that Lincoln was killed by an assassin before he could carry out his plans to bring the South back into the Union.

Lincoln's true greatness was not recognized by many people until after his death. He was a homely, rather awkward man who did not pay a great deal of attention to his clothes. He had grown up on the frontier and did not have the elegant manners nor the social graces that many people expected of a President. Lincoln was misjudged and misunderstood by men who should have known better. In Washington he not only had to face sharper criticism than any President before him, but even ridicule. His own cabinet members disagreed with his decisions about the conduct of the war and criticized him freely. As time went on, many people began to see the qualities of mind and of character that made him stand out among ordinary men. When the war was won at last, Americans realized that this man with his determination and his belief in the right as he saw it possessed true greatness.

Lincoln and Douglas Debating

Americans Honor Abraham Lincoln

Today we know the fine mind and great heart of Abraham Lincoln. We recognize the patience, the will power, the noble character, and the understanding of others that made him one of the world's great men. Lincoln's most outstanding achievement was the preservation of the Union. As you learned in Chapter 7, his Gettysburg Address contains the finest statement of the principles of our democracy ever made.

Our nation has many shrines and memorials to the memory of Lincoln. The most important are the Lincoln Memorial in Washington, D. C., and his tomb in Springfield, Illinois. Lincoln is also one of the four great

A group of students tour the Lincoln Museum in Washington, D. C. This Museum has a famous collection of books, papers, and other things relating to Lincoln.

Americans represented at Mt. Rushmore in South Dakota. These three Lincoln shrines have been described in Chapter 6. In Kentucky there are two famous Lincoln shrines. The old log cabin where Lincoln was born now stands in a memorial building at Hodgenville. The cabin where his parents were married has been preserved at Harrodsburg. In Washington, Ford's Theater where Lincoln was shot is now a Lincoln Museum, and the house across the street where he died is also a memorial.

Everywhere in our country are reminders of Lincoln. Almost every city has a Lincoln school. Towns, buildings and streets have been named after him. Some of you may have traveled on the Lincoln Highway which crosses our country.

Abraham Lincoln is enshrined in the hearts of the American people as perhaps no other man is. We have set aside his birthday as a special day to remember him and do him honor.

Washington's Birthday

February 22 (1732)

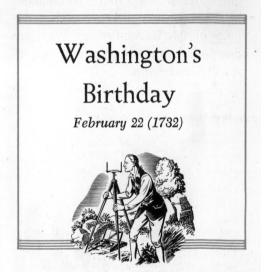

Washington is the only American whose birthday is more widely celebrated in our country than Lincoln's. Washington was born in Virginia in

1732. He was fortunate in belonging to a well-to-do family of Southern planters. Unlike Lincoln, Washington had a good schooling. He studied geometry and trigonometry and became a surveyor of public lands at the age of sixteen. When Washington was twenty, his half brother died, leaving him the Mt. Vernon estate. In 1759 he married Martha Custis, a widow with two children.

How George Washington Served Our Nation

Washington spent much of his lifetime in military service or public office. During the French and Indian War he served with the British Army under General Braddock. As we know, Washington was a member of the Continental Congress from Virginia and later was made commander of the Continental Army. The winning of the Revolutionary War was due in large part to Washington's inspiring leadership.

George Washington at Mt. Vernon

After the war Washington took part in the Constitutional Convention. Later he was elected as our first President and served for two terms. During these early years, our new nation owed much to his wise and firm guidance. He spent his last years at Mt. Vernon, where he died in 1799.

Washington was a tall, well-dressed man, with a dignified and rather severe manner. When at home he lived the life of a country gentleman. He was especially fond of children and loved to have them about him. The qualities that made Washington great as a military leader were his excellent judgment, his courage and calmness in times of danger, and his ability to inspire confidence in those under him. The same qualities made him an excellent President for our new nation. When he retired from public life, Washington was the most admired and honored American of his time.

Celebrating Washington's Birthday

Washington's birthday was celebrated by the nation while he was still living. Even during the Revolutionary War there were parades and festivities on his birthday. In 1784, after the British troops had left New York City, a dinner was held in Washington's honor on a ship in the harbor. From those early days to the present, February 22 has been one of the nation's patriotic holidays. Today all the states and possessions of the United States observe as a legal holiday the birthday of George Washington, patriot, soldier, and statesman.

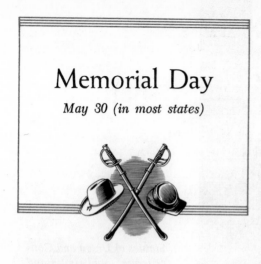

Memorial Day

May 30 (in most states)

Sleep, comrades, sleep and rest
On this Field of the Grounded Arms,
Where foes no more molest,
Nor sentry's shot alarms!

. . . .

Your silent tents of green
We deck with fragrant flowers;
Yours has the suffering been,
The memory shall be ours.

From *Decoration Day*
by Henry W. Longfellow

How Memorial Day Started

Memorial Day is a day for remembrance, and a day to honor servicemen who gave their lives for their country. Memorial Day was first set aside in memory of those who died in the War Between the States. The idea began in the South three years after the war, when a group of women decorated the graves of both Confederate and Union soldiers with flowers. The day they chose was May 30, a time when spring flowers were in bloom. The generous gesture of the Southern women touched the hearts of the people of the North, and helped the nation to forget the bitterness of war.

As a result, the National Commander of the Grand Army of the Republic (veterans of the Northern Army) asked that May 30 be set aside "for the purpose of strewing with flowers or otherwise decorating the graves of comrades who died in defense of their country." Although his order was addressed only to the Grand Army, Memorial Day became a day for all Americans to honor the soldier dead by placing flowers on their graves. Many adult Americans remember the Memorial Day ceremonies in their home towns in years gone by. The veterans of the War Between the States, fewer with each passing year, proudly marched or rode to the cemetery and spoke in quavering old voices of that conflict so long ago.

In 1938, the 75th anniversary of the Battle of Gettysburg, a very special celebration was held on the battleground. From all over the country eighteen hundred veterans of the war were brought to Gettysburg at the expense of the government. A monument was dedicated at this time. It is a shaft of marble fifty feet high with a flame burning at the top which can be seen twenty miles away. On the monument are inscribed these words:

AN ENDURING LIGHT TO GUIDE
US IN UNITY AND FELLOWSHIP

This Eternal Light Peace Memorial was unveiled by two old soldiers, one from the Union army, the other from

Statues of Union and Confederate soldiers stand side by side on this monument at Gettysburg National Park.

the Confederate, as a symbol that old differences are forgotten, and that our nation is one and indivisible.

Celebrating Memorial Day

Today, the soldiers of the Blue and the Gray are no longer with us, but Memorial Day will go on in remembrance of all our fallen heroes. In the national cemeteries where many veterans of the war between the North and South lie, there are special programs every year on May 30. The beautiful Memorial Day ceremony at Arlington National Cemetery is attended by thousands every year. Nor are the American heroes who were buried in foreign lands forgotten. Many who fought in World Wars I and II lie buried in American cemeteries in France and other countries in Western Europe. It is touching to know that their graves are still decorated by the people of these lands in grateful remembrance.

Memorial Day is now a legal holiday in most states in the Union. Certain of the Southern states observe a Confederate Memorial Day. Some celebrate April 26 or May 10, and still others June 3rd, 6th, or 9th. But no matter what the date, the idea is the same — to honor the men who died in battle. Official Flags are placed at half-mast until noon in honor of the dead. When Memorial Day comes round with its holiday from school, let us take time to remember the meaning of the day. You should display your Flag in front of your home. If your school is asked to contribute flowers for soldiers' graves, do your share in memory of those who died in battle.

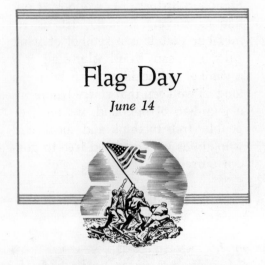

Flag Day

June 14

Lift it high, our glorious banner;
Let it wave upon the breeze;
Freedom's starry emblem ever,
Lift it high o'er land and seas.
By Lena E. Faulds

On June 14 the Star-Spangled Banner flies from public buildings and homes throughout the land. June 14 is Flag Day, set aside each year to honor the Flag which is the symbol of our nation. This particular day was chosen because it was on June 14, 1777, that the Continental Congress ordered the nation's new Flag. Flag Day is not a legal holiday except in Pennsylvania, but each year the President by proclamation asks that June 14 be celebrated as Flag Day.

The Story of Our Flag

You remember that before 1775 there was no one colonial flag for the Americans (see Chapter 2). Congress in 1775 appointed a committee to decide on a flag for the united colonies. The committee investigated the various flags in use in the colonies and reported their recommendations for a national flag. The Congress accepted their recommendations and in 1777 adopted this resolution: "Resolved, That the Flag of the United States be thirteen stripes, alternate red and white, that the 'Union' [upper left quarter] be thirteen stars, white in a blue field, representing a new constellation."

There is no record of why the committee chose this particular flag with the white stars on a blue field, but we can make a pretty good guess at the reasons. You remember that the Navy had been using the "Grand Union" flag, which had thirteen red and white stripes, with the British emblem in the upper left-hand corner. The stripes were kept to signify the thirteen states. What should take the place of the British emblem in the corner? The Americans looked upon their new nation as a "new constellation," so it was fitting to show the Union by thirteen stars. The blue of the heavens would be a natural background for the new constellation.

George Washington himself said this about the Flag: "We take the star from Heaven, the red from our mother country, separating it by white stripes, thus showing that we have separated from her, and the white stripes shall go down to posterity representing liberty." As we know, Congress later made provisions for adding a new star to the Flag for each new state which entered the Union. It is a beautiful flag, our Stars and Stripes, beautiful in design and color, and beautiful as the symbol of the land that we love.

What Flag Day Means to Us

Our Flag Day is not very old as patriotic holidays go. On June 14, 1877, the hundredth anniversary of the Flag's birthday, Congress asked that the Flag be flown from all public buildings to celebrate the centennial. In 1894 a Flag Association was organized to encourage a national Flag Day. From that time on more and more cities began to observe Flag Day, and soon the boys and girls in public schools were also celebrating it. The Pledge of Allegiance came into use about this time. Today all schools display the Flag when school is in session, and children join in the salute at the opening of the school day and at special exercises.

Flag Day is the day to display the Stars and Stripes. As we look at our banner waving proudly, let us remember that it is a symbol of what America means to us. Above all, it is a symbol of the liberty we love. So long as we keep that starry banner as a guardian of our land, we are free people, free to think and speak and worship as we wish, and free to govern ourselves.

Americans display their Flag on all occasions of national importance. Here, paratroopers proudly carry the Flag in the parade marking the Presidential inauguration of 1961.

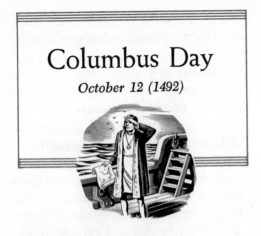

Columbus Day

October 12 (1492)

What a stir in the earth and air
As the mighty truth unfurled,
Three great ships and a crew and a great, great soul—
Columbus—had found a world![1]

Why We Celebrate Columbus Day

Columbus, as we all know, discovered the American continents by accident and died without knowing that he had discovered them. He was seeking a short route to Asia by sailing westward. When he landed on an island in the West Indies which he called San Salvador, Columbus believed he was near the coast of Asia. He never learned that two great continents blocked the westward passage to Asia which he was looking for. What is more, Columbus cannot truthfully be called *the* discoverer of America, since we know that the Northmen reached the coast of North America hundreds of years earlier.

Why, then, do we celebrate the day on which Columbus reached land in the Western Hemisphere? Because Columbus *did* find the American continents whether he knew it or not, and because his voyages led to the settlement of the New World by European countries. For this reason October 12 is celebrated not only in the United States, but in most of the twenty Latin American republics.

In celebrating Columbus Day we are honoring a man who had qualities that all men admire. Columbus was convinced that the world was round and that he could reach Asia by sailing westward. He spent many years of his life trying to find someone who would furnish him with ships and money, so that he could prove his amazing belief. He had the faith to keep trying in spite of disappointment and failure and ridicule. When his chance came at last through the King and Queen of Spain, it required unyielding courage and determination to keep his ships headed westward into unknown seas. Every schoolboy knows the story of how Columbus set out from Palos, Spain, on his first voyage with three ships, the *Niña*, the *Pinta*, and the *Santa Maria*. After an anxious voyage of

Columbus at the Spanish Court

[1] From "Palos, Spain, 1492," by Annette Wynne. Reprinted by permission of the publisher, J. B. Lippincott Company, from *For Days and Days*, by Annette Wynne. Copyright 1919 by J. B. Lippincott Company.

Two boys visit the tomb of Columbus in the city of Ciudad Trujillo (see-oo-dahd' troo-hee' yoh), formerly called Santo Domingo.

several weeks, Columbus arrived at the island he called San Salvador.

The New World Honors Columbus

It is tragic that the man who discovered a hemisphere ended his life in neglect and bitterness. Although he made three more trips to the New World, Columbus failed to find the riches he had promised the Spanish rulers. After the death of his friend the Queen, he was ignored by the country which he had served. When Columbus died in 1506, he asked to be buried on the lovely island of Hispaniola, or Haiti, which he had discovered. Many years later, when his importance was recognized, his body was taken to the city of Santo Domingo and buried in the cathedral.

In 1795, when Hispaniola was taken over by the French, what was thought to be the coffin of Columbus was sent to Havana in Cuba. Later the coffin was returned to Spain and placed in a tomb in the cathedral in Seville. But it now appears that the remains of Columbus are still in the cathedral at Santo Domingo. When repairs were being made there some years ago, an old casket was found which bore a Spanish inscription, "Discoverer of America — First Admiral." "First Admiral" was the title given to Columbus. Authorities believe that this coffin holds the remains of Christopher Columbus. So the great man still rests where he wished to be, in the beautiful isle he called *Española*, or "Little Spain."

Christopher Columbus has not been forgotten in the New World. Although neither of the continents was named for him, the Republic of Colombia bears his name. For many years our own country was called Columbia unofficially, although the name is no longer used. The District of Columbia was named for him, as well as towns, cities, parks, and streets in North and South America. Many statues have been erected in his honor. On San Salvador there is a small memorial shaft with the inscription: "On this spot Christopher Columbus first set foot on the soil of the New World." About forty states now observe October 12 as a legal holiday. Although his momentous discovery was not recognized while he was alive, Columbus has been given his rightful place in history.

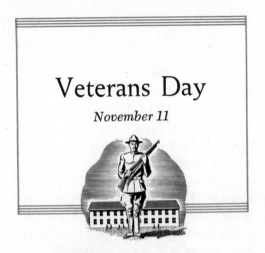

Veterans Day

November 11

November 11, 1918! Never before in the history of the world had there been such a day of rejoicing. In England and France and the United States and many other countries, people crowded the streets, laughing, crying, shouting, waving flags. Whistles blew and bells tolled. World War I had ended. Peace had come at last to a world weary and sick of war. The nations had laid down their arms; the killing was over. After four years of the most terrible warfare the world had ever known, the Germans had agreed to an armistice (or cease-fire agreement) to end the war. The armistice went into effect on the eleventh hour of the eleventh day of the eleventh month of the year 1918.

World War I

Many of you have heard your grandfathers tell about their part in World War I. You can read the story of the war in any American history, so we will give only a brief account here to explain the importance of November 11. World War I began in Europe in 1914, in the days when most European countries had kings. The incident that started the fighting grew out of bad feeling between Austria-Hungary and Serbia. (Serbia today is part of Yugoslavia.) On June 28, the heir to the throne of Austria-Hungary was shot and killed. The man who fired the shot sympathized with Serbia. Austria threatened vengeance on little Serbia, but Russia took Serbia's part.

The various great powers of Europe were bound by treaty to aid each other, as well as smaller countries, in case of war. One by one they took sides with Austria or with Russia until almost all of Europe was divided into two armed camps. Germany, Austria and Turkey (the Central Powers) lined up against Russia, France, England, and Italy (the Allies). Of course, war could not have resulted from one little incident if the big countries had

In this picture, taken on the first Armistice Day in 1918, cheering crowds jam New York's Fifth Avenue to hail the end of the World War.

not feared and distrusted each other. They had been preparing for war for many years.

By autumn of 1914 the powerful German army had crossed over neutral Belgium into France. With the help of Britain great battles were fought to hurl back the Germans. There was fighting on other fronts, too. It was not long before every important country in the world was in the war against the Central Powers — Japan, the countries of Latin America, Australia, New Zealand, Canada, and finally, even the United States. The United States tried to remain neutral, that is, not to take sides officially. We were forced, however, by Germany's submarine attacks on American ships to declare war in April, 1917. (Chapter 7 gave part of President Wilson's War Message.)

Never before had American soldiers been sent to Europe to fight. In a few months the United States was pouring men and supplies into the war. By fall of 1918 the Germans were defeated and ready to accept an armistice. The cost in lives had been tremendous. Out of 65 million men on both sides, almost 9,000,000 had been killed, and 30,000,000 more were either wounded or missing! The United States lost about 130,000 men, and over 200,000 more wounded or missing. Great numbers of American soldiers were buried in cemeteries in France.

The Unknown Soldiers

People continued to remember and to observe Armistice Day on November 11 each year in honor of the millions of men who died in World War I. In 1920 both England and France in solemn ceremonies buried an unknown soldier as a symbol of all their soldier dead. The Unknown Soldier of France was buried under the great Arch of Triumph in Paris. An everlasting flame burns in his honor, and a sentry is always on guard there. In London, the Unknown Soldier was given a resting place of honor in Westminster Abbey, where the kings and queens of Britain are buried.

About a year later, on November 11, 1921, the United States also buried an unknown American soldier. From each of the four American cemeteries in France the body of an unidentified soldier had been removed. The four coffins were taken to the city hall of a nearby French town and placed in a room draped with American flags. A World War veteran, a sergeant of the 59th infantry, placed a wreath of white roses on one of the coffins. In this way the Unknown Soldier was chosen. The coffin was then taken to Washington, and placed in the rotunda of the Capitol. For three days Americans came by the thousands to pass by the coffin in silent reverence. On Armistice Day the Unknown Soldier was buried in Arlington Cemetery in a beautiful ceremony. The coffin was heaped with flowers from all over this nation and from foreign countries as well.

Then, in 1958, two unknown servicemen who died in World War II and the Korean War were also buried at Arlington. Together, these three he-

The Tomb of the Unknown Soldiers, simple and dignified, lies before the entrance to the Memorial Amphitheater at Arlington.

roes symbolize the many brave men who have died for their country.

Armistice Day Becomes Veterans Day

Until 1938 the President each year proclaimed Armistice Day a national holiday at the request of Congress. In May of that year Congress passed an act asking that the day be made a legal holiday throughout the nation. The day was to be set aside not only to honor the soldier dead of World War I, but to show "our belief that peace can be . . . made enduring only by respect for the rights of others and good-will among the nations of the world." In 1954, a bill was passed changing Armistice Day to Veterans Day in honor of all the servicemen and women who have served America.

In the United States and England, Veterans or Armistice Day is observed by a two-minute silence at eleven o'clock, the hour when war ceased in 1918. Ceremonies are held at the tombs of the Unknown Soldiers in France, England, and America. The President of the United States lays a wreath on the memorial in Arlington National Cemetery. Thus do nations remember their war heroes.

The Meaning of Veterans Day

Unfortunately, the peace after World War I did not last. Twenty years later, Germany plunged the world into World War II. In 1941 the United States was forced into this world-wide conflict because of an attack on Pearl Harbor by Germany's ally, Japan. World War II ended in 1945. But the world has not yet found a way to lasting peace, for there are nations that still do not respect the rights of other nations. One of the great tasks for the future is to maintain peace among the nations of the world.

A young Canadian soldier who gave his life in World War I has left us a beautiful poem which we all should read on Veterans Day. John McCrae fought in the terrible battles in Flanders, a part of Belgium. His poem brings home to us our obligation to the soldier dead.

IN FLANDERS FIELDS

In Flanders fields the poppies blow
Between the crosses, row on row,
That mark our place; and in the sky
The larks, still bravely singing, fly
Scarce heard amid the guns below.

We are the Dead. Short days ago
We lived, felt dawn, saw sunset glow,
Loved and were loved, and now we lie,
In Flanders fields.

Take up our quarrel with the foe!
To you from failing hands we throw
The torch. Be yours to hold it high!
If ye break faith with us who die,
We shall not sleep, though poppies grow
In Flanders fields.

So deep was the impression made by McCrae's poem, that several poems were written in answer to it. The following answer pledges us to keep faith with those who died so that we might live in freedom.

AMERICA'S ANSWER

Rest ye in peace, ye Flanders dead,
The fight that ye so bravely led
We've taken up. And we will keep
True faith with you who lie asleep
With each a cross to mark his bed,
And poppies blowing overhead,
Where once his own lifeblood ran red.
So let your rest be sweet and deep
In Flanders fields.

Fear not that ye have died for naught,
The torch ye threw to us we caught.
Ten million hands will hold it high,
And Freedom's light shall never die!
We've learned the lesson that ye taught
In Flanders fields.

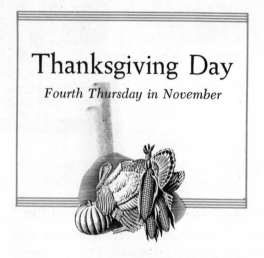

America's Answer, by R. W. Lillard, reprinted by permission of "Current History" magazine, holder of the copyright.

Thanksgiving Day

Fourth Thursday in November

The purpose of Thanksgiving Day is suggested by its name. Americans have been celebrating this day for over 300 years. Thanksgiving Day is our oldest national holiday, dating back to 1621. It was on that day that Governor Bradford of the Plymouth Colony ordered a day for giving thanks to God. Church services were held, followed by a feast of wild turkey and quail. The Pilgrims invited the neighboring Indians and their Chief Massasoit to the celebration. However, Thanksgiving did not become a nation-wide celebration until Lincoln's day. Mrs. Sarah Hale, editor of a woman's magazine called "Godey's Lady's Book," is largely responsible for our national Thanksgiving holiday. Because of her urging, President Lincoln in 1862 proclaimed the last Thursday in November as a national holiday.

Today Thanksgiving Day is a legal holiday in every state and territory and possession of the United States. It has become the custom for the President to issue each year a Thanksgiving Proclamation for the District of Columbia and our possessions. Then the governors of the states proclaim the day a state holiday. People frequently travel long distances by car, plane, or train to celebrate Thanksgiving Day with their families. Like the Pilgrims of olden times, we feast on turkey and give thanks to God for our many blessings.

GALLOWAY

In homes all across our nation, families gather to celebrate Thanksgiving.

Other American Holidays

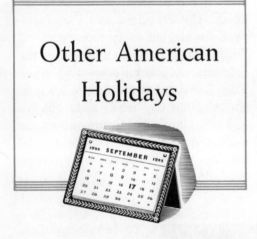

The days you have been reading about are the most important and most widely celebrated patriotic holidays. There are a few other holidays, however, which we Americans celebrate, and you would probably like to know why we do so. Some of these holidays are not legal holidays, but are observed in public schools or by clubs and other organizations.

Armed Forces Day — the third Saturday in May. Before 1947 our Armed Forces each celebrated a separate day — Air Force Day, Army Day, and Navy Day. Now that the Department of Defense includes all the Armed Forces, one day has been set aside as Armed Forces Day.

V–E Day — May 8, 1945. V–E stands for victory in Europe. This day marks the unconditional surrender of Germany to the Allies in World II. Although the war in Europe ended on May 8, 1945, the war in the Pacific against Japan continued.

V–J Day — September 2, 1945. V–J stands for victory over Japan. Japan surrendered on August 14, but the formal surrender was signed on board the battleship U.S.S. *Missouri* on September 2, thus ending World War II.

Labor Day. Although Labor Day does not commemorate any single historical event, it should be mentioned here because it has become one of our important national holidays. Labor Day is celebrated on the first Monday in September, and is a legal holiday throughout the United States. It was started in this country in 1882 to emphasize the importance of labor and to honor American workmen. Labor Day celebrations usually include speeches by important leaders.

Citizenship Day — September 17. This is one of our newest holidays. In 1951 Congress asked the American people to celebrate September 17 each year as Citizenship Day. This day is the anniversary of the signing of the Constitution of the United States in Independence Hall in 1787. So it is a fitting day to honor our new citizens, the young people who reached voting age in the year past. As first-time voters they will have the stirring experience of taking part in our democratic government. On this day we also welcome those new citizens from other lands who fulfilled the requirements of our laws and became naturalized citizens within the past year.

September 17 is a fitting day also for all Americans to pledge their allegiance to our Constitution. We should remember, too, the ideals of liberty, justice, and equality on which our country was founded. We should ask ourselves if we are doing our part toward keeping these ideals alive.

General Election Day. General Election Day is important to all Americans, because it is then that we choose the men and women who represent us. Congress has named the Tuesday after the first Monday in November as Election Day, when offices in the national government are filled. The President and Vice-President are elected every four years; all Representatives and one third of the Senators are chosen every two years. This Tuesday has also become a general election day when state officials and often local officials are chosen. In most states, Election Day is a legal holiday when Presidential elections are held.

Workers stream in and out of busy factories all over America. Labor Day recalls what workers have done to help build our industrial might.

CHAPTER 10

Good Americans Make Democracy Work

Visitors to the Capitol at Washington, D. C., marvel at the rich and beautiful paintings which decorate the walls and ceilings of the building. These paintings portray the very spirit of American liberty and democracy. They seem even more remarkable when we learn that they were done by an Italian artist who did not come to America until he was almost fifty years old! (See page 98.)

The artist, Constantino Brumidi, was forced to flee from Italy to escape persecution because of his political beliefs. Brumidi arrived in the United States in 1852, and became a citizen as soon as he was able.

Brumidi was eager to be of service to his adopted country, and in 1855 he got his wish. He was given the job of decorating the still unfinished Capitol Building. Brumidi said of his work, "My one ambition and my daily prayer is that I may live long enough to make beautiful the Capitol of the one country on earth in which there is liberty." He was so proud of his American citizenship that he signed one of his paintings, "Constantino Brumidi, Citizen of the U.S."

Six Presidents came and went while Brumidi worked at decorating the Capitol. At the age of 74, when he was painting the ceiling of the

AMERICA, PRESENT AND PAST: *From the time the Pilgrims set up their own government to the present day, Americans have cherished self-rule.*

Rotunda, he fell. Although Brumidi managed to hang onto a piece of scaffolding until he was rescued, the shock of the accident caused his death a few months later. The painting on which he was working was finally completed in 1953 by another artist. Brumidi's grave is marked by a stone set up by Congress in grateful recognition of his services to America.

Constantino Brumidi, "Citizen of the U.S.," was a good American. He used his time and skill to show his gratitude to America. Good American citizens do more than just believe in liberty and democracy; they help to keep these ideals strong. American citizens, both young and old, have the job of *making democracy work.* You may think, "I can't do much about it until I can vote." But you would be mistaken, for there is a great deal that you can do to practice democracy and to prepare yourself for the day when you will be of voting age.

You have been reading in previous chapters about your heritage. You have read about the things we Americans hold dear. You have learned how our democratic government came to be, and about the ideals on which it is founded. This last chapter of our book will explain more about your rights and responsibilities as citizens of the United States. It will point out what you can do as young citizens to make our democracy work.

Brumidi at Work in the Capitol

Democracy Has Become Our Way of Life

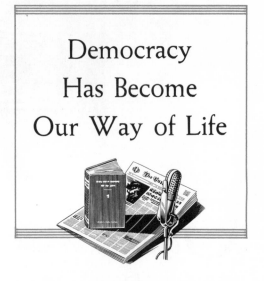

Back in 1787, when the Constitutional Convention had at last finished its work of planning a new government for the United States, a citizen of Philadelphia asked Dr. Franklin, "What have you given us?" The wise old gentleman replied, "A republic, if you can keep it." Franklin gave this answer because he and the other Founding Fathers were not sure that a government in which the people had a voice could succeed. But we have not only kept our republic; we have made it more democratic by adding to our rights and privileges through the years.

If Dr. Franklin could look in on us today, he would be amazed to see how our democracy has developed. In his day only men who were free and

The opportunity to attend school is an important part of the American way of life.

who owned property were allowed to vote in most states. Today almost all men and women over twenty-one have the right to vote, regardless of their race or their color or whether they are property owners. Franklin would also notice that Senators and Presidential electors are no longer chosen by the state legislatures, but by the direct vote of the people. We can be sure that he would approve these changes that have made our nation more democratic.

Franklin would also be interested to see how our ways of living and thinking have changed. We have done a good deal toward putting into practice our ideals of equality and opportunity. We have come to believe that all children should have an education. Free schools in every community, paid for by taxes, are part of our way of life. We also believe that people should be able to earn a living, to live decently, and to receive help in misfortune. In fact, during the last century and a half we Americans have worked out a *way of life* based on our belief in liberty and equality.

What Is Our American Way of Life?

A teacher was explaining to her American history class about our democratic way of living, which goes hand in hand with our democratic government. She told her students that the American way of life includes not only our political liberties, but the personal privileges and opportunities we enjoy in our daily lives and the way we feel toward our fellow men and toward the community in which we live. The teacher then asked the students to name some of the privileges that make up our free American way of life. Here is the list they made:

1. We have the right to speak or write our thoughts and opinions

This scene shows a vital step in winning freedom of the press in America. Peter Zenger, a New York printer and editor, was tried in 1735 for criticizing the governor in his newspaper. Zenger won his case.

freely as long as we do not injure others.

2. We are free to worship in any way we please and at any church we choose.

3. We have the right to vote by secret ballot for the men who are to represent us in the government.

4. We have the opportunity to obtain a free education at least through high school, and a chance to develop our abilities and talents.

5. We can start a business, take up a profession, or work at any job we choose.

6. We have the right to own a home, an automobile — in fact, as much property as we wish, or can afford to buy.

7. We have the right to be safe and secure in our homes. No officer of the law may enter a citizen's home without a search warrant (permission from a court).

8. We can move freely about our own state or country. No American has to ask permission to take his family into any state of the Union.

9. We are free to join any organizations we wish and to attend their meetings, except, of course, those that work against our country's welfare.

10. We are free to read what we wish and listen to what we wish. We are free to find the facts on any subject.

11. We believe that every person deserves respect as a human being, no matter who he is. We believe in fair play and in justice for all.

How Our Way of Life Works

Let us look in on an average American family on a Sunday morning. Parents and children are on their way to the church they have chosen as their place of worship. After church, Dad settles down with the Sunday paper, the boys look at their favorite television program, and Mother prepares Sunday dinner. A neighbor drops in, and he and Dad discuss a recent action taken by the government. Dad disagrees with the government's stand and says so in no uncertain terms. Mother calls out from the kitchen to remind Dad that their Current Events Club will meet the next night. As the family sits down to dinner, they all start to talk about the vacation trip they are planning to a neighboring state.

There is nothing unusual about this description of an American family. It is familiar to all of us. Yet almost everything done or said by the family represents one of the rights or privileges that make up our American way of life. Check the list on page 208 carefully. Which of these privileges are included in the family story?

Our Freedom Has Limits

As you can see, all the items in this list add up to a great deal of freedom. In fact we Americans are free to do just about as we wish in our personal lives. But our freedom has limits. We cannot interfere with the rights of others. For instance, freedom of speech does not mean that we have the right to place lives in danger by shouting "Fire!" in a crowded theater just for fun. It does not mean that we are free to make remarks that hurt another person's reputation, or to play our radio so loudly that it disturbs the neighbors. Respect for the rights of others is part of our way of life in our democracy. You can see that when people live and work together, they have to give up some of their liberty for the common good.

Our freedom is limited in another way. A scientist working for our government, for instance, cannot use his freedom of speech to give away military secrets. We cannot use our liberty in such a way as to place in danger our country's welfare.

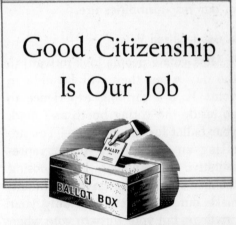

Good Citizenship Is Our Job

Some of us are apt to believe that our democracy will go on even though we take no responsibility for making it work. That is not true. A democratic government does not run itself; the people must run it. In a dictatorship, where one person makes the decisions, the people have very little responsibility for the government. But they also have very little freedom or equality and often very little justice. We citizens of a democracy can't "have our cake and eat it, too." We can't enjoy our freedom and at the same time do nothing to keep it. If we took that attitude, our democracy would break down and our freedoms disappear. As Tom Paine, famous writer of Revolutionary days, once said, "Those who expect to reap the blessings of freedom, must, like men, undergo the fatigues [labor] of supporting it." In other words, it is our job to accept willingly the responsibilities that go with being free citizens in a democratic government. You will find that every right we Americans have carries with it a responsibility. Let us see what some of our responsibilities are.

A Good Citizen Votes

Most young people look forward to the day when they will be able to vote. It is a thrilling experience to go inside the voting booth and mark your ballot for the first time! You are taking an actual part in our representative government by choosing the men who run our government and make our laws. It is not only your privilege, but your duty to vote when you are of age, because our representative government is based on the ballot. Only by voting do we have a voice in choosing candidates or settling an important question of government. Yet many adult Americans do not take time to go to the polls on election day. Do you know that there have been national elections in which only a little over half of our citizens voted, and state and local elections in which still fewer voted? Think of having in our hands the precious right of self-government that men have struggled for centuries to gain, only to toss it carelessly away!

Sometimes people think, "My one vote is not important. It can't possibly make a difference in the outcome of the election." You may remember the familiar old verse:

Little drops of water, little grains of sand
Make the mighty ocean and the pleasant land.

In many school elections, pupils follow closely the voting methods used in electing our government officials.

Listening to campaign speeches is one way voters can learn about the candidates and what they stand for.

Just as little drops of water make the ocean, individual votes determine an election. Many a good candidate has been defeated because not enough citizens turned out to vote. Let us remember that every vote is important and that the vote of the humblest citizen counts as much as that of the President!

You can prepare for the time when you will be a voter by taking part in the elections held by your school, your church groups, and your clubs and organizations. As good citizens we should vote at every election in which we have a part, whether it be for President of the United States or president of the student body at Ourtown Junior High School. You can also do your part as a citizen by urging your parents to vote and by staying with the younger children so your mother can go to the polls. One eighth grade teacher asks her pupils to write notes to their parents, urging them to go to the polls on election day, and explaining why it is important to vote.

A Good Citizen Is Informed about Candidates

Of course, a citizen's vote has little meaning if he does not know something about the people who are running for office or the important questions to be decided by the election. It is not difficult these days to get information about the candidates for office. In your school, you may know personally the students who are seeking office. If not, you can easily find out their qualifications. In small towns, also, people are fairly well acquainted with the candidates for local office. But in state and national elections we often do not know as much about the candidates and what they stand for.

A good way to learn about candidates is to read papers and magazine articles, both for and against them. We may listen to the candidates themselves on the radio, or both see and hear them on television. It is also possible to look up the voting record of men who have already held office and are running for re-election. Men who were not capable and honest citizens have sometimes been elected to Congress or to state and local offices. They were elected because the voters did not bother to find out the facts about them.

Voters should not forget that our government is no better than the men we elect to represent us. If we want good government, we need to be sure that the men who receive our votes will work for the welfare of all the people in the community, the state, or the nation, and not for the selfish interests of certain groups.

A Good Citizen Respects and Obeys the Law

Students sometimes ask a teacher, "If we have freedom of speech, why can't all of us talk in class whenever we want to?" The teacher usually explains, "Liberty doesn't mean doing just as you please without regard for the rights of others. Our American idea of liberty is *liberty under law*. Laws protect our rights and the rights of the other fellow. Unlimited talking disturbs the class, so we need 'laws' in the classroom to make sure that people will speak only at the proper times. Then, too, we must see that everyone will have an equal right to speak." In school, as in the outside world, our freedom must have certain limits.

Wherever people live together, laws are necessary for their protection. "Liberty under law" and "equal justice under law" are the watchwords of our government. We can enjoy our many liberties as long as we don't interfere with the liberties of others. Then the law steps in. For instance, parking laws are necessary to see that all have equal opportunity to park. If you park longer than your fair share of time, you are cheating someone else out of his right to park. So the law says you must pay a fine. If you exceed the speed limit set by your community, you are endangering others. Laws against speeding protect us all from "speed demons" on the highway. The good citizen knows that laws are made to protect all citizens and to provide equal justice to all of us.

People who respect the law do not try to get out of the fine or punishment which comes from breaking it. We sometimes hear a man boasting that he had a traffic ticket "fixed" by a friend who has influence. Let us stop to think what it means when we evade the law. It means that we do not believe in equal justice for all. We believe that it is all right for the other fellow to be punished for breaking the law, but that the law doesn't apply to us. Every time a citizen evades the law he is helping to break down the idea of equal justice on which our democracy is founded. Let's make democracy work by respecting the law!

The Good Citizen Does His Share

Besides voting and obeying the law, the good citizen has other political

These volunteer workers are citizens doing an important job in civilian defense.

duties in a democracy. If he is asked to run for an office which he is capable of filling, he should be willing to do so. If honest, capable citizens refuse to accept public office, then others not so honest and not so capable may be chosen.

Another way in which the citizen does his share to make democracy work is to serve on a jury. As you know, we Americans have the right to be tried by a jury of twelve persons from the community. This means that all citizens are expected to take their turn on the jury if called upon. If people of good judgment and experience are too busy to serve, what happens? Less able people are chosen and the accused man may not get a fair trial. The citizen called for jury duty should ask himself, "Suppose I were the one being tried, what kind of jury would I want?" One citizen who served on a jury said, "It was an experience I shall never forget. For the first time, I understand how our courts operate and why they are a necessary branch of our goverment. I feel proud to have had a share in carrying out justice."

Still another duty of a citizen is to defend his country. We Americans hate war, but as patriotic citizens we must be willing to take part in our country's defense. In former days the defense of our country was largely the job of the military forces. But today war is fought on such an enormous scale that the help of every citizen, not just those in the Armed Forces, is required. In time of war, millions of citizens are needed to turn out the materials of war — weapons, equipment, clothing, food, and all the other requirements of modern fighting forces. Millions, too, both young and old, are needed to help in the many jobs of civilian defense. All Americans must be ready to do their share in the defense of our country.

Communism Threatens Our Freedom

It has been easy for us Americans to take our freedom for granted and to believe that we shall continue to enjoy our democratic way of life. But in recent years our democracy has faced the serious threat of Communism, and we have come to realize that the struggle for freedom never ends. The growing danger of Communism has divided much of the world into two opposing sides — the free world led by the United States, on one side; the Communist world led by Soviet Russia, on the other. Because Communism is dangerous to democratic governments such as ours, it is important for us to know what Communism is, why it threatens our freedom, and how we can combat it.

The Communist Way of Life

Communism and democracy are as different as night and day. To learn how Communism works, let us look at Soviet Russia, the leading Communist country. Russia's government is a dictatorship in the hands of a small group of men. These men hold complete power in the government and complete power over the people. The state (or central government) owns all the land. It also owns and manages the farms, banks, stores, factories, and mines. In other words, there is little private ownership in Russia. Under Communism, moreover, workers have little say about where they work; the state assigns them their jobs and sets their wages.

Communism allows few of the rights which we Americans take for granted. There is only one party, the Communist Party. A citizen may vote, but he has no choice of candidates. He merely votes "yes" for each candidate on a prepared list. Not many would dare to vote "no"! Freedom of speech and press is unheard of. For instance, in the United States we are free to criticize the government, but in Russia criticizing the government is a crime. Newspapers and magazines are allowed to print only what the government wants them to print. As a result, the people get very little accurate information about their own country or the rest of the world. What they read about the United States is often untrue. As for religion, Communists do not believe in God. Although Russians are not forbidden to go to church, few churches are open.

Secret police are part of the Communist way of life. Citizens are spied upon and may be arrested without a warrant. The people do not have the right to trial by jury, nor are they protected against "cruel and inhuman punishment" as Americans are. For political crimes, such as criticizing the state, Russians may be sentenced to prison or to "slave" labor camps.

To sum up, Communism is more than a form of government. It is a way of life in which people live not as they choose to but as their government says they must.

The Spread of Communism

Government under Communism is fairly new in the world. The first Communist government was set up in Russia in 1917, following a revolution against the czar (emperor). Later, by adding several nearby territories, Russia formed the Union of Soviet Socialist Republics. The Soviet Union is the largest country in the world, spreading across eastern Europe and northern Asia to within a few miles of the coast of Alaska. After World War II, the Russians extended their Communist system beyond their own borders. They seized several countries of eastern Europe, and forced Communist governments upon the people.

The Russians have devoted their energies and resources to building a strong industrial nation and a powerful military force. Today the Soviet Union is a leading world power. Although its industrial production is not yet equal to ours, it has become our rival in such important fields as developing atomic weapons and exploring outer space.

After World War II, Communists came into power in other parts of the world. Chinese Communists took over most of China and set up a new government. Red China has the world's largest population — well over 650 million people. By forcing these millions to work for the state, the Chinese leaders are building a Communist nation which may become more dangerous to the world than the Soviet Union. In the meantime, Red China, like a greedy and restless giant, threatens other countries of Asia.

Why Is Communism a Threat to Democracy?

A Russian leader, speaking to Americans, clearly expressed the Communist threat when he said: "We will bury you." He meant, of course, that Communists plan to destroy our democratic government and way of life. Communists believe it is their duty to spread their system throughout the world. Their leaders are tough and ruthless, and they are determined to take over other governments by one means or another.

Communist agents are at work today in almost every country. They are especially active in the undeveloped countries of Asia and Latin America and in the new nations of Africa. Their promises of food and jobs for all workers appeal to those who are hungry and poor and have no hope for the future. These people often turn to Communism thinking they have nothing to lose. But they do not know the other side of the picture — the lack of freedom, the stern

GALLOWAY

Large numbers of workers' cars lined up outside factories like the one in the picture suggest the high standard of living enjoyed by Americans.

discipline, and the dreary lives of most workers in Communist countries.

There are countless ways by which Communists try to gain a foothold in a country. For example, if there is discontent among the people, they may secretly stir up a revolution against the government. If a nation is poor, they may offer to lend money or to supply needed goods and equipment through trade. Another method is to send technicians and skilled workers to build roads, dams, hospitals, and so on. But whatever means the Communists use, their purpose is always the same. They are taking the first steps toward getting control of a country and its government.

In stronger nations, Communists use other methods. They try to build a strong Communist Party and to elect members to government offices. Although the Communist Party has been outlawed in the United States, secret agents work to win Americans to their cause. We know that it is not possible to be a Communist and a loyal American at the same time, because the aim of Communism is to destroy our government. Soviet agents are experts in trickery and underhanded methods. They try to weaken our democracy by encouraging labor troubles or exaggerating cases of injustice. Our government keeps constant watch for Soviet activities in our country.

How Can We Meet the Communist Challenge?

As we have seen, the followers of Communism are determined to make this a Communist world. If they succeed in taking over one nation after another, the free nations will in time be outnumbered. If this happens, the Communists might be able to "bury" us as they have threatened. The United States and other free nations are in a contest with the Communists for survival. As leader of the free world, our nation must meet the Communist challenge with all the resources at its command.

The free world nations have taken steps to protect themselves against Communist aggression. Our government, for instance, has formed alliances with many countries in Europe and Asia. The United States and Canada have joined with several nations of western Europe and with Greece and Turkey in the North Atlantic Treaty Organization (NATO). The purpose of NATO is to hold strong forces in readiness in case of a Soviet attack. As protection against Red China, the United States, Great Britain, France, and several countries of Asia have formed the Southeast Asia Treaty Organization (SEATO). Members of SEATO are pledged to aid a member nation if it should be attacked. The United States has established a ring of air and sea bases around the Communist lands to protect the free world nations. On our own side of the world, the United States and the Latin American nations have warned the Communists not to interfere in the Western Hemisphere.

As long as Communists continue to threaten the world, we have no choice but to maintain strong military forces at home and abroad. Since we cannot afford to give the Soviet Union the lead in military strength, we must continue to develop modern weapons for defense. Even more important, we must not let the Communists get ahead of us in the rivalry for leadership of the world. To meet the growing power of the Soviet Union and Red China, we shall need to move forward in industry, in scientific research, and in education. If they get ahead of us in these fields, the Communists could dominate the world, and our way of life would be buried just as effectively as if they had defeated us in war! Let us remember that we are competing against a system whose people take education very seriously. We shall need trained minds if we are to compete with Communism.

Although the United States must be prepared for possible attack, our government at the same time is working for peace. The fears and tensions in the world might at any time explode into real war. And total war in this atomic age could destroy our way of life. Even a limited war could use up our resources and thus weaken our country. To lessen the danger of war, the United States is working for gradual disarmament. An agreement to ban dangerous atomic tests has been

Under Communism
Freedom of Speech Disappears.

proposed. Although the Soviet Union claims to favor such a plan, the two sides have not been able to reach an agreement.

Many thoughtful Americans believe that to avoid war the free nations and the Communist nations must learn to live together in peace. This idea is called *co-existence*. Under co-existence, each nation would decide how it is to be governed, but would not force its system on others, as Communists now do.

Our Democracy Can Be Improved

At home, Americans can meet the challenge of Communism by improving our democracy. We do not claim that our system works perfectly. Sometimes a citizen loses faith in our government because he did not get a square deal. We must remember that it is not possible for any government to be perfect. Government officials are human beings, and all humans make errors. Citizens may also criticize our democracy because there are Americans who are not given equal rights in the community where they live, or because a government official is found to be dishonest.

We know that there are weaknesses in our democracy. But we should not lose faith in democracy because some officials do not do a good job or because our government does not always work smoothly. Instead, we should do our best as loyal citizens to see that every American receives justice and fair treatment. For we believe that in spite of its imperfections, our form of government gives more opportunity for people to develop their talents and abilities and to live freely and decently and happily than any other kind of government.

Making Democracy Work in Our Daily Lives

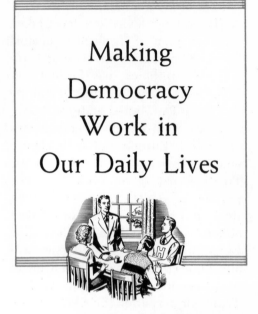

Every one of us can do a great deal to make our democracy work. Political duties, you know, are only part of the job of being good citizens: Democracy is all around us. It is up to us to make democracy work at home, at school, and in the community where we live. By practicing democracy in their daily lives, young people can learn to be good citizens. Here are some of the things you can do.

Practicing Freedom of Speech

At a certain junior high school some boys were discussing the candidates for student president. Most of them were sounding the praises of Johnny

Baker. Then one boy spoke up for the first time. "How about Fred Brown? I think he would make a better president. He's a good speaker and has done a fine job on the student council." The others interrupted him with yells of, "You don't know what you're talking about!" and, "You're all wrong!"

Bob had been exercising his right to express his own opinions, but the other students shouted him down. If we believe in freedom of speech for ourselves, we must allow the other fellow the same privilege. We need not agree with him, but we must respect his right to free speech. If we do not, we are helping to destroy that right. We are saying, "I have the right to free speech, but you haven't." The real meaning of freedom of speech was perfectly expressed by a famous Frenchman, who said, "I disapprove of what you say, but I will defend to the death your *right* to say it." You can help make democracy work by respecting the other fellow's right to express his thoughts when you are at home with your family, at school among your classmates, and wherever else you may be.

Practicing Freedom of Religion

Religious freedom is also part of our way of life. Most of us respect our neighbor's right to worship as he pleases. But freedom of religion means more than that. It means not discriminating against any person because he happens to belong to a different faith than the majority of our schoolmates. It means not letting a person's religion influence the way we feel about him as an individual. For example, some girls in a certain neighborhood were organizing a skating club. One of them suggested Sally Smith for a member. Another girl spoke up, "I don't think we should ask her. She goes to the . . . Church" (naming a religious faith to which none of the group belonged). Then Jane said, "I don't see what difference that makes. We all like Sally and she loves to skate. These are the things we should consider in choosing club members."

Jane not only understood the true meaning of religious freedom; she was putting it into practice. Making an unkind remark about another's religion is to show religious prejudice, and is against our democratic ideals. Remember that no one is any less an

Talking things over together and giving each person the chance to express an opinion is the American way.

American because he goes to a different church than we do.

Respecting the Rights of Others

In our democracy we also believe in equal rights for all people. Young people can put this idea into practice very easily. One simple way is being willing to take your turn in a store, in a ticket line, in playing games. We have all seen the person who tries to get in ahead of others. Such a person is not practicing democracy because he considers himself entitled to more than the other fellow. It is not democratic, either, to expect special privileges because of wealth or position. There is a story about one of our ex-Presidents who stopped to watch some firemen fighting a fire. He got too close for safety and was told by a policeman to "get back." Without mentioning who he was, the man who had been President walked away. He did not expect special rights because he was a famous American. That is the American way.

Let us learn to respect others as human beings with the same rights we have. This principle is expressed in our Declaration of Independence by the statement that "all men are created equal." Stephen Vincent Benét, an American poet who believed deeply in our democracy, expressed this idea in four lines of verse:

Remember that when you say
"I will have none of this exile and this stranger
For his face is not like my face and his speech is strange,"
You have denied America with that word.[1]

We are a land of many races and nationalities, and we are proud that this is so. This is the wonderful and different thing about America. Men from many countries have helped to build our nation. They have become Americans with the rights and privileges of Americans. There is no room in our way of life for racial prejudice. We are all Americans, living and working together in this great democracy of ours.

Respecting Property

A schoolboy is carving his initials on the desk in the classroom; another marks the wall with his pencil as he walks along. Children, and grown-ups, too, drop banana peelings or candy wrappers from their cars onto the city streets. A family visits the park for a picnic lunch, and leaves food and papers on the table or grass. Careless campers fail to put out a fire, and many acres of forest burn. We could go on with dozens of examples of carelessness with public property.

Why do we do these things? Probably because we know there is no one

"This Is the Land Where Hate Should Die"

This is the land where hate should die —
No feuds of faith, no spleen of race,
No darkly brooding fear should try
Beneath our flag to find a place.

DENIS A. MCCARTHY

[1] Lines from *Western Star* by Stephen Vincent Benét, published by Rinehart & Company, Inc. Copyright, 1943, by Rosemary Carr Benét.

to scold or punish us. Certainly none of us would carve on the furniture at home, or smash up his bicycle. Yet if we stop to think about it, we should not destroy or spoil property that belongs to all the people of a community or state, or to the nation — property that we have helped pay for. Our parents, for example, have a good deal of tax money invested in school buildings.

In some countries, as you learned early in this chapter, people are not allowed in government buildings, and what they say, read, and do is closely watched by the police. But in our country we expect people to do the right thing without being watched or spied upon. Someone has said, "The price of freedom is self-discipline." Our democratic system calls for a good deal of self-control and respect for the rights of others. It is the responsibility of good citizens to treat public property as though it were their own. All of us have a fine opportunity to show that we are responsible citizens by taking good care of our school buildings and other public property, and by helping to keep parks and city streets clean.

Breaking Camp

We Pledge Ourselves to Be Good Americans

As we have seen, there is no better way for young people to serve their country than by making democracy work. Below is a pledge which clearly states what each one of you can do to be a good citizen of America.

A PLEDGE FOR AMERICANS

Because I love my country and believe in its government and the American way of life, I will try to carry out this pledge of a good American:

1. I will respect my Flag and be loyal to the government of the United States.

2. I will do my duty when I become an adult citizen by voting in all elections. I will remember that government is no better than the men who run it, and do my best to vote for able and honest men who believe in the ideals of our democracy.

3. I will defend my country in time of war.

4. I will be willing to serve on a jury, and to run for government office if I am qualified to do so.

5. I will obey and respect the laws of my country, state, and community.

6. I will respect private and public property as I want others to respect my property.

7. I will judge a person by what he is, not by his race or religion. I will not let prejudice affect my ideas of justice and fair play.

8. I will respect the opinions and the rights of others. I will try to see both sides of a question.

9. I will be honest and honorable in my dealings with other people as I would have others be honest and honorable toward me.

10. I will be a good citizen in my home and share in the family responsibilities just as I share in the family privileges.

11. I will do my share in school and church and community activities so that my town will be a better place to live in.

★ ★ ★ ★ ★ ★ ★ ★

If you can live up to this pledge, now as well as when you are older, you will be doing your share to keep our democracy strong and our freedom safe. *America Is My Country* has pointed out not only your rights but your duties as citizens of our democracy. Be loyal to your country,

At Iwo Jima

Here lie men who loved America because their ancestors generations ago helped in her founding, and other men who loved her with equal passion because they themselves or their own fathers escaped from oppression to her blessed shores. Here lie officers and men, Negroes and whites, rich men and poor — together. Here are Protestants, Catholics, and Jews — together. Here no man prefers another because of his faith or despises him because of his color. Here there are no quotas of how many from each group are admitted or allowed. Among these men there is no discrimination. No prejudice. No hatred. Theirs is the highest and purest democracy.

The moving words above beautifully express our ideals of equality and the brotherhood of man. They are from a memorial address given by Rabbi Roland B. Gittelsohn in March, 1945. He dedicated a cemetery for the marines who fell in the battle for the Japanese-held island of Iwo Jima in World War II.

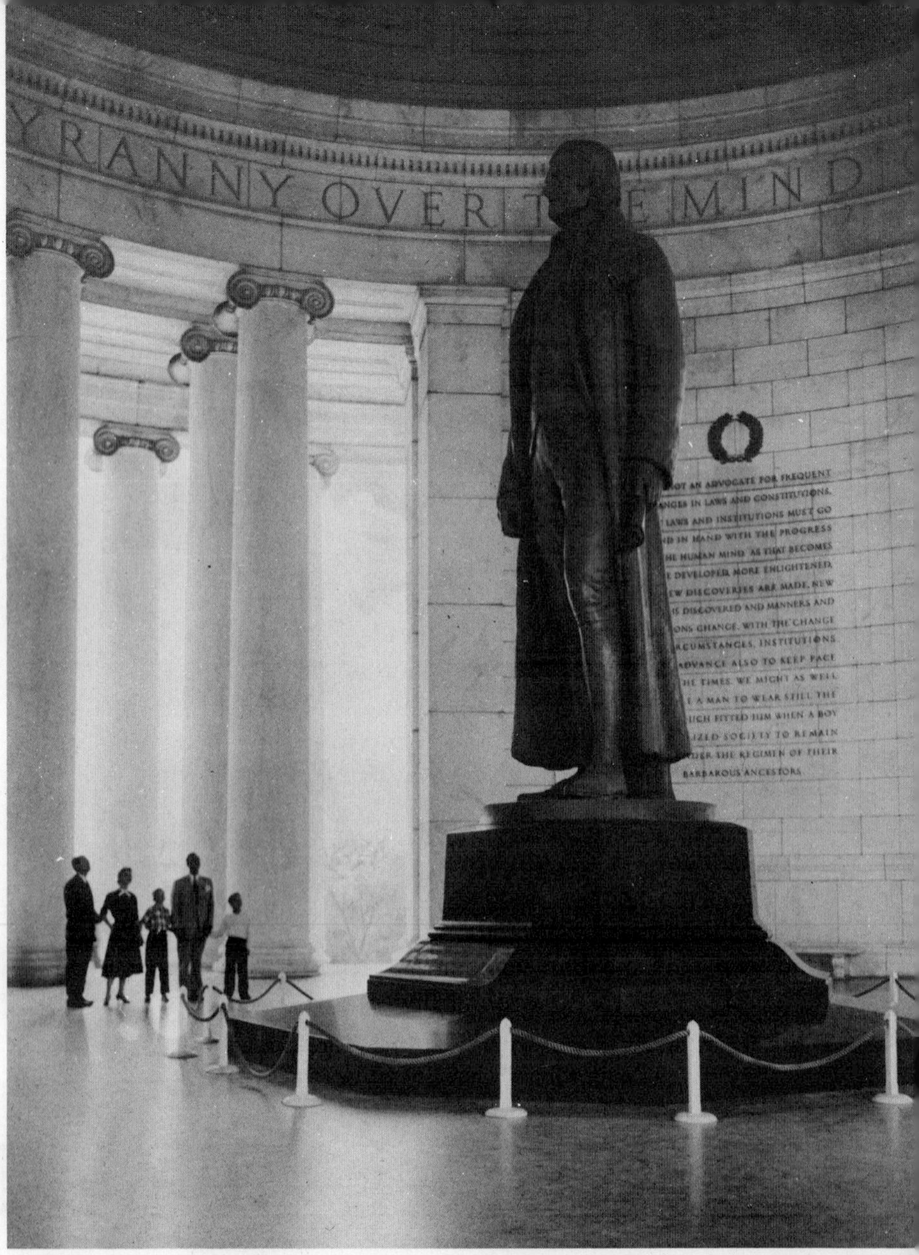

Visitors study the massive statue in the Jefferson Memorial. Thomas Jefferson's intense love of liberty and firm belief in the worth of the individual challenge each of us to keep America great.

have faith in what it stands for, serve it in every way you can. It is in your power to help build not only a better America, but a better world, where all men may have the freedoms we enjoy. With millions of young people doing their jobs as good citizens, we can face the future with faith that our democracy and our free way of life will endure.

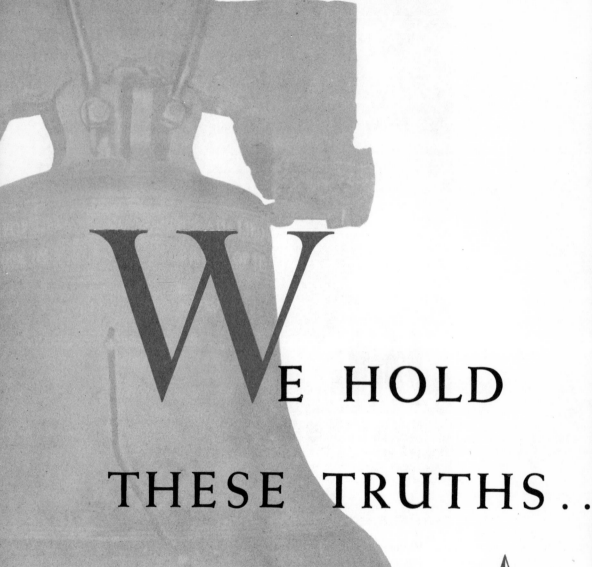

WE HOLD THESE TRUTHS . .

THE DECLARATION OF INDEPENDENCE

After 185 years, the Declaration of Independence still has the power to inspire those who read it. This famous American document is more than an announcement of the separation of the colonies from Great Britain. It is a declaration of our belief in the "unalienable rights" of mankind. In beautiful and unforgettable phrases it states the ideals of liberty and equality on which our government is founded. Indeed, our Declaration of Independence holds out hope of "life, liberty, and pursuit of happiness" to all men everywhere. It is one of the world's great documents of freedom.[1]

Reasons for the Declaration. When in the Course of human events, it becomes necessary for one people to dissolve the political bands which have connected them with another, and to assume among the powers of the earth, the separate and equal station to which the Laws of Nature and of Nature's God entitle them, a decent respect to the opinions of mankind requires that they should declare the causes which impel them to the separation.

The right of the people to control their government. We hold these truths to be self-evident, that all men are created equal, that they are endowed by their Creator with certain unalienable Rights, that among these are Life, Liberty and the pursuit of Happiness. That to secure these rights, Governments are instituted among Men, deriving their just powers from the consent of the governed, That whenever any Form of Government becomes destructive of these ends, it is the Right of the People to alter or to abolish it, and to institute new Government, laying its foundation on such principles and organizing its powers in such form, as to them shall seem most likely to effect their Safety and Happiness. Prudence, indeed, will dictate that Governments long established should not be changed for light and transient causes; and accordingly all experience hath shown, that mankind are more disposed to suffer, while evils are sufferable, than to right themselves by abolishing the forms to which they are accustomed. But when a long train of abuses and usurpations, pursuing invariably the same Object evinces a design to reduce them under absolute Despotism, it is their right, it is their duty, to throw off such Government, and to provide new Guards for their future security. Such has been the patient sufferance of these Colonies; and such is now the necessity which constrains them to alter their former Sys-

[1] The boldface headings and footnotes here, and in the Constitution which follows, are added for help in reading. Otherwise the text follows accepted sources.

tems of Government. The history of the present King of Great Britain is a history of repeated injuries and usurpations, all having in direct object the establishment of an absolute Tyranny over these States. To prove this, let Facts be submitted to a candid world.

Tyrannical acts of the British King. He has refused his Assent to Laws, the most wholesome and necessary for the public good.

He has forbidden his Governors to pass Laws of immediate and pressing importance, unless suspended in their operation till his Assent should be obtained; and when so suspended, he has utterly neglected to attend to them.

He has refused to pass other Laws for the accommodation of large districts of people, unless those people would relinquish the right of Representation in the Legislature, a right inestimable to them and formidable to tyrants only.

He has called together legislative bodies at places unusual, uncomfortable, and distant from the depository of their Public Records, for the sole purpose of fatiguing them into compliance with his measures.

He has dissolved Representative Houses repeatedly, for opposing with manly firmness his invasions on the rights of the people.

He has refused for a long time, after such dissolutions, to cause others to be elected; whereby the Legislative powers, incapable of Annihilation, have returned to the People at large for their exercise; the State remaining in the mean time exposed to all the dangers of invasion from without, and convulsions within.

He has endeavoured to prevent the population of these States; for that purpose obstructing the Laws for Naturalization of Foreigners; refusing to pass others to encourage their migrations hither, and raising the conditions of new Appropriations of Lands.

He has obstructed the Administration of Justice, by refusing his Assent to Laws for establishing Judiciary powers.

He has made Judges dependent on his Will alone, for the tenure of their offices, and the amount and payment of their salaries.

He has erected a multitude of New Offices, and sent hither swarms of Officers to harass our People, and eat out their substance.

He has kept among us, in times of peace, Standing Armies without the Consent of our legislatures.

He has affected to render the military independent of and superior to the Civil power.

He has combined with others to subject us to a jurisdiction foreign to our constitution, and unacknowledged by our laws; giving his Assent to their Acts of pretended Legislation:

For quartering large bodies of armed troops among us:

For protecting them, by a mock Trial, from Punishment for any Murders which they should commit on the Inhabitants of these States:

For cutting off our Trade with all parts of the world:

For imposing Taxes on us without our Consent:

For depriving us in many cases, of the benefits of Trial by Jury:

For transporting us beyond Seas to be tried for pretended offences:

For abolishing the free System of English Laws in a neighbouring Province, establishing therein an Arbitrary government, and enlarging its Boundaries so as to render it at once an example and fit instrument for introducing the same absolute rule into these Colonies:

For taking away our Charters, abolishing our most valuable Laws, and altering fundamentally the Forms of our Governments:

For suspending our own Legislatures, and declaring themselves invested with power to legislate for us in all cases whatsoever.

He has abdicated Government here, by declaring us out of his Protection and waging War against us.

He has plundered our seas, ravaged our Coasts, burnt our towns, and destroyed the lives of our people.

He is at this time transporting large Armies of foreign Mercenaries to compleat the works of death, desolation and tyranny, already begun with circumstances of Cruelty

& perfidy scarcely paralleled in the most barbarous ages, and totally unworthy the Head of a civilized nation.

He has constrained our fellow Citizens taken Captive on the high Seas to bear Arms against their Country, to become the executioners of their friends and Brethren, or to fall themselves by their Hands.

He has excited domestic insurrections amongst us, and has endeavoured to bring on the inhabitants of our frontiers, the merciless Indian Savages, whose known rule of warfare, is an undistinguished destruction of all ages, sexes and conditions.

Efforts of the colonies to avoid separation. In every stage of these Oppressions We have Petitioned for Redress in the most humble terms: Our repeated Petitions have been answered only by repeated injury. A Prince, whose character is thus marked by every act which may define a Tyrant, is unfit to be the ruler of a free people.

Nor have We been wanting in attentions to our British brethren. We have warned them from time to time of attempts by their legislature to extend an unwarrantable jurisdiction over us. We have reminded them of the circumstances of our emigration and settlement here. We have appealed to their native justice and magnanimity, and we have conjured them by the ties of our common kindred to disavow these usurpations, which, would inevitably interrupt our connections and correspondence. They too have been deaf to the voice of justice and of consanguinity. We must, therefore, acquiesce in the necessity, which denounces our Separation, and hold them, as we hold the rest of mankind, Enemies in War, in Peace Friends.

The colonies are declared free and independent. We, therefore, the Representatives of the united States of America, in General Congress, Assembled, appealing to the Supreme Judge of the world for the rectitude of our intentions, do, in the Name, and by Authority of the good People of these Colonies, solemnly publish and declare, That these United Colonies are, and of Right ought to be Free and Independent States; that they are Absolved from all Allegiance to the British Crown, and that all political connection between them and the State of Great Britain, is and ought to be totally dissolved; and that as Free and Independent States, they have full Power to Levy War, conclude Peace, contract Alliances, establish Commerce, and to do all other Acts and Things which Independent States may of right do. And for the support of this Declaration, with a firm reliance on the protection of divine Providence, we mutually pledge to each other our Lives, our Fortunes and our sacred Honor.

WE THE PEOPLE . . .

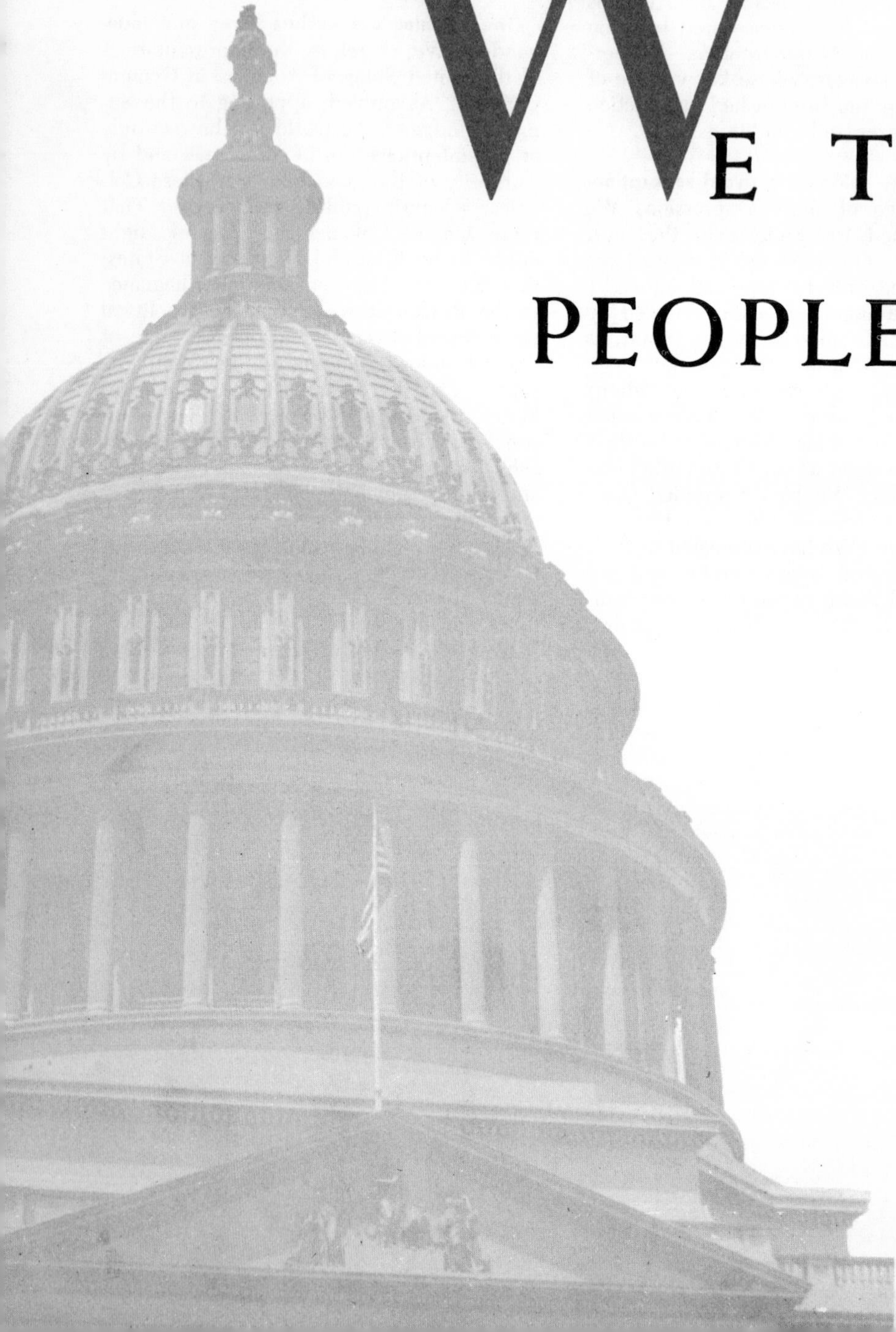

THE CONSTITUTION OF THE UNITED STATES

In these times it is more important than ever before for all Americans to know our Constitution. For about 175 years the Constitution with its Bill of Rights has served the American people both as a plan of government and as a safeguard of our rights and liberties. Written for a small nation of less than 4 million inhabitants, it has kept pace with America's tremendous growth and progress. Today the Constitution serves our great nation of over 180 million people.

So that you may read the Constitution more easily and understand it better, headings in boldface type have been added for Articles, Sections, important paragraphs, and Amendments. Parts of the Constitution no longer in effect are printed in italics. In addition, there is a table on page 230 which will help you to locate certain important topics in the Constitution.

PREAMBLE

WE THE PEOPLE of the United States, in order to form a more perfect union, establish justice, insure domestic tranquillity, provide for the common defense, promote the general welfare, and secure the blessings of liberty to ourselves and our posterity, do ordain and establish this Constitution for the United States of America.

Article I

Legislative Department

Section 1. **Congress in General**

All legislative powers herein granted shall be vested in a Congress of the United States, which shall consist of a Senate and House of Representatives.

Section 2. **The House of Representatives**

a. Election and term of members. The House of Representatives shall be composed of members chosen every second year by the people of the several States, and the electors in each State shall have the qualifications requisite for electors of the most numerous branch of the State Legislature.

b. Qualifications of members. No person shall be a Representative who shall not have attained to the age of twenty-five years, and been seven years a citizen of the United States, and who shall not, when elected, be an inhabitant of that State in which he shall be chosen.

c. Apportionment of representatives and of direct taxes. Representatives and direct taxes shall be apportioned among the several States which may be included within this Union, according to their respective

(Continued on page 231)

Guide to the Study of the Constitution

Important Topics in the Constitution		Where to Find Them [1]
Purpose	Why the Constitution was drawn up.	*Preamble*
Congress	How Congress is organized; qualifications of members; how Senators and Representatives are chosen; how Congress does its business; how laws are passed; when sessions are held; what powers Congress has; what powers are denied the federal government.	*Article I; Amendments 16, 17, 20*
The President	How he is elected; what his qualifications are; what his powers are; how long he may serve.	*Article II; Amendments 12, 22*
The Courts	How federal courts are established; what cases are tried in federal courts; how judges are appointed.	*Article III; Amendment 11*
Relations Between the Federal Government and the States	How a state shall treat citizens of another state; how Congress may govern territories and admit new states; what the federal government guarantees to the states; what powers states may or may not exercise.	*Article IV; Article I, Section 10; and Amendment 10*
Amendments	How the Constitution may be amended.	*Article V*
Supremacy of the Constitution	The supremacy of the Constitution; its support by all federal and state officers.	*Article VI, b*
Ratification	What steps were required to put the Constitution into operation.	*Article VII*
Basic Rights of Citizens	Our rights to freedom of religion, press, speech, assembly, and fair trial; protection of life, liberty, and property; freedom from search and unusual punishment; guarantees against slavery; grounds upon which citizens may not be deprived of the right to vote.	*Bill of Rights (Amendments 1–10); Amendments 13, 14, 15, 19; Article I, Section 9; Article III, Section 2*

[1] You may notice that Amendments 18 and 21 are not mentioned in the right-hand column above. Amendment 18 established Prohibition in 1919; Amendment 21 (1933) repealed the 18th Amendment, returning control of liquor to the states.

numbers, *which shall be determined by adding to the whole number of free persons, including those bound to service for a term of years, and excluding Indians not taxed, three fifths of all other persons.*[1] The actual enumeration shall be made within three years after the first meeting of the Congress of the United States, and within every subsequent term of ten years, in such manner as they shall by law direct. The number of Representatives shall not exceed one for every thirty thousand, but each state shall have at least one representative; *and until such enumeration shall be made, the state of New Hampshire shall be entitled to choose three; Massachusetts, eight; Rhode Island and Providence Plantations, one; Connecticut, five; New York, six; New Jersey, four; Pennsylvania, eight; Delaware, one; Maryland, six; Virginia, ten; North Carolina, five; South Carolina, five; and Georgia, three.*

d. Filling vacancies. When vacancies happen in the representation from any State, the Executive authority thereof shall issue writs of election to fill such vacancies.

e. Officers; impeachment. The House of Representatives shall choose their Speaker and other officers; and shall have the sole power of impeachment.

Section 3. The Senate

a. Number and election of members. The Senate of the United States shall be composed of two Senators from each state, chosen *by the legislature thereof,*[2] for six years, and each Senator shall have one vote.

b. Classification. Immediately after they shall be assembled in consequence of the first election, they shall be divided as equally as may be into three classes. *The seats of the Senators of the first class shall be vacated at the expiration of the second year, of the second class at the expiration of the fourth year, and of the third class at the expiration of the sixth year,* so that one third may be chosen every second year; *and if vacancies happen by resignation, or otherwise, during the recess of the legislature of any State, the Executive thereof may make temporary appointments until the next meeting of the legislature, which shall then fill such vacancies.*

c. Qualifications of members. No person shall be a Senator who shall not have attained to the age of thirty years, and been nine years a citizen of the United States, and who shall not, when elected, be an inhabitant of that State for which he shall be chosen.

d. President of Senate. The Vice President of the United States shall be President of the Senate, but shall have no vote, unless they be equally divided.

e. Other officers. The Senate shall choose their own officers, and also a President pro tempore, in the absence of the Vice President, or when he shall exercise the office of President of the United States.

f. Trial of impeachment. The Senate shall have the sole power to try all impeachments. When sitting for that purpose, they shall be on oath or affirmation. When the President of the United States is tried, the Chief Justice shall preside; and no person shall be convicted without the concurrence of two thirds of the members present.

g. Judgment in case of conviction. Judgment in cases of impeachment shall not extend further than to removal from office, and disqualification to hold and enjoy any office of honor, trust or profit under the United States; but the party convicted shall nevertheless be liable and subject to indictment, trial, judgment and punishment, according to law.

Section 4. How Senators and Representatives shall be chosen and when they are to meet

a. Method of holding elections. The times, places and manner of holding elections for Senators and Representatives shall be prescribed in each State by the Legislature thereof; but the Congress may at any time by law make or alter such regulations, except as to the places of choosing Senators.

b. Meeting of Congress. The Congress shall assemble at least once in every year, *and such meeting shall be on the first Monday in December,* unless they shall by law appoint a different day.[1]

[1] Changed by Amendment XIV.

[2] This method of election has been changed by Amendment XVII.

[1] The time of meeting was changed by Amendment XX.

Section 5. **Rules of Procedure**

a. Organization. Each house shall be the judge of the elections, returns and qualifications of its own members, and a majority of each shall constitute a quorum to do business; but a smaller number may adjourn from day to day, and may be authorized to compel the attendance of absent members, in such manner, and under such penalties, as each house may provide.

b. Rules of proceedings. Each house may determine the rules of its proceedings, punish its members for disorderly behavior, and, with the concurrence of two thirds, expel a member.

c. Journal. Each house shall keep a journal of its proceedings, and from time to time publish the same, excepting such parts as may in their judgment require secrecy; and the yeas and nays of the members of either house on any question shall, at the desire of one fifth of those present, be entered on the journal.

d. Adjournment. Neither house, during the session of Congress, shall, without the consent of the other, adjourn for more than three days, nor to any other place than that in which the two houses shall be sitting.

Section 6. **Compensation, Privileges, and Restrictions**

a. Pay and privileges of members. The Senators and Representatives shall receive a compensation for their services, to be ascertained by law, and paid out of the Treasury of the United States. They shall in all cases except treason, felony and breach of the peace, be privileged from arrest during their attendance at the session of their respective houses, and in going to and returning from the same; and for any speech or debate in either house, they shall not be questioned in any other place.

b. Holding other offices prohibited. No Senator or Representative shall, during the time for which he was elected, be appointed to any civil office under the authority of the United States which shall have been created, or the emoluments whereof shall have been increased during such time; and no person holding any office under the United States shall be a member of either house during his continuance in office.

Section 7. **Mode of Passing Laws**

a. Revenue bills. All bills for raising revenue shall originate in the House of Representatives; but the Senate may propose or concur with amendments as on other bills.

b. How bills become laws. Every bill which shall have passed the House of Representatives and the Senate shall, before it become a law, be presented to the President of the United States; if he approve he shall sign it, but if not he shall return it, with his objections to that house in which it shall have originated, who shall enter the objections at large on their journal, and proceed to reconsider it. If after such reconsideration two thirds of that house shall agree to pass the bill, it shall be sent, together with the objections, to the other house, by which it shall likewise be reconsidered, and if approved by two thirds of that house, it shall become a law. But in all such cases the votes of both houses shall be determined by yeas and nays, and the names of the persons voting for and against the bill shall be entered on the journal of each house respectively. If any bill shall not be returned by the President within ten days (Sundays excepted) after it shall have been presented to him, the same shall be a law, in like manner as if he had signed it, unless the Congress by their adjournment prevent its return, in which case it shall not be a law.

c. Approval or disapproval by the President. Every order, resolution, or vote to which the concurrence of the Senate and House of Representatives may be necessary (except on a question of adjournment) shall be presented to the President of the United States; and before the same shall take effect, shall be approved by him, or being disapproved by him, shall be repassed by two thirds of the Senate and House of Representatives, according to the rules and limitations prescribed in the case of a bill.

Section 8. **Powers Granted to Congress**

The Congress shall have power

a. To lay and collect taxes, duties, imposts, and excises, to pay the debts and provide for the common defence and general welfare of the United States; but all duties, imposts and excises shall be uniform throughout the United States;

b. To borrow money on the credit of the United States;

c. To regulate commerce with foreign nations, and among the several States, and with the Indian tribes;

d. To establish an uniform rule of naturalization, and uniform laws on the subject of bankruptcies throughout the United States;

e. To coin money, regulate the value thereof, and of foreign coin, and fix the standard of weights and measures;

f. To provide for the punishment of counterfeiting the securities and current coin of the United States;

g. To establish post offices and post roads;

h. To promote the progress of science and useful arts by securing for limited times to authors and inventors the exclusive right to their respective writings and discoveries;

i. To constitute tribunals inferior to the Supreme Court;

j. To define and punish piracies and felonies committed on the high seas and offences against the law of nations;

k. To declare war, grant letters of marque and reprisal, and make rules concerning captures on land and water;

l. To raise and support armies, but no appropriation of money to that use shall be for a longer term than two years;

m. To provide and maintain a navy;

n. To make rules for the government and regulation of the land and naval forces;

o. To provide for calling forth the militia to execute the laws of the Union, suppress insurrections, and repel invasions;

p. To provide for organizing, arming and disciplining the militia, and for governing such part of them as may be employed in the service of the United States, reserving to the States respectively the appointment of the officers, and the authority of training the militia according to the discipline prescribed by Congress;

q. To exercise exclusive legislation in all cases whatsoever, over such district (not exceeding ten miles square) as may, by cession of particular States, and the acceptance of Congress, become the seat of the government of the United States, and to exercise like authority over all places purchased by the consent of the legislature of the State, in which the same shall be, for the erection of forts, magazines, arsenals, dock-yards, and other needful buildings; — and

r. To make all laws which shall be necessary and proper for carrying into execution the foregoing powers, and all other powers vested by this Constitution in the government of the United States, or in any department or officer thereof.

Section 9. **Powers Denied to the Federal Government**

a. *The migration or importation of such persons as any of the States now existing shall think proper to admit, shall not be prohibited by the Congress prior to the year one thousand eight hundred and eight, but a tax or duty may be imposed on such importation, not exceeding ten dollars for each person.*

b. The privilege of the writ of habeas corpus shall not be suspended, unless when in cases of rebellion or invasion the public safety may require it.

c. No bill of attainder or ex post facto law shall be passed.

d. No capitation, or other direct, tax shall be laid, unless in proportion to the census or enumeration herein before directed to be taken.

e. No tax or duty shall be laid on articles exported from any State.

f. No preference shall be given by any regulation of commerce or revenue to the ports of one State over those of another: nor shall vessels bound to, or from, one State be obliged to enter, clear, or pay duties in another.

g. No money shall be drawn from the Treasury, but in consequence of appropriations made by law; and a regular statement and account of the receipts and expenditures of all public money shall be published from time to time.

h. No title of nobility shall be granted by the United States: and no person holding any office of profit or trust under them shall, without the consent of the Congress, accept of any present, emolument, office, or title, of any kind whatever, from any king, prince, or foreign state.

Section 10. **Powers Denied to the States**

a. No State shall enter into any treaty, alliance, or confederation; grant letters of marque and reprisal; coin money; emit bills of credit; make any thing but gold and silver coin a tender in payment of debts; pass any bill of attainder; ex post facto law, or law impairing the obligation of contracts, or grant any title of nobility.

b. No State shall, without the consent of the Congress, lay any imposts or duties on imports or exports, except what may be absolutely necessary for executing its inspection laws; and the net produce of all duties and imposts, laid by any State on imports or exports, shall be for the use of the treasury of the United States; and all such laws shall be subject to the revision and control of the Congress.

c. No State shall, without the consent of Congress, lay any duty of tonnage, keep troops, or ships of war in time of peace, enter into any agreement or compact with another State, or with a foreign power, or engage in war, unless actually invaded, or in such imminent danger as will not admit of delay.

Article II

Executive Department

Section 1. **President and Vice President**

a. Term of office. The executive power shall be vested in a President of the United States of America. He shall hold his office during the term of four years, and together with the Vice President, chosen for the same term, be elected as follows:

b. Electors. Each State shall appoint, in such manner as the legislature thereof may direct, a number of electors, equal to the whole number of Senators and Representatives to which the State may be entitled in the Congress; but no Senator or Representative, or person holding an office of trust or profit under the United States, shall be appointed an elector.

Former method of electing President and Vice President. *The electors shall meet in their respective States, and vote by ballot for two persons, of whom one at least shall not be an inhabitant of the same State with themselves. And they shall make a list of all the persons voted for, and of the number of votes for each; which list they shall sign and certify, and transmit sealed to the seat of government of the United States, directed to the President of the Senate. The President of the Senate shall, in the presence of the Senate and House of Representatives, open all the certificates, and the votes shall then be counted. The person having the greatest number of votes shall be the President, if such number be a majority of the whole number of electors appointed; and if there be more than one who have such majority, and have an equal number of votes, then the House of Representatives shall immediately choose by ballot one of them for President; and if no person have a majority, then from the five highest on the list the said house shall in like manner choose the President. But in choosing the President the votes shall be taken by States, the representation from each State having one vote; a quorum for this purpose shall consist of a member or members from two thirds of the States, and a majority of all the States shall be necessary to a choice. In every case, after the choice of the President, the person having the greatest number of votes of the electors shall be the Vice President. But if there should remain two or more who have equal votes, the Senate shall choose from them by ballot the Vice President.*[1]

c. Time of elections. The Congress may determine the time of choosing the electors, and the day on which they shall give their votes; which day shall be the same throughout the United States.

d. Qualifications of the President. No person except a natural born citizen, *or a citizen of the United States, at the time of the adoption of this Constitution,* shall be eligible to the office of President; neither shall any person be eligible to that office who shall not have attained to the age of thirty-five years, and been fourteen years a resident within the United States.

e. Vacancy. In case of the removal of the President from office or of his death, resig-

[1] Changed by Amendment XII.

nation, or inability to discharge the powers and duties of the said office, the same shall devolve on the Vice President, and the Congress may by law provide for the case of removal, death, resignation, or inability, both of the President and Vice President, declaring what officer shall then act as President, and such officer shall act accordingly, until the disability be removed, or a President shall be elected.

f. The President's salary. The President shall, at stated times, receive for his services, a compensation, which shall neither be increased nor diminished during the period for which he shall have been elected, and he shall not receive within that period any other emolument from the United States, or any of them.

g. Oath of office. Before he enter on the execution of his office, he shall take the following oath or affirmation: —"I do solemnly swear (or affirm) that I will faithfully execute the office of President of the United States, and will to the best of my ability, preserve, protect and defend the Constitution of the United States."

Section 2. Powers of the President

a. Military powers; reprieves and pardons. The President shall be commander in chief of the army and navy of the United States, and of the militia of the several States, when called into the actual service of the United States; he may require the opinion, in writing, of the principal officer in each of the executive departments, upon any subject relating to the duties of their respective offices, and he shall have power to grant reprieves and pardons for offences against the United States, except in cases of impeachment.

b. Treaties; appointments. He shall have power, by and with the advice and consent of the Senate, to make treaties, provided two thirds of the Senators present concur; and he shall nominate, and by and with the advice and consent of the Senate, shall appoint ambassadors, other public ministers and consuls, judges of the Supreme Court, and all other officers of the United States, whose appointments are not herein otherwise provided for, and which shall be established by law; but the Congress may by law vest the appointment of such inferior officers as they think proper, in the President alone, in the courts of law, or in the heads of departments.

c. Filling vacancies. The President shall have power to fill up all vacancies that may happen during the recess of the Senate, by granting commissions which shall expire at the end of their next session.

Section 3. Duties of the President

He shall from time to time give to the Congress information of the state of the Union, and recommend to their consideration such measures as he shall judge necessary and expedient; he may, on extraordinary occasions, convene both houses, or either of them, and in case of disagreement between them with respect to the time of adjournment, he may adjourn them to such time as he shall think proper; he shall receive ambassadors and other public ministers; he shall take care that the laws be faithfully executed, and shall commission all the officers of the United States.

Section 4. Impeachment

The President, Vice President and all civil officers of the United States shall be removed from office on impeachment for, and conviction of, treason, bribery, or other high crimes and misdemeanors.

Article III

Judicial Department

Section 1. The Federal Courts

The judicial power of the United States shall be vested in one Supreme Court, and in such inferior courts as the Congress may from time to time ordain and establish. The judges, both of the Supreme and inferior courts, shall hold their offices during good behavior, and shall, at stated times, receive for their services, a compensation, which shall not be diminished during their continuance in office.

Section 2. Jurisdiction of the Federal Courts

a. Federal courts in general. The judicial power shall extend to all cases, in law and equity, arising under this Constitution, the laws of the United States, and treaties made or which shall be made, under their authority; — to all cases affecting ambassadors, other public ministers and consuls; — to all cases of admiralty jurisdiction; — to controversies to which the United States shall be a party; — to controversies between two or more States; — *between a State and citizens of another State;* — between citizens of different States; — between citizens of the same State claiming lands under grants of different States, and between a State, or the citizens thereof, and foreign states, citizens or subjects.[1]

b. Supreme Court. In all cases affecting ambassadors, other public ministers and consuls, and those in which a State shall be a party, the Supreme Court shall have original jurisdiction. In all the other cases before mentioned, the Supreme Court shall have appellate jurisdiction, both as to law and fact, with such exceptions, and under such regulations as the Congress shall make.

c. Rules respecting trials. The trial of all crimes, except in cases of impeachment, shall be by jury; and such trial shall be held in the State where the said crimes shall have been committed; but when not committed within any State, the trial shall be at such place or places as the Congress may by law have directed.

Section 3. **Treason**

a. Definition of treason. Treason against the United States shall consist only in levying war against them, or in adhering to their enemies, giving them aid and comfort. No person shall be convicted of treason unless on the testimony of two witnesses to the same overt act, or on confession in open court.

b. Punishment of treason. The Congress shall have power to declare the punishment of treason, but no attainder of treason shall work corruption of blood, or forfeiture except during the life of the person attainted.

Article IV

The States and the Federal Government

Section 1. **State Records**

Full faith and credit shall be given in each State to the public acts, records, and judicial proceedings of every other State. And the Congress may by general laws prescribe the manner in which such acts, records, and proceedings shall be proved, and the effect thereof.

[1] This clause has been modified by Amendment XI.

Section 2. **Privileges and Immunities of Citizens**

a. Privileges. The citizens of each State shall be entitled to all privileges and immunities of citizens in the several States.

b. Extradition. A person charged in any State with treason, felony, or other crime, who shall flee from justice, and be found in another State, shall, on demand of the executive authority of the State from which he fled, be delivered up, to be removed to the State having jurisdiction of the crime.

c. Fugitive workers. *No person held to service or labor in one State, under the laws thereof, escaping into another shall in consequence of any law or regulation therein, be discharged from such service or labor, but shall be delivered upon claim of the party to whom such service or labor may be due.*

Section 3. **New States and Territories**

a. Admission of new States. New States may be admitted by the Congress into this Union; but no new State shall be formed or erected within the jurisdiction of any other State; nor any State be formed by the junction of two or more States, or parts of States, without the consent of the legislatures of the States concerned, as well as of the Congress.

b. Power of Congress over territory and property. The Congress shall have power to dispose of and make all needful rules and regulations respecting the territory or other property belonging to the United States; and nothing in this Constitution shall be so construed as to prejudice any claims of the United States, or of any particular State.

Section 4. **Guarantees to the States**

The United States shall guarantee to every State in this Union a republican form of government, and shall protect each of them against invasion; and on application of the legislature, or of the executive (when the legislature cannot be convened) against domestic violence.

Article V

Method of Amendment

The Congress, whenever two thirds of both houses shall deem it necessary, shall propose amendments to this Constitution, or, on the application of the legislatures of two thirds of the several States, shall call a convention for proposing amendments, which, in either case shall be valid to all intents and purposes, as part of this Constitution, when ratified by the legislatures of three fourths of the several States, or by conventions in three fourths thereof, as the one or the other mode of ratification may be proposed by the Congress; provided that *no amendments which may be made prior to the year one thousand eight hundred and eight shall in any manner affect the first and fourth clauses in the ninth section of the first article, and that* no State, without its consent, shall be deprived of its equal suffrage in the Senate.

Article VI

General Provisions

a. Public debt. All debts contracted and engagements entered into, before the adoption of this Constitution, shall be as valid against the United States under this Constitution, as under the Confederation.

b. Supremacy of the Constitution. This Constitution, and the laws of the United States which shall be made in pursuance thereof; and all treaties made, or which shall be made, under the authority of the United States, shall be the supreme law of the land; and the judges in every State shall be bound thereby, anything in the Constitution or laws of any State to the contrary notwithstanding.

c. Oath of office; no religious test. The Senators and Representatives before mentioned, and the members of the several State legislatures, and all executive and judicial officers, both of the United States and of the several States, shall be bound by oath or affirmation, to support this Constitution; but no religious test shall ever be required as a qualification to any office or public trust under the United States.

Article VII

Ratification of the Constitution

The ratification of the conventions of nine States shall be sufficient for the establishment of this Constitution between the States so ratifying the same.

AMENDMENTS TO THE CONSTITUTION

Amendment I (adopted 1791)

Freedom of Religion, Speech, and the Press; Right of Assembly

Congress shall make no law respecting an establishment of religion, or prohibiting the free exercise thereof; or abridging the freedom of speech, or of the press; or the right of the people peaceably to assemble, and to petition the government for a redress of grievances.

Amendment II (adopted 1791)

Right to Keep and Bear Arms

A well-regulated militia, being necessary to the security of a free State, the right of the people to keep and bear arms, shall not be infringed.

Amendment III (adopted 1791)

Quartering of Troops

No soldier shall, in time of peace be quartered in any house, without the consent of the owner, nor in time of war, but in a manner to be prescribed by law.

Amendment IV **(adopted 1791)**

Limiting the Right of Search

The right of the people to be secure in their persons, houses, papers, and effects, against unreasonable searches and seizures, shall not be violated, and no warrants shall issue but upon probable cause, supported by oath or affirmation, and particularly describing the place to be searched, and the persons or things to be seized.

Amendment V **(adopted 1791)**

Guaranty of Trial by Jury; Private Property to be Respected

No person shall be held to answer for a capital, or otherwise infamous crime, unless on a presentment or indictment of a grand jury, except in cases arising in the land or naval forces, or in the militia, when in actual service in time of war and public danger; nor shall any person be subject for the same offense to be twice put in jeopardy of life or limb; nor shall be compelled in any criminal case to be a witness against himself, nor be deprived of life, liberty, or property, without due process of law; nor shall private property be taken for public use without just compensation.

Amendment VI **(adopted 1791)**

Rights of Accused Persons

In all criminal prosecutions, the accused shall enjoy the right to a speedy and public trial, by an impartial jury of the State and district wherein the crime shall have been committed, which districts shall have been previously ascertained by law, and to be informed of the nature and cause of the accusation; to be confronted with the witnesses against him; to have compulsory process for obtaining witnesses in his favor, and to have the assistance of counsel for his defense.

Amendment VII **(adopted 1791)**

Rules of the Common Law

In suits at common law, where the value in controversy shall exceed twenty dollars, the right of trial by jury shall be preserved, and no fact tried by a jury, shall be otherwise re-examined in any court of the United States than according to the rules of common law.

Amendment VIII **(adopted 1791)**

Excessive Bail, Fines, and Punishment Prohibited

Excessive bail shall not be required, nor excessive fines imposed, nor cruel and unusual punishments inflicted.

Amendment IX **(adopted 1791)**

Rights Retained by the People

The enumeration in the Constitution of certain rights, shall not be construed to deny or disparage others retained by the people.

Amendment X **(adopted 1791)**

Powers Reserved to States and People

The powers not delegated to the United States by the Constitution, nor prohibited by it to the States, are reserved to the States respectively, or to the people.

Amendment XI **(adopted 1798)**

Limiting the Powers of Federal Courts

The judicial power of the United States shall not be construed to extend to any suit in law or equity, commenced or prosecuted against one of the United States by citizens of another State, or by citizens or subjects of any foreign state.

Amendment XII **(adopted 1804)**

Election of President and Vice President

The electors shall meet in their respective States, and vote by ballot for President and Vice President, one of whom, at least, shall not be an inhabitant of the same State with themselves; they shall name in their ballots the person voted for as President, and in distinct ballots the person voted for as Vice President, and they shall make distinct lists of all persons voted for as President, and of all persons voted for as Vice President, and of the number of votes for each, which lists they shall sign and certify, and transmit sealed to the seat of government of the United States, directed to the President of the Senate; — the President of the Senate shall, in the presence of the Senate and House of Representatives, open all the certificates and the votes shall then be counted; — the person having the greatest number of votes for President shall be the President, if such number be a majority of the whole number of electors appointed; and if no person have such majority, then from the persons having the highest numbers not exceeding three on the list of those voted for as President, the House of Representatives shall choose immediately, by ballot, the President. But in choosing the President, the votes shall be taken by States, the representation from each State having one vote; a quorum for this purpose shall consist of a member or members from two thirds of the States, and a majority of all the States shall be necessary to a choice. And if the House of Representatives shall not choose a President whenever the right of choice shall devolve upon them, *before the fourth day of March next following*, then the Vice President shall act as President, as in the case of the death or other constitutional disability of the President. — The person having the greatest number of votes as Vice President, shall be the Vice President, if such number be a majority of the whole number of electors appointed, and if no person have a majority, then from the two highest numbers on the list, the Senate shall choose the Vice President; a quorum for the purpose shall consist of two thirds of the whole number of Senators, and a majority of the whole number shall be necessary to a choice. But no person constitutionally ineligible to the office of President shall be eligible to that of Vice President of the United States.

Amendment XIII **(adopted 1865)**

Slavery Abolished

Section 1. **Abolition of Slavery**

Neither slavery nor involuntary servitude, except as a punishment for crime whereof the party shall have been duly convicted, shall exist within the United States, or any place subject to their jurisdiction.

Section 2. **Enforcement**

Congress shall have power to enforce this article by appropriate legislation.

Amendment XIV **(adopted 1868)**

Citizenship Defined

Section 1. **Definition of Citizenship**

All persons born or naturalized in the United States, and subject to the jurisdiction thereof, are citizens of the United States and of the State wherein they reside. No State shall make or enforce any law which shall abridge the privileges or immunities of citizens of the United States; nor shall any State deprive any person of life, liberty, or property, without due process of law; nor deny to any person within its jurisdiction the equal protection of the laws.

Section 2. **Apportionment of Representatives**

Representatives shall be apportioned among the several States according to their respective numbers, counting the whole number of persons in each State, excluding Indians not taxed. But when the right to vote at any election for the choice of electors for President and Vice President of the United States, Representatives in Congress, the executive and judicial officers of a State, or the members of the legislature thereof, is denied to any of the male inhabitants of such State, being twenty-one years of age, and citizens of the United States, or in any way abridged, except for participation in rebellion, or other crime, the basis of representation therein shall be reduced in the proportion which the number of such male citizens shall bear to the whole number of male citizens twenty-one years of age in such State.

Section 3. **Disability Resulting from Insurrection**

No person shall be a Senator or Representative in Congress, or Elector of President and Vice President, or hold any office, civil or military, under the United States, or under any State, who, having previously taken an oath, as a member of Congress, or as an officer of the United States, or as a member of any State legislature, or as an executive or judicial officer of any State to support the Constitution of the United States, shall have engaged in insurrection or rebellion against the same, or given aid or comfort to the enemies thereof. But Congress may by vote of two thirds of each house, remove such disability.

Section 4. **Public Debt of the United States Valid; Confederate Debt Void**

The validity of the public debt of the United States, authorized by law, including debts incurred for payment of pensions and bounties for services in suppressing insurrection or rebellion, shall not be questioned. But neither the United States nor any State shall assume or pay any debt or obligation incurred in aid of insurrection or rebellion against the United States, or any claim for the loss or emancipation of any slave; but all such debts, obligations, and claims shall be held illegal and void.

Section 5. **Enforcement**

The Congress shall have power to enforce by appropriate legislation the provisions of this article.

Amendment XV **(adopted 1870)**

Right of Suffrage

Section 1. **The Suffrage**

The right of citizens of the United States to vote shall not be denied or abridged by the United States or any State on account of race, color, or previous condition of servitude.

Section 2. **Enforcement**

The Congress shall have power to enforce this article by appropriate legislation.

Amendment XVI **(adopted 1913)**

Income Tax

The Congress shall have power to lay and collect taxes on incomes, from whatever source derived, without apportionment among the several States, and without regard to any census or enumeration.

Amendment XVII **(adopted 1913)**

Direct Election of Senators

a. Election by the people. The Senate of the United States shall be composed of two Senators from each State, elected by the people thereof, for six years; and each Senator shall have one vote. The electors in each State shall have the qualifications requisite for electors of the most numerous branch of the State legislatures.

b. Vacancies. When vacancies happen in the representation of any State in the Senate, the executive authority of such State shall issue writs of election to fill such vacancies: Provided that the legislature of any State may empower the executive thereof to make temporary appointments until the people fill the vacancies by election as the legislature may direct.

c. Not retroactive. This amendment shall not be so construed as to affect the election or term of any Senator chosen before it becomes valid as part of the Constitution.

Amendment XVIII **(adopted 1919)**

National Prohibition

Section 1. **Prohibition of Intoxicating Liquors**

After one year from the ratification of this article the manufacture, sale, or transportation of intoxicating liquors within, the importation thereof into, or the exportation thereof from the United States and all territory subject to the jurisdiction thereof for beverage purposes is hereby prohibited.

Section 2. **Enforcement**

The Congress and the several States shall have concurrent power to enforce this article by appropriate legislation.

Section 3. **Limited Time for Ratification**

This article shall be inoperative unless it shall have been ratified as an amendment to the Constitution by the legislatures of the several States, as provided by the Constitution, within seven years from the date of the submission hereof to the States by the Congress.

Amendment XIX **(adopted 1920)**

Extending the Vote to Women

Section 1. **Woman Suffrage**

The right of citizens of the United States to vote shall not be denied or abridged by the United States or by any State on account of sex.

Section 2. **Enforcement**

The Congress shall have power to enforce this article by appropriate legislation.

Amendment XX **(adopted 1933)**

Beginning of Presidential and Congressional Terms

Section 1. **Terms of President, Vice President, and Congress**

The terms of the President and Vice President shall end at noon on the 20th day of January, and the terms of Senators and Representatives at noon on the 3d day of January, of the years in which such terms would have ended if this article had not been ratified; and the terms of their successors shall then begin.

Section 2. **Sessions of Congress**

The Congress shall assemble at least once in every year, and such meeting shall begin at noon on the 3d day of January, unless they shall by law appoint a different day.

Section 3. **Presidential Succession**

If, at the time fixed for the beginning of the term of the President, the President elect shall have died, the Vice President elect shall become President. If a President shall not have been chosen before the time fixed for the beginning of his term, or if the President elect shall have failed to qualify, then the Vice President elect shall act as President until a President shall have qualified; and the Congress may by law provide for the case wherein neither a President elect nor a Vice President elect shall have qualified, declaring who shall then act as President, or the manner in which one who is to act shall be selected, and such person shall act accordingly until a President or a Vice President shall have qualified.

Section 4. **Choice of President by the House**

The Congress may by law provide for the case of the death of any of the persons from whom the House of Representatives may choose a President, whenever the right of choice shall have devolved upon them, and for the case of the death of any of the persons from whom the Senate may choose a Vice President whenever the right of choice shall have devolved upon them.

Section 5. **Date Effective**

Sections 1 and 2 shall take effect on the fifteenth day of October following the ratification of this article.

Section 6. **Limited Time for Ratification**

This article shall be inoperative unless it shall have been ratified as an amendment to the Constitution by the legislatures of three fourths of the several States within seven years from the date of its submission.

Amendment XXI **(adopted 1933)**

Repeal of Prohibition

Section 1. **Repeal of Amendment XVIII**

The eighteenth article of amendment to

the Constitution of the United States is hereby repealed.

Section 2. **States Protected**

The transportation or importation into any State, territory or possession of the United States for delivery or use therein of intoxicating liquors in violation of the laws thereof, is hereby prohibited.

Section 3. **Limited Time for Ratification**

This article shall be inoperative unless it shall have been ratified as an amendment to the Constitution by conventions in the several States, as provided in the Constitution, within seven years from the date of the submission hereof to the States by the Congress.

Amendment XXII **(adopted 1951)**

Two Term Amendment

Section 1. **Presidential Term Limited**

No person shall be elected to the office of the President more than twice, and no person who has held the office of President, or acted as President, for more than two years of a term to which some other person was elected President shall be elected to the office of the President more than once. But this article shall not apply to any person holding the office of President when this article was proposed by the Congress, and shall not prevent any person who may be holding the office of President, or acting as President, during the term within which this article becomes operative from holding the office of President, or acting as President during the remainder of such term.

Section 2. **Limited Time for Ratification**

This article shall be inoperative unless it shall have been ratified as an amendment to the Constitution by the legislatures of three-fourths of the several States within seven years from the date of its submission to the States by the Congress.

FOR GREATER APPRECIATION OF "AMERICA IS MY COUNTRY"

★ Chapter 1 ★

Do You Know These Words?

Note: Though you have heard and read most of the words in this book before, each chapter offers worthwhile opportunities for word study. Sometimes you will come across familiar words which you think you understand but which you might find difficult to explain. Occasionally you will come across an unfamiliar word which has been used because there is no good substitute for it. Here is a list of such words from Chapter 1. Find in the dictionary the meaning which *best* explains each word as it is used in the chapter. On a sheet of paper, write the word and beside it give the meaning. Then add a sentence from Chapter 1 in which this word is used.

citizen	patriotism
nation	Constitution
nationality	ideals
democracy	heritage
government	loyalty
birthright	

Checking Your Understanding

The following questions will help you check what you read in Chapter 1.

1. What is the official name of your country?
2. When was its birthday?
3. How does the American nationality differ from most other nationalities?
4. What things have made the United States a leader in the world?
5. What are the ideals America stands for?
6. What is expected of a patriotic citizen?
7. What is our American heritage?

What Do You Think?

These questions will help you think through the material in Chapter 1.

1. In what ways do you think America has gained by having citizens with different national backgrounds?
2. Why do many nations today look to the United States for leadership?
3. Can the people of America believe in freedom and equality for themselves, but not for people of other nations? Explain your answer.
4. How can young citizens prove their patriotism?

5. Why is it important for Americans to know about our American heritage?

For Further Study

Here are some suggestions for library or other work for those who would like to learn more about topics mentioned in this chapter. The work can be done by individual students or committees.

1. Find out what important minerals the United States does not have, and why they are needed in our industry.

2. Consult the *World Almanac* or *Information Please Almanac* for figures on the number of people of various national backgrounds included in our population. How many nationalities are represented? Which nationalities are in the majority?

3. Find figures on the amount or value of farm crops and manufactured goods produced in a recent year in the United States. How does U. S. production compare with that of other countries?

4. Report to the class on some American who gave outstanding service to our country. You will find the necessary information in your school or community library.

5. Bring to class newspaper or magazine stories about people who are serving our country in some way today.

6. Tell the class about a radio or television program which deals with American history.

7. Write an essay or poem on "What America Means to Me."

Books You Will Like

The books listed here will tell you more about the topics discussed in this chapter.

America's Stamps, by Maud and Miska Petersham. Macmillan. What our postage stamps tell us about our country.

An American ABC, by Maud and Miska Petersham. Macmillan. Easy stories of America, illustrated in color.

The Man Without a Country, by Edward Everett Hale. Houghton Mifflin. What happened to a man who said he never wanted to hear the words "United States" again.

They Were Strong and Good, by Robert Lawson. Viking. The story of the two parents and four grandparents of a typical American.

★ Chapter 2 ★

Do You Know These Words?

Find in the dictionary the meaning which *best* explains each word as it is used in the text. On a sheet of paper write the word and beside it give this meaning. Then add a sentence from Chapter 2 in which the word is used.

symbol	etiquette
reveille	insignia
indivisible	relic
documents	monument
significance	centennial

Checking Your Understanding

1. Can you describe the Flag of the United States? What is the union?

2. Can you explain this saying, "Every star a state, and every state a star"?

3. What are some ways in which we show respect for the Flag?

4. Why does a nation have a seal?

5. Describe the coat of arms of the United States.

6. Why is the Liberty Bell sacred to Americans?

7. What does the Statue of Liberty mean to us?

8. What does Uncle Sam symbolize?

9. Can you give three different names for our Flag?

What Do You Think?

1. Why should every citizen respect his country's flag?

2. Do you think that knowing the symbols of our nation will help us to be more patriotic? Why?

3. What do the lines from the poem by Emma Lazarus (page 32) mean to you?

4. Why should Americans, if possible, go to see the Liberty Bell and the Statue of Liberty?

For Further Study

1. Find the star in the Flag that stands for your state (page 18). Prepare a report on the history of your state up to the time it entered the Union.

2. Report to the class on your state flag and its story.

3. Look up your state seal. What do its parts mean?

4. Read and report on one of the following: Betsy Ross; Frances Hopkinson, designer of the American Flag; the bald eagle; the story of how the Flag came to be called "Old Glory."

5. What are the rules about flying the Flag over schoolhouses? Consult the *World Almanac* or the *Information Please Almanac.* Find out, if you can, whether the Flag is flown over all schoolhouses in your state.

6. Make a study of the coins and paper money of the United States and the symbols used on them.

7. For stamp collectors: Consult your stamps and stamp catalog to find how stamps have commemorated our national symbols: the Flag, the Liberty Bell, the Statue of Liberty, the eagle, the Great Seal.

8. Make a collection for your notebook or bulletin board of cartoons, advertisements, pictures, or short articles on our national symbols. Watch the daily newspapers and the weekly and monthly magazines.

9. Write a poem on any one of our national symbols.

10. Write a newspaper article which might have appeared when the Statue of Liberty was dedicated, or when the Liberty Bell was first hung in the Statehouse.

Books You Will Like

Big Miss Liberty, by Francis Rogers. Lippincott. A French boy tells the story of the Statue of Liberty.

"New Stars for Old Glory," by Lonnelle Aikman. *The National Geographic,* July, 1959.

Old Abe, the American Eagle, by Lorraine Sherwood. Scribner's. The story of a real eagle who took part in the War Between the States.

The Flag of the United States, by James A. Moss. United States Flag Association. A book full of poems, stories, and other material on the Flag.

Uncle Sam of America, by Philip Jordan. Webb. How Uncle Sam became the symbol of America.

★ Chapter 3 ★

Do You Know These Words?

Find in the dictionary the meaning which *best* explains each word as it is used in the chapter. On a sheet of paper write the word and beside it give the meaning. Then add a sentence from Chapter 3 in which this word is used.

independence	amendments
declaration	preamble
constitution	parchment
convention	compromise
continental	adoption
militia	resolution

Checking Your Understanding

1. What two documents contain our American idea of government?
2. What did the Declaration of Independence proclaim to the world?
3. What great ideas about the rights of all men are found in the Declaration of Independence?
4. Why is July 2 an important date in American history?
5. Name several important signers of the Declaration of Independence.
6. What important men helped make the Constitution?
7. What reasons are given in the Preamble for writing the Constitution?
8. Why was a Bill of Rights added to the Constitution?

What Do You Think?

1. Why do you think Philadelphia has been called the "cradle of liberty"?
2. Our Declaration of Independence states that "all men are created equal." Are all men equal? What do you think the statement means?
3. Could there be a national law forbidding Americans to criticize the government? Why?
4. There is only one way that our rights under the Constitution could legally be taken away from us. What is it? Do you think this could ever happen?
5. Why do you think the Founding Fathers made it difficult to amend the Constitution?

For Further Study

1. If you live in one of the thirteen original states, find out what men from your state helped write the Constitution.
2. Report to the class on famous signers of the Declaration of Independence. Pictures, a brief biography, and anecdotes will help to make your talk interesting.
3. Report in the same way on "Our Founding Fathers."
4. Memorize the Preamble to the Constitution and recite it to the class. Be sure you know what all the words mean.
5. Who are American citizens? Read Amendment XIV, Section 1, of the Constitution.
6. Find information about the National Archives Building and report to the class.
7. Make a list of the different topics covered by the twenty-two amendments

to our Constitution. Which ones have to do with our rights as citizens?

8. Watch newspapers and magazines for references to the Constitution, the Declaration of Independence, or our ideals of justice and equality and freedom. Read the selections you find to the class or put them on your bulletin board.

9. Write a letter that might have been written by one of the delegates to Congress or the Constitutional Convention after one of these events: the vote on Lee's resolution for independence; the signing of the Constitution; the public reading of the Declaration; the first meeting of the Constitutional Convention.

10. Draw cartoons illustrating: the weakness of the Articles of Confederation; King George reading the Declaration of Independence; the argument between the large and small states in the Constitutional Convention; the demand for a Bill of Rights.

Books You Will Like

Our Independence and the Constitution, by Dorothea Fisher. Random House. The writing of our great documents as seen through the eyes of a Philadelphia family.

The Fourth of July Story, by Alice Dalgliesh. Scribner's. How the Declaration of Independence was written and the first copies distributed.

You and the Constitution of the United States, by Paul Witty and Julilly Kohler. Children's Press. Our Constitution with pictures and story.

★ Chapter 4 ★

Do You Know These Words?

Find in the dictionary the meaning which *best* explains each word as it is used in the chapter. On a sheet of paper write the word and beside it give the meaning. Then add a sentence from Chapter 4 in which this word is used.

executive	budget
judicial	violation
qualifications	majority
representative	supreme
legislative	oath
republic	

Checking Your Understanding

1. Which government represents the people of the United States as a whole?

2. What special qualifications must a citizen have to be President?

3. What are the President's main responsibilities?

4. What are the symbols of the Presidency? Of the House? Of the Senate?

5. What personal sacrifices must a President make?

6. What two groups make up Congress and how are they chosen?

7. What are the main duties of Congress as a whole? Of the Senate? Of the House?

8. What are the steps a bill goes through to become a law?

9. What kinds of cases does the Supreme Court judge?

10. How many members does the Supreme Court have? How are they chosen?

11. Who are the Capitol pages?

What Do You Think?

1. Why do you think we have more than one political party?

2. When a newspaper uses this expression, "The White House sent congratulations to Churchill on his birthday," what does it mean?

3. Why do you think the Justices for the Supreme Court are not elected?

4. Why do we have age and residence requirements for the President and members of Congress? Why are the requirements for President stricter than for members of Congress?

5. No man may serve as President for more than two full terms (eight years). Do you think this is a wise law?

6. Do you think the President should be elected by popular vote instead of by electors? Give reasons for your answer.

7. Can you explain why Election Day is never later than November 8?

For Further Study

1. Check in a recent *World Almanac* or *Information Please Almanac* under "Congress" to find how many members your state sends to the House of Representatives.

2. Who are the Senators from your state?

3. Who is the Representative from your district?

4. Who is the President of the Senate?

5. Who is Speaker of the House?

6. Why is our nation called a republic and also a democracy? Consult the dictionary and encyclopedia for information.

7. List some things your father is free to do that the President is not.

8. Find pictures and articles on the President, the Cabinet members, Congress, or the Supreme Court to display on your bulletin board.

9. Plan a "Parade of Presidents." Each student will choose a President and prepare a brief report on his life and achievements.

Books You Will Like

Pathways of Our Presidents, by Floyd I. McMurray. Bobbs-Merrill. Interesting stories of our Presidents.

Thirty-Two Roads to the White House, by Alberta Graham. Nelson. The lives of thirty-two men who became President.

We Are the Government, by Mary Elting. Doubleday. Simple story of how our government works.

★ Chapter 5 ★

Do You Know These Words?

Find in the dictionary the meaning which best explains each word as it is used in the chapter. On a sheet of paper write the word and beside it give the meaning. Then add a sentence from Chapter 5 in which this word is used.

architect	portico
statuary	diagonal
mural	terrace
massive	capital
site	capitol

Checking Your Understanding

1. How was our national capital located? Who planned the city?

2. How much of Washington does the United States Government own today?

3. What is meant by the "Federal Triangle"?

4. What is the White House? How did the White House get its name?

5. Who was the first President to occupy the White House?

6. What is the Capitol?

7. What is the Rotunda?

8. What are the main wings of the Capitol?

9. What is the purpose of Statuary Hall?

10. Where does the Supreme Court meet?

11. Who was Constantino Brumidi?

12. What do you have to do to visit a session of Congress?

What Do You Think?

1. Should the people of Washington, D. C., be given the right to vote in Presidential elections? To send representatives to Congress? Give reasons for your answers.

2. Would you like to live in the White House as the President's son or daughter? Why?

3. Why are tourists allowed to visit the White House and Capitol?

For Further Study

1. Read and report on the life and work of L'Enfant.

2. Look at pictures and write a description of some room in the White House.

3. Make a scale model of the White House, Capitol, or the Supreme Court Building.

4. Find additional information on the Supreme Court Building, the Capitol, or the White House. Report on the interesting points not told in this chapter.

5. Report to the class on the Statue of Freedom above the Capitol dome.

6. Draw your own plan of Washington showing the chief government buildings and monuments.

7. For stamp collectors: Look through a stamp album or a stamp catalogue and report on how our national capital and its buildings have been commemorated with special stamps.

8. Write to the Congressman from your district and ask who from your state is represented in Statuary Hall. (See page 76: How to Address Congressmen.)

Books You Will Like

Adventure on the Potomac, by Dorothy Leavitt. Little, Brown. A Congressman's family sees Washington, D. C.

Articles on and illustrations of our national capital in "The National Geographic" magazine. January, 1953, and August, 1952.

Mistress of the White House, by Helen L. Morgan. Westminster Press. Dolly Madison becomes the first lady of the land.

Pictures of the White House. *The National Geographic*, January, 1961.

The Real Book About Our National Capital, by E. John Long. Garden City. A good guide to Washington.

They Built a City, by Janice Holland. Scribner's. Pictures and stories of Washington, D. C.

★ Chapter 6 ★

Do You Know These Words?

Find in the dictionary the meaning which best explains each word as it is used in the chapter. On a sheet of paper write the word and beside it give the meaning. Then add a sentence from Chapter 6 in which this word is used.

obelisk	engraved
vigil	landmark
monument	sentry
cornerstone	inscription
memorial	sculptor

commemorate

Checking Your Understanding

1. What three great Americans are honored by national memorials in Washington?
2. What makes the Washington Monument unusual?
3. What famous speeches are engraved in the Lincoln Memorial?
4. What is Arlington National Cemetery?
5. Why are so many of our better-known landmarks located in the eastern United States?
6. What event do the Lexington and Concord Memorials mark?
7. How did *Old Ironsides* earn its name?
8. What Presidents does the Mount Rushmore Memorial honor?
9. What is Plymouth Rock?
10. Name as many events as you can that took place in Independence Hall.

What Do You Think?

1. What are two good reasons for visiting Mt. Vernon and Monticello today?
2. What does the inscription in the Jefferson Memorial mean to you?
3. Which one of the national monuments or landmarks described in this chapter would you most like to visit? Why?
4. Why do we pay honor to the Unknown Soldiers?

For Further Study

1. Check the "Reader's Guide" magazine index for articles about the monuments described in this chapter. Read and report on one of them.
2. Find information for a report on some monument or landmark illustrated in this chapter but not fully explained.
3. Report to the class on the inventions of Thomas Jefferson.
4. Have you any historical landmarks or monuments in your state? If so, report on them to the class. If you live in a state rich in historic landmarks, you might choose a committee to study and report on them.
5. Show the landmarks and memorials on an outline map of your state.
6. Follow the dimensions given in this chapter and make a scale model of the Washington Monument.
7. For stamp collectors: Prepare a bulletin board display of stamps commemorating our national monuments and landmarks. See books on stamps in your library.
8. Draw a large outline map of the United States and locate important landmarks and memorials.

9. Using the *World Almanac*, locate all the memorials and monuments to Abraham Lincoln.

10. Draw one of the monuments or memorials described in the chapter.

Books You Will Like

Abraham Lincoln, by Clara Judson. Wilcox and Follett. Excellent story telling how a pioneer boy became President.

Abraham Lincoln, by Ingri and Edgar d'Aulaire. Doubleday. Easy-to-read story of Lincoln with colored pictures.

George Washington, by Clara Ingram Judson. Wilcox and Follett. Interesting story of a great American.

Patsy Jefferson of Monticello, by Marguerite Vance. Dutton. Story of Jefferson and his daughter.

Robert E. Lee, by Guy Emery. Messner. The story of the famous general.

The First Book of National Monuments, by Norman Labsenz. Watts. Historic places, forts, battlefields, etc.

Thomas Jefferson, by Genevieve Lisitzky. Viking. A fine picture of Jefferson and his times.

★ Chapter 7 ★

Do You Know These Words?

Find in the dictionary the meaning which best explains each word as it is used in the chapter. On a sheet of paper write the word and beside it give its meaning. Then add a sentence from Chapter 7 in which this word is used.

slogan	dedicate	inhuman
creed	proposition	cultivate
pledge	consecrate	destiny
submission	hallow	sovereign
prospects	tribute	strike (the colors)
inseparable	principles	

Checking Your Understanding

1. Why did Patrick Henry give his famous speech on liberty?

2. When Washington talked to his troops before the Battle of Long Island, what choices did he say the Americans had?

3. How did Lincoln happen to make the Gettysburg Address? What makes it one of the world's greatest speeches? One of the great documents on democracy?

4. In his Second Inaugural Address, what tasks did Lincoln outline for the years following the War Between the States?

5. In his War Message, what did Wilson say the United States would fight for?

6. In his last speech, what did Franklin Roosevelt say that the nations must do if civilization is to survive?

7. What did Dwight Eisenhower say in his First Inaugural Address about the part each of us plays in serving America?

8. Write down from memory as many as you can of the slogans and watchwords given in this chapter. How many did you remember?

9. What American freedoms are named in the Freedom Pledge?

10. What happened to make Jacob Riis realize that he was a true American?

11. What is the "immortal second sen-

tence" of the Declaration of Independence referred to in "What Is an American?"

What Do You Think?

1. Which of the famous speeches did you enjoy most? Why?

2. Which creed or pledge do you like best? Why?

3. Do you believe that reading and thinking about patriotic quotations will help young Americans become more patriotic? Why?

4. In what ways does Webster's "Liberty or Union" speech differ from most present-day speeches?

For Further Study

1. Read and report to the class on the life and deeds of one of the famous Americans mentioned in this chapter.

2. Learn the Freedom Pledge. Perhaps your class would like to recite the pledge together at the beginning of your history period.

3. Find out which phrases of the American's Creed are in the Declaration of Independence, in the Preamble of the Constitution, and in the Gettysburg Address.

4. Find in the Gettysburg Address the phrases that describe our democracy and our ideals.

5. Find other good quotations or slogans and present them to the class. The books on quotations and mottoes listed below will help you. Your library may have others.

6. Write a poem on one of the exciting events mentioned in this chapter, bringing in the slogan or watchword that goes with it. The death of Nathan Hale or the defense of the Alamo would make a good poem.

7. Draw cartoons illustrating patriotic slogans or watchwords for your bulletin board.

8. Plan a class discussion on the short quotations featured on pages 143 and 151. Each student may be responsible for one quotation and be prepared to tell the class in his own words what it means.

9. List all the suggestions for being good citizens given in the quotations on citizenship, page 157.

10. Present to your class a dramatization of "The Man Without a Country." You can find the play in drama collections in your library.

11. Plan a news broadcast, using the most interesting events in the chapter as news.

Books You Will Like

American Mottoes and Slogans, by George Earlie Shankle. Wilson. Famous slogans of famous people.

Keep My Flag Flying, by Mary T. Carroll. Longmans. Good story of Daniel Webster's life.

My American Heritage, collected by Ralph Henry and Lucile Pannell. Rand McNally. A fine collection of poems, speeches, and sayings dear to Americans.

Quotations for Special Occasions, by Maud Van Buren. Wilson. Excellent quotations given under *patriotism.*

Ships That Made U. S. History, by Helen Mitchell and William Wilson. Whittlesey House. Famous ships and famous trips in our history.

Shrine of Liberty, by Olga Hall-Quest. Dutton. The story of the Alamo and the battle that took place there.

Watchwords of Liberty, by Robert Lawson. Little, Brown. Exciting stories of exciting words and deeds.

★ Chapter 8 ★

Do You Know These Words?

Here are only a few of the difficult words contained in the poems and songs. As you reread each selection, look up the words you do not know. The selection will mean much more to you if you do.

hymn	caissons
anthem	spangled
hallelujah	reverence
ensign	perilous
convenes	ramparts
screed	stress

alabaster

Checking Your Understanding

1. What good trait does the author of the poem *Columbus* emphasize?
2. Why did Paul Revere wait for a signal from the church tower?
3. In *O Captain! My Captain!*, what is meant by the ship mentioned in the first and last verses? Who is the captain? What "fearful trip" do you think Whitman is referring to?
4. What answer did you find to the question in the title of the poem, "*What Makes a Nation?*"
5. What idea about our American people does the author bring out in the poem, *I Am an American?*
6. Who wrote our national anthem? How did it come to be written?
7. What two songs were popular in the South and the North during the War Between the States?
8. Why should young Americans be familiar with some of our well-known patriotic poems?

What Do You Think?

1. Can you explain in a sentence the idea in Whitman's poem on democracy?
2. What do you think the last three verses of *Yankee Doodle* describe?
3. What ideas does the song *America the Beautiful* express?
4. Which of the patriotic poems in this chapter do you like best? Why?
5. Which of our patriotic songs do you think best expresses the spirit of America?

For Further Study

1. Read and report on the true story of Paul Revere's ride.
2. In an encyclopedia look up *Old Ironsides.* How does it compare in size and weight to modern ships?
3. Check in library books for poems on our flag or country. Pick one to present to the class.
4. Look up other songs about our country. Which ones would you add to this chapter? Why?
5. Write an additional verse for *Yankee Doodle,* and read it to the class. You might imagine a visit to a modern army camp with tanks, planes, and so forth, instead of the camp described in the poem.
6. Write a poem with the title, *Land We Love,* or *My Country.*
7. Find pictures for a bulletin board display to illustrate the first verse of *America the Beautiful.*
8. Draw a series of cartoons depicting Paul Revere's sighting of the signal

lanterns and his ride through the countryside.

9. Write a paragraph explaining the thoughts expressed in the poem, *"What Makes a Nation?"*

10. Learn one or more verses of a poem selected from this chapter.

11. Draw sketches to illustrate one of the poems or songs.

Books You Will Like

American History in Verse for Boys and Girls, edited by Burton Stevenson. Houghton Mifflin. Poems that tell our history from Columbus through World War I.

Freedom's Flag, by Rupert S. Holland. Macrae. The story of *The Star-Spangled Banner.*

My American Heritage, collected by Ralph Henry and Lucile Pannell. Rand McNally. Songs, poems, speeches, and quotations dear to America.

Sing for America, by Opal Wheeler. Dutton. Stories, pictures, and songs from every part of America.

Stories of Our American Patriotic Songs, by John H. Lyons. Vanguard. The stories, words, and music of ten of our best-known patriotic songs.

★ Chapter 9 ★

Do You Know These Words?

Find in the dictionary the meaning which best explains each word as it is used in the chapter. On a sheet of paper write the word and beside it give this meaning. Then add a sentence from Chapter 9 in which this word is used.

armistice	solemn
preservation	commemorate
remembrance	coincidence
principles	achievements
proclamation	union (of flag)

Checking Your Understanding

1. Why do we celebrate the Fourth of July as a legal holiday?

2. Who are the two Americans whose birthdays our nation celebrates?

3. What does Memorial Day stand for?

4. What do we celebrate on Flag Day?

5. How have we honored Christopher Columbus in America?

6. What is the story of Armistice Day? How did it become Veterans Day?

7. Why is General Election Day important?

8. Whom does Citizenship Day honor? Why was September 17 chosen as the date?

9. What is our oldest national holiday and why do we celebrate it?

10. Why do we celebrate Labor Day?

11. Why is it important to know what our holidays stand for?

What Do You Think?

1. Do you think we should observe our patriotic holidays by special programs in assembly or in the classrooms? Why?

2. Do you think all families should fly our Flag outside their homes on our patriotic holidays? Why?

3. What can young people do to keep alive the meaning of our patriotic holidays at school, at home, and in the community?

For Further Study

1. What is the Salute to the Union? See the *World Almanac.*

2. Prepare a report on what happened on V–E Day.

3. What does V–J Day represent?

4. Report on the first Thanksgiving Day.

5. Make a calendar of your selection of the "Ten Most Important Holidays."

6. Learn a suitable quotation or poem for a class program about our holidays.

7. Many of our holidays fall in the school year. Plan and give a class or assembly program to celebrate the nearest national holiday. Suggestion: the history and meaning of the day; songs and poems honoring the day; great men or events connected with the holiday; original play or skit; displays of pictures, etc.

8. See that your family has a Flag and that it is displayed on important patriotic holidays.

Books You Will Like

Holiday Round Up, by Lucile Pannell and Frances Cavanah. Macrae Smith. A collection of interesting facts about our holidays.

Poems for Red Letter Days, by Elizabeth Hough Sechrist. Macrae Smith. A collection of poems about patriotic and other holidays.

Quotations for Special Occasions, by Maud Van Buren. Wilson. Good quotations on all the holidays.

★ Chapter 10 ★

Do You Know These Words?

Find in the dictionary the meaning which best explains each word as it is used in the chapter. On a sheet of paper write the word and beside it give its meaning. Then add a sentence from Chapter 10 in which this word is used.

jury	privilege
censor	political
rights	responsibilities
endure	Communism
injustice	dictatorship

Checking Your Understanding

1. What special ideas represent the American way of life?

2. What are the political duties of good citizens?

3. How can young people practice good citizenship?

4. What are the chief differences between the Communist way of life and ours?

5. How does Communism threaten our democracy?

6. What responsibilities go with freedom of speech and religion?

What Do You Think?

1. Who would have more responsibilities as a citizen, a man in Soviet Russia or in the United States? Why?

2. Why do you think there is so little freedom in a Communist country?

3. What can you do to help our democracy grow and improve?

4. What does lack of respect for public property show?

5. In what ways do the Boy and Girl Scouts, the Rangers, the 4–H Clubs, and similar groups help young people to become better citizens?

6. What organizations in your community help to make your town a better place to live in?

7. What could you and other young people do to make your neighborhood a better place to live in?

8. Which parts of the Pledge for Americans do you think will be hardest to live up to? Why?

For Further Study

1. Make a chart showing how our various rights and privileges are balanced by duties and responsibilities.

2. Prepare a list of ten rights and privileges you now enjoy which you would lose if Communists controlled our land.

3. Turn to page 236 and find how the Constitution defines treason.

4. Our right to free speech is limited by laws prohibiting libel and slander. Look up the words *libel* and *slander* in a dictionary or encyclopedia, and explain why such laws are needed.

5. Bring to class newspaper reports on people who have given some service to your community, your state, or the nation.

6. Make a list of things you can do to be a good citizen at home or at school.

7. Find pictures and advertisements for a bulletin board display illustrating our privileges and rights (as listed on pages 207 and 208). Write suitable captions on cards.

8. Write an essay on the idea that "Good Citizenship Begins in the Neighborhood and at School."

9. Read and discuss with your class the Pledge for Americans on page 221. Which parts can young people carry out now?

Books You Will Like

Put Democracy to Work, by Ruth H. Wagner and Ivah E. Green. Schuman. Excellent survey of rights and duties in a democracy.

We Are the Government, by Mary Elting. Doubleday. Describes the part we citizens play in our democracy.

You and Democracy, by Dorothy Gordon. Dutton. What living in a democracy is like.

1-L-61.

INDEX

This Index includes references not only to the text but also to pictures, boxes of additional information, charts, and maps. These may be identified as follows:

p refers to a picture
b refers to an information box
c refers to a chart
m refers to a map

ACKNOWLEDGMENTS

The authors and publisher are indebted to Richard Bartlett for the colored drawings on the first three pages and also the drawings used on the cover; to Courtney Allen for the drawings at the beginning of each chapter and all the colored drawings within the chapters; and to Walter Frame for the spot drawings accompanying the section heads within the chapters. Except where credit is given elsewhere, thanks are extended to the following for permission to reproduce pictures.

Page	*Source*
iv	(background) National Archives (inset) Library of Congress
1	H. Armstrong Roberts
3	Santa Fe Railway
4	Standard Oil Company (New Jersey)
6	A. Devaney
7	Harold M. Lambert Studios
12	Philip Gendreau
14	Official Photograph U. S. Navy
16	Department of State
21	Massachusetts Audubon Society — W. Bryant Tyrell Photo
23	Photo Courtesy National Park Service
26	A. Devaney
30	Wide World
36	H. Armstrong Roberts
39	New England Mutual Life Insurance Co.
40	New England Mutual Life Insurance Co.
43	Library of Congress
44	Courtesy of John Hancock Mutual Life Insurance Company
51	Culver Service
53	Culver Service
57	Courtesy of Insurance Company of North America Companies, Philadelphia
59	Chamber of Commerce of U.S.A.
63	United Press (both photos)
68	Photo by Abbie Rowe — Courtesy National Park Service
69	United Press International Photo
71	Wide World Photos
73	United Press
74	Wide World
79	Harris & Ewing
81	A. Devaney
84	L. C. Handy Studios
86	Photo Courtesy National Park Service
87	Official U. S. Air Force Photo
91	Photo by Abbie Rowe — Courtesy National Park Service
94	Photo by Abbie Rowe — Courtesy National Park Service
95	Photo by Abbie Rowe — Courtesy National Park Service
97	L. C. Handy Studios
98	Library of Congress
100	National Archives
103	Harold M. Lambert Studios
104	Massachusetts Department of Commerce
106	Chamber of Commerce of U.S.A.
107	Photo Courtesy National Park Service
109	Photo by Abbie Rowe — Courtesy National Park Service
110	A. Devaney
111	Photo by Abbie Rowe — Courtesy National Park Service
112	L. C. Handy Studios
114	Photo Courtesy National Park Service
115	Mount Vernon Ladies' Association
117	Thomas Jefferson Memorial Foundation
118	Thomas Jefferson Memorial Foundation
119	Massachusetts Department of Commerce
121	Massachusetts Department of Commerce
122	Courtesy Philadelphia Electric Company
125	Official Photograph U. S. Navy
127	Illinois Department of Conservation — Herbert Georg Photo
128	(upper) Courtesy National Park Service (middle) Courtesy National Park Service (lower) The Alamo
129	(upper left) Indiana Department of Conservation, Division of State Parks (upper right) H. Armstrong Roberts (middle) Courtesy National Park Service (lower) Commercial Studios
130	Eastman Kodak
131	Harold M. Lambert Studios
132	Library of Congress
136	(background) Library of Congress (inset) H. Armstrong Roberts
139	Library of Congress
141	International News
142	Harris & Ewing
145	Wide World
148	Library of Congress
150	Alburtus — Yale News Bureau
153	Library of Congress
154	Library of Congress
155	San Jacinto Museum of History
156	U. S. Army Photograph
159	Harris & Ewing
160	H. Armstrong Roberts
161	New England Mutual Life Insurance Co.
163	Brown Brothers
164	Massachusetts Department of Commerce
167	Official Photograph U. S. Navy
168	Courtesy of John Hancock Mutual Life Insurance Company
179	Harris & Ewing
184	A. Devaney
185	Acme Photo
191	Photo by Abbie Rowe — Courtesy National Park Service

194 Harold M. Lambert Studios
196 Magnum Photos
198 Owen, Black Star
199 Brown Brothers
201 Chamber of Commerce of U.S.A.
204 A. Devaney
205 A. Devaney
207 Lew Merrim from Monkmeyer
208 Federal Hall Memorial Museum
210 Courtesy of Gamaliel Bradford Senior High School, Wellesley, Mass.
211 Lieberman, Black Star
213 Boston Civil Defense — Crocker Photo
219 Courtesy of Gamaliel Bradford Senior High School, Wellesley, Mass.
223 Courtesy of Insurance Company of North America Companies, Philadelphia
224 Photo Courtesy National Park Service
238 National Archives

Selections in copyright have been acknowledged on the pages where they occur, with a few possible exceptions where diligent search failed to discover the existence of copyrights.